Economic Governance and the Challenge of Flexibility in East Asia

Economic Governance and the Challenge of Flexibility in East Asia

Edited by
Frederic C. Deyo, Richard F. Doner,
and Eric Hershberg

ROWMAN & LITTLEFIELD PUBLISHERS, INC.
Lanham • Boulder • New York • Oxford

ROWMAN & LITTLEFIELD PUBLISHERS, INC.

Published in the United States of America
by Rowman & Littlefield Publishers, Inc.
4720 Boston Way, Lanham, Maryland 20706
www.rowmanlittlefield.com

12 Hid's Copse Road, Cumnor Hill, Oxford OX2 9JJ, England

This is a project sponsored by the Social Science Research Council with funds provided by the Ford Foundation and the Chiang Ching-kuo Foundation for International Scholarly Change.

British Library Cataloguing in Publication Information Available

Library of Congress Cataloging-in-Publication Data
Economic governance and the challenge of flexibility in East Asia / edited by Frederic C. Deyo, Richard F. Doner, and Eric Hershberg.
    p. cm.
    A collection of 9 papers by the editors and other scholars.
    Includes bibliographical references and index.
    ISBN 0-7425-0943-5 (alk. paper) — ISBN 0-7425-0944-3 (pbk. : alk. paper)
    1. Industrial management—East Asia—Case studies. 2. Industrial policy—East Asia—Case studies. 3. Decentralization in management—East Asia—Case studies. 4. Flexible manufacturing systems—East Asia—Case studies. 5. Industries—East Asia—Case studies. I. Deyo, Frederic C. II. Doner, Richard F. III. Hershberg, Eric.

HD70.E22 E34 2001
338.95—dc21   00-062653

Printed in the United States of America

♾™ The paper used in this publication meets the minimum requirements of American National Standard for Information Sciences—Permanence of Paper for Printed Library Materials, ANSI/NISO Z39.48-1992.

Contents

Contents

Introduction

Economic Governance and Flexible Production in East Asia

Frederic C. Deyo and Richard F. Doner

Some years ago, Charles Sabel explored the possibility that developing countries would move toward "changing models of economic efficiency." Sabel speculated that a shift from mass to more flexible forms of production could result from the internal decentralization of large firms and from the evolution of firms in the informal sector to some variant of what came to be known as the Third Italy (Sabel 1986: 41–50). This volume explores the issues first raised by Sabel, albeit in much changed economic conditions, through a more explicit institutional and political theoretical lens and with a focus on a variety of sectors in what, until its widespread late 1990s economic crisis, was the most successful developing region in the world—East and Southeast Asia.[1]

Recent years have witnessed profound transformations in the nature of the challenges facing developing countries seeking to promote economic growth and equity. A combination of technological advances, external market liberalization, and transformations in the nature of product markets has imposed powerful constraints on firms in developed and developing countries alike, while creating new opportunities for firms and entire sectors to enter markets from which they had previously been excluded. The Asian economic crisis intensified these pressures and opportunities in part by increasing pressure for liberalization in both factor and product markets. But it also complicated responses to these conditions by destabilizing macroeconomic conditions and financial flows and stimulating major changes in corporate governance.

This volume seeks to enhance our understanding of the factors that account for the success or failure of economic actors seeking to achieve competitiveness in these new circumstances. More specifically, the volume analyzes the role of economic governance institutions in facilitating competitive performance in the developing market economies of East and Southeast Asia. Drawing on case studies of a variety of industries, the authors demonstrate the significance of productive flexibility for achieving success across a wide range of economic sectors. Equally important, they highlight the critical role of institutional factors—especially networks—in shaping actors' capacities to adapt to rapid changes in markets, technologies, and consumer demand.

While "getting governance institutions right" may not be sufficient to sustain competitiveness or to ensure economic development, these elusive outcomes appear implausible absent such institutional underpinnings. But if coordinating mechanisms are necessary, there is neither one magic institutional formula for success nor any functionalist guarantee that an economic need will lead to supportive mechanisms. We instead find different institutional configurations within and across different industries. And we find that sociopolitical factors weigh heavily on the kinds of arrangements that do emerge. This introductory chapter begins by outlining the challenges confronting developing countries and the utility of East Asian cases for understanding both the challenges and the institutional and political responses to them.

FLEXIBILITY PRESSURES

Firms in the industrializing as well as industrially advanced countries are now confronting a combination of exogenous pressures—transformed markets, external market liberalization, and accelerating technological change. Global oversupply in many industries has resulted in buyers' markets where customers enjoy expanded choices. Today, global buyers stress competitive price, good quality, quick delivery time, and heightened responsiveness to changing demand requirements. Fleury noted this pattern in his study of industrial change in Brazil during the 1990s, when unlike the earlier period in which firms were "[a]ccustomed to a restricted product variety and relatively high prices, the opening to the global market had a different impact: markets became segmented, and a confusing pattern of price, quality and diversity emerged as requisites of demand" (Fleury 1995).

In addition, firms throughout the developing world are forced to contend with more liberalized external markets. This process has been especially extensive in East Asia. The economic crisis there was in part the result of liberalized capital markets, and the region's product markets had already been relatively open by the early 1990s. Many of the region's countries are now facing further tariff reductions as part of imminent World Trade Organization membership, as well as tariff reforms through the Asia Pacific Economic Cooperation process and under the ASEAN Free Trade Area (AFTA) agreements.[2] Combined with significant levels of foreign investment, these reforms collectively transmit cost and quality pressures with ever greater force to local firms.[3]

What will be the impact of market liberalization on production? There is of course the possibility that liberalization will encourage mass, as opposed to more flexible, production. As McKeown has argued with regard to developed-country firms, increased access to large export markets for firms with small domestic markets means greater opportunities for longer production runs (McKeown 1999). This point was certainly borne out by South Korean success prior to the crisis, as suggested by Ernst's contribution to this volume. But even where liberalization promotes longer production runs of standardized goods, successful firms will have to enhance their operational capabilities with regard to product diversification (Kotha 1995) and change, continual process improvements *(kaizen)*,[4] enhanced quality and timeliness of delivery of products, and, in some cases, product development and innovation. In this volume, we refer to these various performance capabilities as instances of the more general concept of production *flexibility*.[5]

The range of industry cases covered in this volume suggest several specific patterns of flexibility-inducing market pressures in East and Southeast Asia. For firms in export-oriented textile/garment and athletic footwear industries (Lui and Chiu, Appelbaum and Smith, and Cheng, this volume), pressures are for quick-response and supply-chain management to meet volatile demand for a wide range of products and relatively short production runs, a pattern described by Boyer and Hollingsworth (1997: 457–458) as "customized production." A similar pattern might obtain for firms that cannot compete in mass exports and opt to become domestic "niche" players. Firms in industries such as autos and semiconductors (Deyo and Doner, Rasiah, and Ernst, this volume) are pushed toward strategies of "diversified quality mass production," in which increasing returns to scale obtain but in which high-volume goods also undergo constant modification.[6] Still another related pattern, "adaptive production," is seen in the hard disk drive industry, where firms must shift rapidly from one mass-produced "high-technology commodity" to another (Wong, this volume).[7] Although differing in some important ways, each of these strategies requires continually improving production processes in order to meet cost and quality pressures imposed by others trying similar strategies.[8]

PERFORMANCE DEMANDS AND THE COMPETITIVE STRATEGIES OF FIRMS

Are heightened demands for flexibility actually reflected in the strategies of less-developed country (LDC) firms, and are these firms successful in pursuing new strategies of flexibility? Here we find much variability, since firms compete in part by selecting and continually redefining the market niches in which they operate. The possibility of strategic choice implies as well diversity in the performance requirements to which firms attend, although it is also clear that firms may simultaneously compete in multiple ways. Attention to a *set of interrelated performance demands* suggests the usefulness of attending to performance *profiles*, as firms seek to establish an effective balance among various complementary and/or competing objectives (including, inter alia, cost containment and achievement of scale economies).

We can, nevertheless, identify clear tendencies in the responses of firms to external pressures. At one extreme, Fleury (1995) shows that, in response to the new demands of global markets, some Brazilian firms have in fact regressed to a predominant emphasis on price, having found that previously competitive cost structures were no longer adequate in the face of foreign competition. And, indeed, a case can be made that *very* high levels of competition may have the effect of discouraging the sorts of long-term investments necessary for high degrees of flexibility, diverting attention to more immediate concerns for price-cutting and survival (see Crouch and Streeck 1997: 8). Similarly, in the face of increasing demands for flexibility, companies can move down to more standard-technology market niches, or, alternatively, into other product markets (Hollingsworth and Streeck 1994: 284). The chapter by Lui and Chiu notes the tendency for Hong Kong clothing manufacturers to respond to growing competitive pressures through relocation of production to lower-cost mainland Chinese production sites, on the one hand, and a shift into nonmanufacturing activities, on the other. More common are the mixed cases of firms which have successfully improved their performance capabilities relating to quality improvement and shortened/customized production runs, but which still largely react to existing market opportunities rather than seek to create new ones. Cheng's discussion (this volume) of "design-sensitive" and "cost-sensitive" footwear market segments further suggests diversity in the strategic responses of firms even within a single country and industry to these external pressures.

In response to new competitive pressures, a smaller number of developing-country firms have upgraded into process engineering and moderate product development. In this volume, Rasiah's analysis of Penang's machine tool firms describes significant process innovations undertaken in coordination with foreign semiconductor firms. Wong's discussion of the disk drive industry in Singapore suggests that process engineering among local subsidiaries there may indeed be more advanced than in the home country plants of these multinational firms. Similarly, Deyo and Doner's study of a Thai auto supplier firm reveals a combination of process and product innovation in automotive jigs.

Far fewer are cases where LDC firms have engaged in significant *product innovation*. There are exceptions to be sure. Wong, for example, notes the recent development of a new disk drive product by a transnational corporation (TNC) subsidiary in Singapore, albeit in consultation with the TNC's U.S.-based design team. But more representative is Fleury's observation that Brazilian manufacturers have in some cases moved successfully into market niches demanding high levels of quality and dependability, but not of product innovation (Fleury 1995). This general absence of strategies of innovation may be explained in several ways.

The first views performance demands as cumulative and developmental, thus suggesting that LDC firms have not yet progressed to the level necessary for innovation. David Soskice's distinction between "radical innovations" and "incremental improvements in existing technologies" suggests that the latter are the most relevant for developing-country firms (Soskice 1994). Amsden (1989) similarly stresses the greater importance of "learning" (adopting and adapting existing technologies, achieving higher skill levels) than of innovation, even in industrially advanced South Korea. A second, *structural,* view stresses *(a)* the reluctance of TNC's to share leading-edge technology with local firms, or to assist them in moving into the innovation-intensive sectors where their own position might be threatened, and *(b)* the TNC-organized sectoral chains of economic activities, valorization, and control, which may consign LDC firms to low-value production niches in the world economy (Gereffi, Korzeniewicz, and Korzeniewicz 1994).

Yet a third explanation stresses the tendency for firms to become "stuck" in non-innovative niches. Such a path-dependency view is reflected in Lui and Chiu's discussion of the way in which cost-based strategies of Hong Kong firms may preclude subsequent, more dynamic flexibility strategies. This approach is most consistent with the institutional focus of this volume, which emphasizes relationships among firms and the institutions that influence those relationships. It is these contexts which in turn influence how firms collectively define the legitimate boundaries of industrial practices and thus identify and pursue strategies of adjustment (Herrigel 1994). As Ernst's contribution to this volume reveals, these three explanations are not mutually exclusive: the problems of Korean *chaebol* in electronics reflect not just the inherent difficulties of major innovations in semiconductors and real rivalry with advanced-country producers, but also institutional constraints of the Korean political economy.

ECONOMIC GOVERNANCE
AND PRODUCTION FLEXIBILITY

What, then, influences the capacity of firms to compete in strategically chosen ways? Firm-specific resources, including the very nature of management and entrepreneurship, are certainly critical. But as the Deyo-Doner study of the Thai auto parts firm illustrates, leadership often involves the capacity to draw on extrafirm resources.[9] And as cross-national differences in modal firm behavior suggest, such capacity in turn depends on much more than individual firm objectives and capacities. Of particular importance are the ways in which economic governance institutions encourage and enhance some performance capabilities over others.

Economic governance refers generally to the socioinstitutional regulation and coordination of economic transactions. Davis and North (1971: 5–6) provide a useful starting point in referring to "an institutional arrangement between economic units that governs the ways in which these units can cooperate and/or compete." Similarly, Hollingsworth, Schmitter, and Streeck (1994: 5) define governance as the "totality of institutional arrangements—including rules and rule-making agents—that regulate transactions inside and across the boundaries of an economic system."

Governance institutions shape and constrain economic transactions in such a way as to influence the sorts of performance goals which may feasibly be pursued. Starting from this premise, debates regarding the relationship between governance institutions and economic performance have by necessity stimulated continuing discussion of types, dimensions, and economic outcomes of governance itself. In particular, three types of governance have been identified and discussed: markets, hierarchies, and networks.[10]

The first of these, markets, is conceptually problematic. Indeed, there is some controversy as to whether it is a form of economic governance at all, as implied by Hollingsworth and Streeck (1994: 270) in their reference to the "institutionally thin" neoclassical order governing world markets. Coleman (1994: 170) similarly asserts that "[n]eoclassical economics is largely institution-free: the perfect market is the one institution recognized in neoclassical theory, and is less an institution than an assumption that institutional problems in arriving at exchanges at market-clearing prices will be solved." But if markets are not themselves institutions, they may usefully be included in governance typologies if used as a shorthand for a set of regulatory institutions within which they function. These institutions include a legal framework, which establishes property rights, contract, relational norms among economic actors, permissible and prohibited market exchanges, and the like. Indeed, without such institutional regulation (largely mediated by the state), markets would quickly degenerate into anarchy (Block 1994: 698).

Using this broadened definition of instituted markets, what can be said about corresponding characteristics of economic transactions and performance outcomes? There has been a general recognition of the superiority of markets relating to short-term responsiveness to shifting economic conditions, and to the achievement of allocative efficiencies in the distribution of resources among competing uses, all within existing resource endowments and organizational capabilities. Williamson (1994: 90) notes in this regard the outstanding adaptive properties of markets to disturbances where adaptations on the part of individual actors are sufficient. Markets encourage high levels of economic flexibility in large measure through the contractual freedom they afford firms and individuals in their economic transactions (see Soskice 1999).

Lacking roots in noneconomic normative or relational obligations, market-governed economic transactions tend to be transitory, fragile, and largely instrumental in nature. For this reason, forms of adaptation requiring more enduring or cooperative transactions become problematic, except in the case of major innovations.[11] The specifically temporal, and thus developmental, deficit in market governance may be understood by reference to the distinction between static flexibility, which is short-term in orientation and reactive in nature, and dynamic flexibility,[12] which seeks to anticipate and alter future markets, to enhance resource endowments in skills and technology, and to continually improve the organization of production. As described by Colclough and Tolbert, "[t]he dynamic approach to flexibility means that productive change is institutionalized, involving an enhancement of corporate capacity to develop and introduce technological advances. [It] is a forward-looking, future-oriented response to the problem of high market uncertainty" (Colclough and Tolbert 1992: 18). The difference is illustrated by Lui and Chiu's discussion of the short-term responsiveness of garment and electronics firms to market volatility, but of the greater difficulties of such firms in matters of process innovation or product development under Hong Kong's "disorganized," market-governed capitalism. Similarly, Deyo and Doner show how Thailand's relatively thin institutional context discourages long-term upgrading by auto parts firms.

A second type of governance, hierarchy, is explicated in the early writings of Coase (1937: 386–405) and Chandler (1977). As further discussed by Williamson, hierarchy is a form of economic governance superior to markets in underwriting longer-term collaboration and developmental investments, critical bases for dynamic flexibility. Williamson's starting point is to note several impediments to collaboration and long-term investments which markets typically fail to address. Such impediments include the mutual vulnerabilities associated with firm-level investments in transaction-specific assets, the possibilities that other firms will appropriate the positive externalities associated with one's own investments, and an inability to assess adequately the reliability of transactional partners or the distribution of benefits associated with collaboration. For Williamson, these various transactional problems are addressed more adequately within hierarchies than in atomistic markets.[13] This is so because hierarchies internalize many of the problematic relationships noted above, and thus create an embedding social order within which authoritative solutions to transactional problems may be imposed. Hy Van Luong notes in this regard that, in response to growing market uncertainty and increased need for production flexibility, Vietnam's textile industry has enhanced coordination between garment manufacturing and textile production through a strategy of state-brokered vertical integration (Luong 1996). Similarly, Appelbaum and Smith find that South Korea's textile industry has enhanced the capacity for quality improvements and customization of production for export markets through tightened coordination between design, production, and marketing within hierarchical *chaebol* structures. These two cases thus suggest a compatibility between hierarchical governance and customized mass production.

But hierarchical governance may itself create further collaborative problems, including oft-noted tendencies toward formalism, verticality, and rigidity, as well as the resistance, secrecy, and subterfuge encouraged among those subject to organizational authority.[14] South Korea's recent problems in electronics illustrate some of these weaknesses (Ernst, this volume). Williamson himself notes some possible tradeoffs in the choice between markets (which encourage short-term, individualistic adaptation) and hierarchies (which provide a means of longer-term, coordinated adaptation), suggesting the possibility of hybrids (especially network-like structures) between the two as actors seek forms of governance which combine elements of each.

If Williamson and others working within a Coasian tradition tend to see such hybrids as relatively unstable and often only transitional,[15] writers working within a third perspective emphasize the stability of looser, more horizontal networks among formally independent actors. Although comprising "softer, more multilateral forms of governance than either markets or hierarchies," networks are nonetheless ubiquitous and potentially superior in performance outcomes under conditions of uncertainty and volatility (Powell and Smith-Doerr 1994: 382).

NETWORK GOVERNANCE AND FLEXIBLE PRODUCTION

Piore and Sabel were among the first to systematically link network governance with flexible performance outcomes. In their now classic discussion of the organization of production among craft-based small firms in northern Italy and elsewhere, Piore and Sabel (1984) showed how dense ties of interdependence and trust, rooted in informal relations and a shared sense of community, permitted firms to cooperate in ways which enhanced flexibility in the production of high-quality, innovative products for specialized and/or volatile markets. This early work, itself tracing lineage to Marshall's discussion of late-nineteenth-century industrial districts in Europe, has spawned a growing literature on the competitive advantages of territorially based clusters of interdependent firms in a variety of sectors and locales (Scott and Angel 1988; Storper and Harrison 1991). This and related literatures on interfirm networks emphasize the competitive advantages of operational collaboration in matters of product design, technology support, machinery maintenance and instruction, and contracting. Highlighted as well is the supportive role of a broader governance context of informal or family relations, coproduction agreements, strategic alliances, interlocking directorships, and preferential relations with local trading houses, business groups, and supplier associations.

Ideally, economic networks enhance production flexibility by facilitating flows of information and resources, often impeded under hierarchy, across the production process. Such flows increase the speed with which new information (e.g., market change) is diffused to those employees and firms from whom change or response will be demanded. In addition, they encourage a sharing of resources necessary for quick reaction or adaptation (e.g., by providing engineering and technology assistance to supplier firms during product changes), and they foster a sharing of ideas for collaborative problem solving among the various actors whose interdependent activities must be altered in a coordinated fashion (e.g., by bringing engineering, design, production, and marketing departments, along with key suppliers, into design planning, or by using cross-level, cross-department production teams to seek ways to improve production). Finally, economic networks facilitate quick, informal cooperation in dealing with unexpected contingencies, as illustrated by the case (described by Deyo and Doner) of an auto supplier firm in Thailand which was able to receive a rush shipment of steel from a Hong Kong supplier prior to negotiation of a formal purchase contract. Stated more generally, denser informational flows and resource sharing help to "tighten" and integrate the whole production process so as to permit quick, coherent change through cooperative action within and across firms. This enhanced system integration is essential for such flexibility-demanding performance outcomes as just-in-time delivery, total quality management, diversified quality production, and rapid product development.[16]

Like hierarchies, networks contribute to the integration of the production process, here by embedding economic transactions in a formal or informal social framework of constraints, incentives, sanctions, and mutual obligations. This framework in turn lends durability, openness, and depth to economic transactions by providing assurances to network members against opportunism, deceit, and other transactional hazards noted by Williamson and others. Formal network structures, such as quality circles, cross-departmental project-planning teams, and supplier clubs, are explicitly constructed to enhance operational flexibility. But more informal relations as well may enhance flexibility within firms by encouraging horizontal cooperation, providing ways around rigid rules, and fostering involvement and commitment to group goals (Powell and Smith-Doerr 1994: 380). Similarly, stable, trust-based relations may encourage process specialization, provide a basis for spreading costs and risks across firms, and encourage cooperation in matters of training, market forecasting, credit, and product development. Dore (1983), for example, discusses the importance of "relational contracting" for enduring, cooperative contractual relations in Japan, a concept akin to Aoki's (1984) "visible handshaking" and Wachter and Williamson's (1978) "obligational contracting." In these and other cases, informal personal relations embed transactions in a broader bond of mutual obligation, which provides each party with sufficient information about and leverage over contracting parties to discourage opportunism. The success of coproduction, research and development, and collaborative agreements among firms may similarly benefit from personal relations and professional networks among engineers or managers.

How common is network governance among LDC firms? The evidence is at best mixed. Based on an extensive literature review, Nadvi and Schmitz (1994) find that while industrial clusters are in fact quite common in developing countries, long-term economic cooperation and information sharing are far from pervasive.[17] Similarly, Ruas et al. (1994) note the absence of significant cooperation among firms in two Brazilian industrial clusters (shoes and automobile parts). On the other hand, the chapter by Cheng argues that Taiwan's footwear industry emerged as a result of geographical clustering and resource sharing. Similarly, the growth of hard disk drive production in Southeast Asia has, according to Wong, resulted in part from the timely provision of personnel, equipment, market opportunities, and learning by proximate firms and institutions. These and other accounts (Hamilton and Woolsey 1988; Whitley 1992; Poon 1994) suggest that extensive networking between firms has, in fact, contributed to the success of many industries in Asia.

The discussion thus far makes clear the need for care in specifying the unit of analysis: Are we seeking to characterize individual firms, or *groups* of networked firms, as more or less flexible? In this volume, Deyo and Doner's description of the operations of a Thai automobile supplier emphasizes the flexibility of an individual firm, although even this case is positioned, as it is in Appelbaum and Smith's account, within a broader context of interfirm linkages and sociopolitical institutions. Conversely, the descriptions by Rasiah and Wong of supplier networks centering on transnational subsidiaries in Malaysia and Singapore emphasize the flexibility not so much of individual firms as of the interfirm networks in which firms are embedded. More generally, many existing accounts of industrial districts or clusters emphasize the ways in which "collective efficiencies" (Schmitz 1992) are achieved not through the aggregated performances of individual firms, which may themselves be quite inflexibly specialized in particular industrial processes, but rather through an ability on the part of the larger groups of interrelated firms to redirect and reconstitute the organization of production and division of labor among firms (also see Bazan and Schmitz 1997). Such a shift in level of analysis provides a useful basis for an understanding of the implications of production flexibility for broader processes of economic development.

This positive portrayal of the competitive advantages of networks must be balanced, of course, by recognition of the negative performance implications of power and collusion within networks as well as of the corresponding competitive advantages of market governance noted earlier. The literature on economic networks has tended to stress cooperative relations among equals to the partial exclusion of considerations of power and resource inequalities among economic actors (Granovetter 1994). While the very notion of networking implies somewhat more symmetrical relations than would be associated with hierarchical governance, there remain clear differences in the degree to which network relations within and across firms are characterized by differences in resources and power. Storper and Harrison (1991: 412–413) explicitly address this issue through a governance typology based on power, itself the outcome of two aspects of interfirm dependency: number of a firm's alternative suppliers (or customers) and specialization in important skills or technology. These two factors, suggest Storper and Harrison, determine the balance of power between any two firms. From this standpoint, the Korean *chaebol* described by Ernst can be understood as a case of highly vertical networks (Hamilton 1999). Similarly, the degree of hierarchy evidenced in Appelbaum and Smith's account of "vertically integrated networks" among Hong Kong's garment firms, as in Deyo and Doner's discussion of auto as-

sembler/supplier networks, is significantly greater than that characterizing relations among Taiwanese shoe producers, as discussed by Cheng. These considerations further suggest the fruitfulness, from the standpoints of both theory and empirical investigation, of abandoning rigid governance typologies in favor of a more
general characterization of governance situations by reference to a common set of
underlying dimensions, including degree of particularism, formalism, verticality,
stability, open-endedness, and multiplexity. This approach suggests one describe a
particular governance arrangement as *more or less* hierarchical or market-like. It
also encourages consideration of the roles of third parties in network relationships, such as the trading companies mediating between global buyers and Taiwanese producers of cost-sensitive athletic footwear, as described by Cheng.

Recognition that economic collaboration may as often be rooted in asymmetri-
cal resource dependency as in coequal cooperation suggests a further question relating to network functioning and performance outcomes: how network inequalities influence information flows and the depth of cooperation across the
production process. There is evidence that inequalities in power and resources
may undercut cooperation in ways not unlike those found within formal hierarchies, with important consequences for production outcomes. Sako (1994), for
example, notes that horizontal networks of firms are associated in Japan with
richer flows of information than are typically found between contractors and the
supplier companies they organize into supplier associations (see also Sabel 1994:
17–42). Most critical for our purposes is early research by Levy and Kuo (1991)
suggesting a link between the verticality of Korean networks and *chaebol* mass
production strategies.

A second concern is the danger of cronyism. Networks can involve more collusion than collaboration. The region under consideration in this volume—East
Asia—was until recently the source of much optimistic theorizing as to the benefits of collaborative institutions (World Bank 1993).[18] The recent economic crisis has clearly shaken that optimism, with many arguing that what passed for collaboration was in essence a form of cronyism. An important consequence of the
crisis has been greater pressure for reform in corporate governance, e.g., trans-
parency and respect for shareholder and stakeholder rights. This development
compels even greater attention to the actual functioning of networks. Most of the
chapters in this volume address cases of relative productive success linked to collaborative but noncollusive network arrangements. Only in Rasiah's examination
of the Kelang Valley do we find important weaknesses, and there, not surprisingly,
one finds more politically motivated collusion. What, then, accounts for variation
in the extent to which collaborative networks are collusive? The cases suggest the
importance of external market pressures: trade liberalization or some functional
equivalent becomes both a source of pain and a necessary ingredient in collective
upgrading.[19]

This brings us to a further criticism: that while network governance can indeed
promote flexibility, it is a second-best option to unfettered market transactions.

One argument in favor of this position has to do with the dangers of collusion. As noted above, however, the option is not simply between markets or networks, for it matters enormously whether networks operate under external market pressure. A second argument has to do with the fact that, as Soskice (1999) has argued in the context of industrialized countries, radical innovations linked to new, evolving technologies (e.g., biotechnology and electronics) are in fact typical of relatively uncoordinated, market economies. Yet this observation is of minor relevance for developing countries. For one thing, the liberal market pattern found in industrialized economies in fact depends on prior and extensive institutional development not common in developing countries. Second, the challenge for developing countries is the ability to make effective use of existing but often noncodifiable, tacit technologies. As theories of endogenous growth and national systems of innovation have shown (Romer 1994; Metcalfe 1995), the capacity of firms to enhance production flexibility depends in part on the nature of transactions and relationships among firms. More specifically, this literature, and the distinct differences in technological capacity among countries exposed to similar exogenous technologies, suggest that network-type governance may provide a superior basis for some types of production flexibility by enhancing flows of information and resources as well as the possibilities for economic collaboration among economic actors. Whether examining "collective efficiencies" in industrial clusters or the benefits of Japanese manufacturing techniques within more vertical arrangements, scholars have emphasized the value of reciprocity and social exchange for firms attempting to contend with demands for higher quality, rapid delivery, and greater product diversity (Kaplinsky with Posthuma 1994; Nadvi and Schmitz 1994).

EXPLAINING ECONOMIC NETWORKS

There are three general approaches to explaining the origins of network governance. The first, a *strategic networking* approach, emphasizes the deliberate efforts of key actors, mainly employers and managers,[20] as they seek to establish a web of intra- and interfirm relationships (as well as to alter the larger institutional environment) in support of their chosen goals and competitive strategies. A second, *emergence* approach draws on social exchange theory to show how ongoing economic relationships, whatever their initial roots and however market-like they are at the outset, may increasingly assume network-like characteristics as continued interaction alters interests, identities, and mutual perceptions of reliability and capability over time. The third, here termed an *environmental-contextual* approach, explains economic governance by reference to the larger sectoral and/or national socioeconomic environment within which governance relations evolve and function. While these three views are not mutually exclusive, and indeed may often represent diverse strands of particular accounts of network origins, they do define the major analytical starting points for most theories of network governance. In this section, we explore these views, emphasizing the importance of the environmental-contextual approach in explaining the relatively attenuated and uneven emergence of network governance in developing countries.[21]

Strategic Networking

When large firms establish associations of their major suppliers in order to encourage better communication, quality improvements, or technology sharing, and when firms enter into long-term joint venture, coproduction, or technology agreements, the resulting network structures are in large measure the direct outcomes of economic strategies which seek to encourage closer cooperation by establishing an institutional basis for information sharing, joint action, collective monitoring, and moral leverage for bringing recalcitrant firms or employees back into line with group standards. These cases may most usefully be understood by reference to strategic networking,[22] analogous to Williamson's transaction-cost approach to hierarchy in assuming that resourceful actors can themselves create governance structures supportive of their economic objectives. Hollingsworth and Streeck (1994: 276) similarly discuss the possibility that economic actors may seek to "reconstruct community" by forming trade, professional, and other business associations. Granovetter attributes the propensity of firms to "construct" networks and alliances largely to economic strategies and to a shared recognition of the utility of networks for resource mobilization (Granovetter 1994: 454). Powell and Smith-Doerr (1994) emphasize strategic considerations in their discussion of the development of business groups and alliances. And Cooper, Perry, LeHeron, and Hayward (1995) explicitly link network governance strategies among New Zealand horticulturalists to shared needs to respond flexibly to external shocks and end-buyer pressures.[23] In this volume, Deyo and Doner discuss the ways in which a small auto supplier firm has systematically created and utilized relations with other firms in order to access new technologies, markets, and capital sources. Similarly, Wong describes the ways in which U.S. disk drive producers construct Southeast Asian-based supplier networks.

Recent work by Sabel provides a particularly interesting, process-oriented view of the way in which economic actors can construct trust-based networks even in the absence of a supportive institutional environment. For Sabel (1994), actors seeking the benefits of collaboration but fearful of the perils of mutual vulnerability may institutionalize cooperation through agreement on constituted rules of engagement. In anticipation of continuing change in the goals, resource endowments, and interests of contracting parties, these rules seek to institutionalize a process of continuous joint problem solving and collective redefinition of production possibilities by empowering those directly involved in production processes to alter them collectively. These "discursive institutions," which provide a means of ongoing monitoring, and thus an alternative to (or basis for) trust in economic relations,[24] are illustrated by Cheng's account of the role of business associations in linking quota allocations to quality standards and industrial up-grading in Taiwan.

Emergence

Sabel's account overlaps with a closely related emergence approach, which seeks to understand network formation by reference to an iterative process of trust building through continuing interaction among economic actors. Game the-ory, a precursor to this approach, models the process whereby players make use of information from earlier trials in deciding whether to engage in subsequent moves which increase both vulnerability and opportunity for mutual gain (See Smith 1974; Axelrod 1984; Coleman 1994). Another precursor, social exchange theory, suggests ways in which social norms and stable social relations (e.g., of coopera-tion and power) emerge from ongoing interaction (Homans 1961; Blau 1964). In more recent work, Sabel (1994) emphasizes the importance of mutual monitoring for the evolution of trust-based cooperation among economic actors. Such moni-toring in fact comprises an essential condition for the deepening of cooperation over time as economic actors engage in initially shallow forms of cooperation which minimize mutual vulnerability, and then move to fuller cooperation in mat-ters of more vital self-interest as mutual confidence increases. Deyo and Doner note, for example, the prolonged period of confidence building which precedes the subcontracting of major projects by auto assemblers to suppliers in Thailand.

As noted earlier, of course, a path-dependency view would argue that initial commitment to a particular governance strategy may inhibit subsequent change of the sort, for example, anticipated by strategic or emergence approaches (Sos-kice 1999: 128–129). To return to the Hong Kong case, the negative influence of cost-focused, expedient, market-governed transactions might reinforce lack of trust and commitment among employees and firms, thus inhibiting the sorts of new relationships necessary for more dynamic strategies.[25]

The Environmental-Contextual View

Important though strategic and emergence approaches are for an understand-ing of network formation, they fail to differentiate adequately the circumstances within which networks emerge across space and time as, for example, between de-veloping and industrially more advanced countries. By contrast, a contextual ap-proach provides a foundation for just such comparisons, in part by suggesting how strategies and interactions are themselves influenced by the economic and so-ciopolitical environments in which firms operate. We begin by noting the network implications of variation in macroeconomic stability and factor markets, following which we turn to the impact of socioinstitutional, policy, and political/coalitional environments in developing countries.

Macroeconomic Conditions

Our focus on developing countries makes it incumbent to take account of the impact of uncertainty and risk associated with inflationary pressures, economic policy volatility, and other aspects of macroeconomic instability so often encountered in these countries and which undermine dynamic flexibility strategies in favor of speculative and short-term strategies. Posthuma (1997) notes, for example, that Brazil's economic instability has discouraged exclusive sourcing contracts between automobile assemblers and suppliers because of concerns about the possible bankruptcy of business partners. She goes on to note the more general disincentive posed by what she terms Brazil's "inflationary culture" for improvements in firm efficiency and productivity, long-term planning, and the assumption of new fixed costs, all essential elements for upgrading and industrial development. However, this relatively gloomy assessment contrasts with an opposed suggestion that flexible production, in the form of Japanese management techniques, is particularly appropriate for such conditions because of its enhanced potential for scaling back production in times of reduced demand (Hoffman and Kaplinsky 1998). This view is consistent with the assumption of "the superior capacity of flexibly specialized firms to accommodate changes in the level and composition of demand (Hirst and Zeitlin 1991: 223). The recent financial crisis in Southeast Asia offers an opportunity to assess these different perspectives. Deyo and Doner, for example, find that a Thai auto supplier was able to cope with the crisis through increased reliance on high-quality, innovative machine tool exports to new, non-Asian markets.

In part, the relationships among governance, flexibility, macroeconomic stability, and competitive success may depend on the degree to which firms have already adopted flexible strategies. Where such practices are weak or nonexistent, it may be difficult to create them under more volatile economic conditions. But other contextual factors, including especially labor factor markets and the sociocinstitutional environment, are important as well.

Labor Markets

Labor markets are an important determinant of the production and governance strategies of local firms. The impact of labor markets may be understood from the standpoint of labor supply as well as the institutional structures through which labor markets operate. We attend here to labor supply, reserving institutional questions for later discussion.

Our key concern is the impact of labor abundance and skill scarcity, conditions relatively typical of developing countries. Even in the face of pressures to move into more demanding product niches, a surplus of unskilled labor and lack of skilled workers are normally assumed to push firms toward price-based market strategies and minimal attention to training (Ruas et al. 1994). Firms obtain skilled workers by poaching from competitors rather than contributing to in-house or collective training schemes. This is precisely what has occurred in the Thai auto industry, forcing the firm described by Deyo and Doner to look to neighboring countries for skilled workers. And yet, as Michael Smitka's (1991) account of Japanese subcontracting suggests, the very scarcity of labor and skills may induce firms to establish employment practices and supplier linkages based on mutual commitment and personal obligation in order to retain skilled workers and suppliers. The resulting network structures may then enable firms to pursue the more dynamic strategies which such networks support. This is consistent with Hollingsworth and Boyer's (1997: 269) argument that flexible production strategies tend to benefit from rigid labor markets external to the firms and flexible labor markets internal to the firm. Whether they in fact do so depends in no small measure on the existence of institutional arrangements capable of coordinating labor market competition among firms.

Institutional Context

This brings us to the *institutional context*—the third major element in discussions of the environmental determinants of economic governance and competitive strategies. This literature starts with a conceptual distinction between two institutional levels: first, the social and institutional framework of governance within which economic transactions are directly embedded and, second, the broader socioinstitutional context within which this framework emerges and functions.[26] As noted below, the analytical linkage between these two institutional levels is typically defined by reference to the ways in which the larger social environment encourages or undercuts one or another governance configuration. Following in this tradition, Herrigel (1994) discusses the governance consequences of what he terms the industrial order, or "the social, political, and legal framework . . . that shapes the way that producers serving given product markets collectively define the legitimate boundaries of industrial practices . . . a framework that creates the conditions under which particular repertoires of governance mechanisms emerge and are employed" (97). Similarly, Soskice refers to the "framework of constraints and incentives set up by the national infrastructural institutions within which companies have to operate," and which determines "whether or not a company can develop appropriate relations with its employees and with other companies to sustain the patterns of work organization required for the product market and innovation strategy it wants to pursue" (Soskice 1994; Powell and Smith-Doerr 1994). Those working within such a perspective thus seek to specify the ways in which a variety of national or sectoral institutions interactively shape economic governance as well as the strategies and performance capabilities which flow from it. What then are some of these institutions?

Factor Market Institutions

Soskice (1999: 130–133) and other researchers document the influence of labor market and industrial relations institutions on company strategies and network structures. We have already noted Hollingsworth's suggestion that flexible production strategies tend to benefit from rigid labor markets external to the firms and flexible labor markets internal to the firm. Similarly, in their discussion of industrial relations systems in Germany and Sweden, Turner and Auer (1996: 233–257) argue that national codetermination rules and relatively strong labor movements have resulted in team-based production and labor-management cooperation in both countries.

Equally important are financial institutions, as in Soskice's suggestion that the need by German banks for a means of monitoring the creditworthiness of firms via the reputation of particular companies within contracting networks has given further impetus to interfirm cooperation. This observation is consistent with the more generally noted association of credit-based financial systems with cooperation and networks, and of capital-based systems with market governance (Zysman 1983; Rademakers 1997). In this volume, Deyo and Doner discuss the consequences for Thai industry of a weakness in factor market institutions, while Wong points to the more positive role of such institutions in Singapore.

Company Law

Company law directly influences relations among firms by proscribing or encouraging business groups and interfirm cooperation in matters of finance, marketing, and research and development. U.S. antitrust legislation, for example, has generally discouraged the sorts of cooperation found among firms in Germany and Japan, while at the same time encouraging mergers and vertical integration (Herrigel 1994; Soskice 1999: 111; Granovetter 1994). Williamson (1994) suggests in this regard an association between three types of contract law (classical, forbearance, and neoclassical) with corresponding types of governance (market, hierarchy, and "hybrids" respectively).

Sectoral Business Linkages

Sectoral business linkages provide another basis for economic networks. Such linkages, exemplified by business associations, employer federations, and professional societies, foster recurrent interaction, standard setting, mutual commitment, interfirm monitoring and regulation, and the provision of collective goods, all of which in turn encourage risk taking and collaboration in business dealings.[27] Cole's account (1989) of the introduction of production quality circles in Sweden and Japan, for example, stresses the lead role of employer associations in this process. Similarly, professional societies may encourage the sharing of information and R&D collaboration by sanctioning norms of confidentiality, reciprocity, and reliability among engineers and technicians (Powell and Smith-Doerr 1994). Wong's description of the Singapore disk drive case is especially illustrative in this regard: the industry's success is in part the result of collaborative efforts among foreign disk drive producers and suppliers, relations which in turn reflect the broader set of intercorporate institutions within Singapore as a whole.

What then explains the high level of collaboration in Singapore, or in Penang for that matter? Primordial loyalties, especially those based on kinship, ethnicity, and locality, may sometimes be important in providing a basis for trust and cooperation. Portes (1994:429–30), for example, shows how ethnicity may provide a basis for cooperation and access to resources. Similarly, Loury (1987) and Coleman (1994) have emphasized the ways in which membership in close-knit communities or informal social networks encourages investment in and mobilization of "social capital" for economic ends. And others (Thompson 1991; Granovetter 1994; Whitley 1992) have noted the ways in which community and group membership may foster trust and cooperation by embedding economic relations in a "moral economy" of shared identity, normative regulation, social sanctions (including threat of exclusion from group-based resources), and group monitoring.[28] That such identities may create a sociocultural foundation for economic networks is suggested in Cheng's study of Taiwan's footwear industry and Rasiah's work on ethnic Chinese networks in Penang's semiconductor industry.

But ascriptive networks may be developmental cul-de-sacs when and if they preclude access to the external resources and information which looser ties might permit. The challenge seems to be to achieve a balance between cohesion on the one hand and developmental openness on the other. This dilemma is similar to what Michael Bratton (1989: 415) has termed the tension between "solidarity and scale" and what Barbara Geddes (1994: 31) terms the "dual strategy" problem, in which members of a smaller group trust each other but not outsiders. What factors explain why some ethnic networks "work," as in Taiwan and Penang, while others tend to be either stifling or simply irrelevant, as in Malaysia's Kelang Valley or in Hong Kong? Here we stress the influence of political factors—the state and its coalitional bases.

State Institutions

State institutions play a significant role in virtually all accounts of the impact of the institutional environment on networks. Without necessarily accepting all assumptions of earlier "statist" accounts (e.g., Wade 1990; Weiss and Hobson 1995) of industrial organization and development, and despite the "destatization" of national economies under neoliberal reforms,[29] it is clear that states continue to have an impact on economic network formation, and indeed have assumed important *new* roles, less regulative and more facilitative, under market reforms (Block 1994). In some cases, the state role is an indirect one, for example that of influencing business groups, financial institutions, associations, and industrial relations practices. State officials can, in this regard, empower business associations to provide selective incentives necessary to achieve interfirm coordination relating to quality standards, R&D, labor practices, and infrastructure (Granovetter

1994; Maxfield and Schneider 1997; Doner and Ramsay 1997). In this volume, Lui and Chiu emphasize the importance of lack of state support for the weakness of interfirm relations in Hong Kong, while Cheng, Wong, and Rasiah describe government programs which have sought to create developmental "linkage" programs between large firms and their suppliers. Similarly, in the early 1990s, the Brazilian government organized Sectoral Chambers to create a forum for industrial negotiation and for discussion of economic policies and collective needs among auto firms and trade unions (Posthuma 1997). The chapters by Appelbaum and Smith, and by Wong, in fact point to explicit industrial district policies in South Korea and Singapore, respectively.

At a more general level, the facilitative role of the state may be understood as that of helping to resolve a number of impediments to collaboration. For example, state underwriting of industrial training programs, research institutes, or industrial parks, even where firms are themselves required to assist in funding them, may help to resolve relational problems regarding transaction-specific investments, the monitoring of benefits, and economic externalities by reducing the scope of hazardous collaboration required for particular joint activities.

Finally, it is important to note that despite growing interest in processes of economic globalization, most accounts of "state" governance continue to be framed at a national level of analysis. This remains the case despite suggestions by some that globalization may be associated with a partial bypassing of national state regulation by global regulative institutions on the one hand, and by local/regional institutions on the other (McMichael 1996: 134–142; also see Hollingsworth and Streeck 1994: 291–292; Crouch and Streeck 1997: 12–16). The literature on industrial districts and locality-based networks in particular suggests the possibility that "state" governance roles are increasingly devolving to local government (see Doner and Hershberg 1999), a position consistent with Rasiah's discussion of the role of local government in the development of Penang's electronics industry.

Macropolitics and Coalitions

If state policy is important for economic governance, it is important to understand differences among states in both policies and institutional outcomes. This volume suggests that coalitional factors are one important factor in explaining this variation (Soskice 1999: 130–133),[30] relating particularly to the relative strength of associational ties among small and large Asian firms. Rasiah's chapter in fact constitutes a natural experiment showing how the political prominence of ethnic Chinese in Penang, in contrast to their position in other Malaysian states, fostered associational linkages among Chinese machine tool firms on the one hand and between small and medium-sized enterprises (SMEs) and transnational electronics firms on the other.

Differences between SME-dominated producer chains in Taiwan and Korea's *chaebol*-dominated interfirm linkages provide an even more striking contrast, and one equally attributable to coalitional factors. Whereas in Korea state policies advantaged a handful of large firms and their associations, in Taiwan tax laws, labor provisions, financial policies, and support for associations were granted across-the-board and actually provided incentives to limit firm size (Deyo, Doner, and Fields 1993: 10).[31] Why do we find this difference between two similarly "strong" states? Part of the reason is ideological: the primary goal of the nationalist Chinese regime since its defeat on the mainland has been to strengthen Taiwan militarily and politically by fostering economic development under conditions of price stability and relative economic equality. But the ideological motive was reinforced by an ethnic-based division of labor that put virtually all political power in the hands of the minority mainlanders and left the private sector open to the local Taiwanese majority. While this mitigated Taiwanese opposition to political subjugation by providing the Taiwanese with economic outlets, it also raised concerns among the political elite that local economic power could be translated into political power. Learning from its defeat on the mainland, and as an exogenous minority regime, the nationalist state sought legitimacy neither from a landed aristocracy nor from a coterie of privileged capitalists, but rather from a multitude of small producers and smallholders who benefited from the state's "growth with equity" policies. This importance of coalitional factors is clear as well in Rasiah's description of the Penang case, where local officials were responsive to the needs of machine tool makers in part because of the importance of these firms for generating employment and exports, and in part because of shared ethnic ties.

Corporate Linkages

Our emphasis up to now—and indeed the focus of most of this volume's cases—has been on institutions at the national or subnational level. Yet these institutions operate within and are themselves influenced by a set of international corporate linkages. Demand by international buyers for high-quality, fashion-responsive products, for example, may favor success among (and select on) network-configured, flexible local firms, as suggested by Cheng in his description of Taiwan's footwear industry (for a general discussion, see Gereffi 1994). And international producers may establish local subsidiaries which themselves influence local production networks through their direct participation as well as through the organization of local supplier firms into supplier groups. Doner, for example, has noted the facilitating and developmental role of supplier clubs organized by Japanese automobile assemblers in Southeast Asia (Doner 1991). Conversely, it has been argued by some (e.g., Borrus and Zysman 1997) that U.S. firms exhibit greater openness to host country participation than do their Japanese counterparts, and are thus better suited to take advantage of nimble Chinese firms in East and Southeast Asia. This would help to explain, for example, the dominance of U.S. firms in the electronics cases described in this volume by Wong and Rasiah.

We stress the importance of understanding how international corporate linkages interact with domestic institutions and local strategies in explaining cross-national variation in the degree to which local industries achieve success in moving into high-value niches in global commodity chains. Such interaction is explored in this volume by Rasiah, who contrasts the semiconductor industries in two Malaysian states, by Wong in his treatment of the sources of success in Singapore's disk drive sector, and by Cheng in his discussion of Taiwan's success in sports shoes.

A Final Note on Trust

The different approaches to network growth suggest somewhat different views of the sources of "trust," a core concept in the network literature. An environmental context position emphasizes the importance of prior normative or associational commitments (e.g., kinship, community ties, professional associations, legal regulation) for the creation either of trust or of institutional safeguards which provide alternatives to trust. A strategic networking approach asserts that economic actors can themselves institute trust-enhancing normative orders. And an emergence approach sees continuing economic collaboration as itself the source of cumulative trust building. Our understanding of the way these various sources of trust together shape governance institutions will depend on greater attention to longitudinal, processual, and comparative case studies of the emergence, evolution, and functioning of economic networks in specific sectoral and national contexts.

SOCIODEVELOPMENTAL CONSEQUENCES OF NETWORK GOVERNANCE: DOMESTIC SMES

It was noted at the outset that one of our initial motivations in embarking on this study was the promise implicit in the network literature of an economic model which combined equity with growth, and which offered a socially beneficial path to economic competitiveness. A stylized depiction of that literature suggests a somewhat optimistic view of the social and political possibilities in economic association based on an assumed trust and cooperation among economic actors who are relatively equally endowed in resources and who willingly enter into economic relations which are at once equitable and economically dynamic. Our earlier discussion of issues of power and exploitation at a minimum suggests caution in making such optimistic assumptions.

While the possibilities for equitable development are not directly addressed in this volume, the chapters do provide a useful vantage point for addressing this issue through an understanding of the sociodevelopmental implications of network governance for SMEs. While SMEs are at the very heart of the network formations discussed by the authors in this volume, just as important, they define critical social and developmental ramifications of those networks. The *social* importance of SMEs follows in part from the large percentage of workers employed and self-employed in this sector across the region. It follows as well from the growing tendency of large firms to outsource production to local suppliers (thus further expanding SME employment), and a corresponding growth in the informal sector resulting from both outsourcing and, most recently, the Asian economic crisis. Finally, SMEs are an important conduit for distribution of the economic gains from industrial and commercial growth, including those to women, minorities, and indigenous peoples. The *developmental* importance of SMEs derives from their numerical preponderance among industrial firms, their significance as a large portion of GDP, and their role in fostering domestic entrepreneurship, providing a supplier infrastructure for international firms and tapping the economic resources and synergies latent in Asian social organization and culture.

What then are some possible links between networks and SME development, particularly among the domestic SME supplier companies that are a focus of much of this volume? First should be noted an observation by some that the literature on networks and flexible production has turned a blind eye to the more exploitative and exclusionary aspects of flexibility, including in this context the "low road," exploitative, sweatshop-like supplier chains of some large firms (Curry 1993: 118). In response to this quite reasonable assertion, we offer four observations, respectively relating to a possible misuse of the term "network," the institutional and strategic dualism of many supplier chains, resource asymmetries within network relations themselves, and the antidevelopmental tendencies of closed, "parochial" networks.

First, the exploitative, sweatshop-sourcing patterns so often discussed in the critical literature on networks are in fact as often characterizable as instances of arms-length, low-trust *market* governance supportive of largely static, numerical flexibility performance capacities as they are of network governance relations per se. The negative SME outcomes engendered by such market-governed supplier relations are emphasized in the chapters by Lui and Chiu and by Appelbaum and Smith.

Second, there is abundant evidence suggesting that supplier chains often present a marked dualism between networked firms and workers in core production processes on the one hand and market-integrated actors outside those core processes on the other. To the extent that network governance enhances the profitability and growth of firms, creates more business for suppliers, and induces larger firms to support supplier development, network participation brings obvious benefits. But having said this, it is important to note the obvious: that networks have boundaries. Thus, a balanced assessment of the social impact of network structures must take into account actors both within and outside those structures, or alternately, must seek to understand how network location and centrality influences outcomes (Powell and Smith-Doerr 1994: 376). Taking this argument a step farther, it should be noted that market-governed supplier relations may be associated not only with exclusion from network benefits. As often, location in the market periphery of networks may actually diminish SME advancement opportunities through exploitation and domination. Such a possibility is suggested by dualistic accounts of economic structure which assume functional interdependencies between core and peripheral industries.[32] The exploitative lower-tier supplier chains which eventuate from such strategies may be seen as compensating for the high costs of more dynamic strategies among core production processes and high-tier suppliers (Sako 1994: 34). The resulting dualism has been noted in studies of Japanese supplier relations, some pointing to a stark dualism in conditions of employment and developmental support across work processes and support firms. Other studies acknowledge dualism, but dispute the view that Japanese lower-tier SME suppliers are becoming technologically weaker, less organized, and poorer (McMillan 1992). Just as state-mandated labor standards cushion all workers from the more severe abuses associated with cost-focused strategies, requirements in areas such as local content and technology transfer that are placed on large firms in their dealings with local suppliers may moderate network exclusivity and the extent of developmental dualism.

Third, to the extent exploitation does characterize *networked* supplier relations, it sometimes reflects the sorts of resource asymmetries and associated tendencies toward verticality discussed earlier. It was noted that even where interfirm relations assume such "network"-like characteristics as stability, multiplexity, open-endedness, and particularism, they may nonetheless be relatively vertical in nature, especially where they are organized by a few large, resourceful firms. Vertically organized supplier chains, as noted by Appelbaum and Smith, position more resourceful actors to structure economic networks to their own advantage and to appropriate for themselves a disproportionate share of the benefits of collaboration. The extent of exploitation, of course, is moderated by several factors. One involves the market-driven tendency toward mutual vulnerability resulting from asset-specific investment driven by "buy" rather than "make" decisions. As illustrated in the electronics and footwear industries (Wong, Rasiah, and Cheng, this volume), some multinational firms have opted to rely on suppliers for key components due to the combination of rapid product life cycles and high costs of capital equipment. The degree to which this tendency in fact strengthens suppliers may depend on a second factor noted earlier—namely, the fewer the available suppliers, the greater is supplier leverage (Storper and Harrison 1991). A further moderating factor is recognition on the part of dominant firms of the need for some degree of trust and mutuality as a condition for network functioning. Paternalistic relations may, in this regard, provide a culturally available "solution" to the inherent tension between verticality and network relations.

It is necessary, of course, to adopt a dynamic, emergence view of networks and their social outcomes, one which highlights the ways in which economic governance patterns and SME developmental possibilities change over time.

For example, to the extent international firms rely increasingly on local suppliers' participation in process engineering, quality control, and even product development, initial resource asymmetries may diminish over time (Sako 1992),[33] thus enabling local SME's to surmount the impediments to upward mobility rooted in market, capital, and technology dependences on international firms. Deyo and Doner note the increased bargaining power afforded a Thai auto supplier by virtue of its growing capacity to produce machine tools outside the competence of assemblers. Conversely, however, Nadvi and Schmitz (1994) note the tendencies within initially relatively egalitarian industrial clusters toward increasing vertical differentiation as some firms benefit cumulatively over time from opportunities not available to other firms. State SME assistance programs, of course, may moderate such a tendency by reducing the technology, market, and capital dependency of small supplier firms on corporate customers, thus enhancing their bargaining position vis-à-vis larger firms.

Finally, network structures can themselves sometimes restrict and suppress the developmental potential of SMEs in ways which confine production to low-value, cost-focused, "sweatshop"-like activities. This unfortunate outcome is related to two further characteristics of networks: closure and content (Granovetter 1994: 465). Closure, and associated lack of internetwork overlap, refers to the extent to which actors become locked into parochial network structures which deny them access to outside information and resources. The question of economic "lock-in" is frequently raised in the context of discussions of ethnic- and kinship-based economic networks (Powell and Smith-Doerr 1994; Portes 1994). As noted earlier, such a possibility is often taken further to suggest that networks which are too closely tied to and encompassed by kinship or other primordial identities may present developmental cul-de-sacs inasmuch as they preclude access to the external resources and information which looser ties might permit (Granovetter 1994). From the standpoint of SMEs, the successful management of the tension between solidarity and scale may require the strategic utilization and transformation of preexisting forms of communal solidarity to create networks supportive of dynamic economic strategies. Alternately, such preexisting solidarities may provide the basis for network forms which through ongoing interaction subsequently evolve into professional and economic relations. In either case, such evolution, if taken too far, may prove self-defeating to the extent that solidarity gives way to opportunistic (strategic) networking.

The problem of closure is in turn associated with that of content. To understand the outcomes of networks for either economic performance or social equity, it is necessary to know what types of relations are involved and what sorts of information and resources flow through them (Powell and Smith-Doerr 1994). Friendship and kinship relations may differ from professional networks, for example, in the extent to which they encourage learning and innovation. Learning and innovation, in turn, may destabilize and transform existing network structures.

NOTES

We are grateful to Jillian Green for her excellent research assistance in the preparation of this introduction, as well as to Alasdair Bowie, Marc Jones, Alvaro Diaz, and Gary Gereffi for helpful comments on an earlier draft.

1. For earlier thoughtful works addressing these issues, see especially Kaplinsky, with Posthuma (1994), Nadvi and Schmitz (1994), and Rabellotti (1994).

2. As part of its landmark "Asian Miracle" study, the World Bank stressed the openness of the East Asian economies measured by the share of exports plus imports in GDP. See World Bank (1993). On the AFTA, see for example, Sirithaveeporn (1999).

3. For discussion of these pressures, see Friedman (1988), also James Womack, Daniel T. Jones, and Daniel Roos (1990).

4. ISO and QSO quality standards may often be required not only for access to particular markets, but as conditions for procuring supplier contracts from other firms.

5. As is reflected in our title, we prefer to organize and frame the discussion by reference to the broad concept of "flexible production," rather than "flexible specialization" in order to capture the *diversity* of technology and market pressures facing firms and the corresponding variety of firm-level responses to those pressures. On "flexible specialization," see the pioneering work of Piore and Sabel (1984). For an argument against the use of flexible specialization as an ideal type, see Zysman (1997).

6. On cost and quality pressures in the auto industry, see Humphrey (1998).

7. On pressures in the disk drive industry for rapid ramp-up and time to market, see McKendrick (1997).

8. In principle, technology and increasing returns can facilitate such capacity. Continuing technology changes, including the availability of more flexible technologies (e.g., CAD/CAM and new communications systems) have supported firm-level efforts to increase organizational flexibility while at the same time forcing companies to meet the competitive challenge of other companies that have already begun to use these new technologies. Similarly, the returns from export markets potentially allow firms to write off innovation costs over more units, thus reducing time between innovations and stimulating investment in multipurpose personnel and equipment capable of meeting changing market pressures.

9. For a similar case, concluding that technological success was the result of "the astute use of . . . relationships with raw material suppliers, and other business contacts," see Girvan and Marcelle (1990).

10. A number of writers place primary emphasis on business-government relations as the core element of economic governance. We here follow a second approach which centers on private sector institutions and views state institutions and policies as elements of the environment within which such governance institutions function.

11. Thus, Soskice (1999) argues that uncoordinated "liberal market economies" such as that of the United States confer real advantages in radical innovation as opposed to incremental changes in existing industries.

12. This distinction is drawn from Colclough and Tolbert (1992). Compare the related distinction between static and dynamic efficiencies as discussed by Storper and Harrison (1991).

13. Cf. Chandler's argument (see Granovetter 1994) regarding the important shift from "attempting to achieve market control through contractual cooperation to achieving it through administrative efficiency."

14. These problems are further discussed below, in the context of the impact of power differentials on cooperation.

15. In more recent writing, Williamson (1991) cites conditions under which hybrids are viable over longer periods of time. Chandler (1990) argues that business groups are transitional and unstable, and generally give way to large, integrated firms.

16. For discussion of the systemic nature of economic flexibility, see Alter and Hage (1993). Also see Hoffman and Kaplinsky's (1988) discussion of what they term "systemofacture."

17. Nadvi and Schmitz (1994). Clusters are typically defined as geographical/sectoral concentrations of industrial activity with varying degrees of cooperative behavior.

18. On the need for fuller attention to alternative network forms of governance in the Asian economies, see Moon and Prasad (1998) and Doner (1991).

19. One functional equivalent would be Korean "contests," in which subsidies are provided in exchange for success in export markets.

20. The role of government agencies is discussed separately below.

21. This emphasis follows from an assumption that strategic and interactional/emergence accounts of network formation would be less likely to differentiate developed from developing countries than would an account centering on socioeconomic contextual differences.

22. This view is causally more defensible than closely related functionalist explanations, which seek to explain business networks by reference to their positive outcomes for economic efficiency or flexibility.

23. Relatedly, Williamson (1991) criticizes "culturalist" interpretations of governance as failing to acknowledge the ways in which culture is itself continually influenced by the economic strategies and interests of key actors.

24. Lui (1996) notes a danger in pushing a strategic approach too far: a tendency to reduce networking to purely calculative economizing, thus in effect denying that networks are socially embedded at all.

25. For a fuller treatment of the issue of path dependency, see Hollingsworth and Boyer (1997).

26. Thus Commons (1934) distinguishes the *institutional* environment, or the "set of fundamental political, social, and legal ground rules that establishes the basis for production, exchange, and distribution," from economic institutional *arrangements*, a distinction followed by Williamson (1991) in his reference to institutional environments on the one hand, and governance institutions on the other.

27. While business associations may be viewed either as part of the environmental context or as an element of interfirm governance itself, it may be most useful to view them as mediating between governance and environment insofar as they function to create a policy and institutional environment supportive of the needs of affiliated firms.

28. Whitley (1992) characterizes these as "background" contextual factors, to be distinguished from other, more "proximate" influences (e.g., industrial relations and financial institutions, business-government relations, educational institutions, and the like). But given the direct bearing of kinship and ethnicity on communally embedded firms such as those discussed by Portes and others, we have chosen not to pursue this distinction.

29. See Haggard and Kauffman (1995) on the negative impacts of economic liberalization on state capacity to influence economic transactions and outcomes.

30. Warren (1994), for example, argues that the "Third Italy's" vaunted social capital is in part the result of an alignment of interests in which the ruling Communist Party has cultivated a base of support among local SMEs against the Christian Democrats and their large corporate constituents. On the coalitional bases of Japan's SME associations, see Calder (1988).

31. For a useful study of Korea's association of large textile firms, see Eui-Young Kim (1993). On the importance of associations in Taiwan, see Kuo Cheng-Tian (1995).

32. Portes's work on informal sectors (1994) suggests precisely such a possibility, as larger firms seek to protect themselves and their core production processes and workers from costly state regulation through increased reliance on unregulated informal-sector suppliers.

33. Also see Ruas et al. (1994) on the gradual development of cooperative links between auto companies and their suppliers in Brazil.

BIBLIOGRAPHY

Alter, Catherine, and Michael Hage. 1993. *Organizations Working Together: Coordination in Interorganizational Networks.* Newbury Park, Calif.: Sage.
Amsden, Alice. 1989. *Asia's Next Giant: South Korea and Late Industrialization.* New York: Oxford University Press.
Aoki, Masahiko, ed. 1984. *The Economic Analysis of the Japanese Firm.* Amsterdam: North-Holland.
Axelrod, Robert. 1984. *The Evolution of Cooperation.* Cowles Commission Monograph 12. New York: Wiley.
Bazan, Luiza, and Hubert Schmitz. 1997. "Social Capital and Export Growth: An Industrial Community in Southern Brazil." Occasional Paper. Copenhagen: Copenhagen Business School, Department of Intercultural Communication and Business.
Blau, Peter. 1964. *Exchange and Power in Social Life.* New York: Harper.
Block, Fred. 1994. "The Roles of the State in the Economy." In *The Handbook of Economic Sociology,* edited by Neil J. Smelser and Richard Swedberg, 691–710. Princeton: Princeton University Press.
Borrus, Michael, and John Zysman. 1997. "Wintelism and the Changing Terms of Global Competition." Berkeley Roundtable on the International Economy Working Paper 96cb.
Boyer, Robert, and J. Rogers Hollingsworth. 1997. "From National Embeddedness to Spatial and Institutional Nestedness." In *Contemporary Capitalism: The Embeddedness of Institutions,* edited by J. Rogers Hollingsworth and Robert Boyer. New York: Cambridge University Press.
Bratton, Michael. 1989. "Beyond the State: Civil Society and Associational Life in Africa." *World Politics* 41, no. 3: 407–430.
Calder, Kent. 1988. *Crisis and Compensation: Public Policy and Political Stability in Japan, 1949–1986.* Princeton: Princeton University Press.
Chandler, Alfred D. 1977. *The Visible Hand: The Managerial Revolution in America.* Cambridge, Mass.: Harvard University Press.
———. 1990. *Scale and Scope: The Dynamics of Industrial Capitalism.* Cambridge, Mass.: Harvard University Press.

Coase, Ronald H. 1937. "The Nature of the Firm." *Economica* 4: 386–405.

Cohen, Stephen S., and John Zysman. 1987. *Manufacturing Matters: The Myth of the Post-Industrial Economy*. New York: Basic.

Colclough, Glenna, and Charles M. Tolbert. 1992. *Work in the Fast Lane: Flexibility, Divisions of Labor and Inequality in High-Tech Industries*. Albany: SUNY Press.

Cole, Robert E. 1989. *Strategies for Learning: Small-Group Activities in American, Japanese and Swedish Industry*. Berkeley: University of California Press.

Coleman, James. 1994. "A Rational Choice Perspective on Economic Sociology." In *The Handbook of Economic Sociology*, edited by Neil J. Smelser and Richard Swedberg, 166–180. Princeton: Princeton University Press.

Commons, John R. 1934. *Institutional Economics*. Madison: University of Wisconsin Press.

Cooper, Ian, Martin Perry, Richard LeHeron, and David Hayward. 1995. Business Networks and Exporting. Occasional Paper No. 31, Department of Geography, University of Auckland.

Crouch, Colin, and Wolfgang Streeck, eds. 1997. *Political Economy of Modern Capitalism*. Thousand Oaks, Calif.: Sage.

Curry, James. 1993. "The Flexibility Fetish." *Capital and Class* 50 (Summer): 99–127.

Davis, Lance E., and Douglass C. North. 1971. *Institutional Change and American Economic Growth*. Cambridge: Cambridge University Press.

Deyo, Frederic, ed. 1996. *Social Reconstructions of the World Automobile Industry*. London: Macmillan.

Deyo, Frederic C., Richard Doner, and Karl Fields. 1993. "Industrial Governance in East and Southeast Asia." Paper presented at the Social Science Research Council Workshop on Industrial Governance and Labor Flexibility in Comparative Perspective in September, New York.

Doner, Richard F. 1991. "Explaining the Politics of Economic Growth in Southeast Asia." *The Journal of Asian Studies* 50, no. 4: 818–849.

Doner, Richard F., and Eric Hershberg. 1999. "Flexible Production and Political Decentralization: Elective Affinities in the Pursuit of Competitiveness?" *Studies in Comparative and International Development*. (Spring): 45–82.

Doner, Richard F., and Ansil Ramsay. 1997. "Competitive Clientelism and Economic Governance: The Case of Thailand." In *Business and the State in Developing Countries*, edited by Sylvia Maxfield and Ben Ross Schneider, 237–276. Ithaca, N.Y.: Cornell University Press.

Dore, Ronald. 1983. "Goodwill and the Spirit of Market Capitalism." *British Journal of Sociology* 34: 459–482.

Fleury, Alfonso. 1995. "Quality and Productivity in the Competitive Strategies of Brazilian Industrial Enterprises." *World Development* 23, no. 1: 73–85.

Friedman, David. 1988. *The Misunderstood Miracle*. Ithaca, N.Y.: Cornell University Press.

Geddes, Barbara. 1994. *Politician's Dilemma: Building State Capacity in Latin America*. Berkeley: University of California Press.

Gereffi, Gary. 1994. "The Organization of Buyer-Driven Global Commodity Chains: How U.S. Retailers Shape Overseas Production Networks." In *Commodity Chains and Global Capitalism*, edited by Gary Gereffi and Miguel Korzeniewicz, 95–122. Westport, Conn.: Praeger.

Gereffi, Gary, Miguel Korzeniewicz, and Roberto P. Korzeniewicz. 1994. "Introduction: Global Commodity Chains." In *Commodity Chains and Global Capitalism*, edited by Gary Gereffi and Miguel Korzeniewicz, 1–14. Westport, Conn: Praeger.

Girvan, Norman, and Gillian Marcelle. 1990. "Overcoming Technological Dependency: The Case of Electric Arc (Jamaica) Ltd.: A Small Firm in a Small Developing Country." *World Development* 18, no. 1: 91–107.

Granovetter, Mark. 1973. "The Strength of Weak Ties." *American Journal of Sociology* 78: 1360–1380.

———. "Business Groups." 1994. In *The Handbook of Economic Sociology*, edited by Neil J. Smelser and Richard Swedberg, 453–475. Princeton: Princeton University Press.

Haggard, Stephen, and Robert Kaufman. *The Political Economy of Democratic Transitions*. Princeton: Princeton University Press.

Hamilton, Gary. 1999. "Asian Business Networks in Transition: or, What Alan Greenspan Does Not Know about the Asian Business Crisis." In *The Politics of the Asian Economic Crisis*, edited by T. J. Pempel. Ithaca, N.Y.: Cornell University Press.

Hamilton, Gary, and Nicole Woolsey Biggart. 1988. "Market, Culture, and Authority: A Comparative Analysis of Management and Organization in the Far East." *American Journal of Sociology* 94, Supplement S: 52–94.

Herrigel, Gary. 1994. "Industry as a Form of Order: A Comparison of the Historical Development of the Machine Tool Industries in the United States and Germany." In *Governing Capitalist Economies*, edited by J. Rogers Hollingsworth, Wolfgang Streeck and R. C. Schmitter, 97–128. New York: Oxford University Press.

Hill, Richard Child, and Kuniko Fujita. 1996. "Japanese Production Networks and Flexible Manufacturing: Matsushita in Southeast Asia." Paper presented at a conference on Economic Governance and Flexible Production in Asia. National Tsing Hua University, Taiwan.

Hirst, Paul, and Jonathan Zeitlin. 1991. "Flexible Specialization versus Post-Fordism: Theory, Evidence, and Policy Implications." *Economy and Society* 20, no. 1: 1–56.

Hoffman, Kurt, and Raphael Kaplinsky. 1988. *Driving Force: The Global Restructuring of Technology, Labor, and Investment in the Automobile and Components Industries*. Boulder, Colo.: Westview.

Hollingsworth, J. Rogers, and Robert Boyer, eds. 1997. *Contemporary Capitalism: The Embeddedness of Institutions*. Cambridge: Cambridge University Press.

Hollingsworth, J. Rogers, Philippe C. Schmitter, and Wolfgang Streeck. 1994. "Capitalism, Sectors, Institutions, and Performance." In *Governing Capitalist Economies*, edited by J. Rogers Hollingsworth, Philippe C. Schmitter, and Wolfgang Streeck, 3–16. New York: Oxford University Press.

Hollingsworth, J. Rogers, and Wolfgang Streeck. 1994. "Countries and Sectors: Concluding Remarks on Performance, Convergence, and Competitiveness." In *Governing Capitalist Economies*, edited by J. Rogers Hollingsworth, Wolfgang Streeck, and R. C. Schmitter, 270–300. New York: Oxford University Press.

Homans, George. 1961. *Social Behavior: Its Elementary Forms*. New York: Harcourt Brace.

Humphrey, John. 1998. "Assembler-Supplier Relations in the Auto Industry: Globalisation and National Development." Sussex, England: Institute of Development Studies, University of Sussex.

Jackson, Karl D. 1999. "Introduction." In *Asian Contagion: The Causes and Consequences of a Financial Crisis*, edited by Karl Jackson. Boulder, Colo.: Westview.

Kaplinsky, Raphael with Anne Posthuma. 1994. *Easternisation: The Spread of Japanese Management Techniques to Developing Countries*. Portland, Ore.: Frank Cass and the UN University Press.

Kim, Eui-Young. 1993. "The Developmental State and the Politics of Business Interest Associations: The Case of the Textile Industry." *Pacific Focus* 8, no. 2: 31–60.

Kotha, Suresh. 1995. "Mass Customization: Implementing the Emerging Paradigm for Competitive Advantage." *Strategic Management Journal* 16: 21–42.

Kuo Cheng-Tian. 1995. *Global Competitiveness and Industrial Growth in Taiwan and the Philippines.* Pittsburgh: University of Pittsburgh Press.

Levy, Brian, and Wen-Jeng Kuo. 1991. "The Strategic Orientations of Firms and the Performance of Korea and Taiwan in Frontier Industries: Lessons from Comparative Case Studies of Keyboard and Personal Computer Assembly." *World Development* 19, no. 4: 363–374.

Loury, Glenn. 1987. "Why Should We Care about Group Inequality?" *Social Philosophy and Policy* 5: 249–271.

Lui, Tai-lok. 1996. "Trust and Chinese Business Behaviour." Paper presented at the 8th International Conference on Socio–Economics in July, Université de Genève, Switzerland.

Luong, Hy Van. 1996. "The Strength of Vietnamese Industrial Fabric: Institutional Mechanisms of Firm Competitiveness in the Textile and Garment Industries of Vietnam." Paper presented at a conference on Economic Governance and Flexible Production at National Tsing Hua University, Taiwan.

Maxfield, Sylvia, and Ben Ross Schneider. 1997. "Business, the State, and Economic Performance in Developing Countries." In *Business and the State in Developing Countries,* edited by Sylvia Maxfield and Ben Ross Schneider, 3–35. Ithaca, New York: Cornell University Press.

McKendrick, David. 1997. "Sustaining Competitive Advantage in Global Industries: Technological Change and Foreign Assembly in the Hard Disk Drive Industry." Data Storage Industry Globalization Project, Report #97–06, University of California, San Diego.

McKeown, Timothy J. 1999. "The Global Economy, Post-Fordism, and Trade Policy in Advanced Capitalist States." In *Continuity and Change in Contemporary Capitalism,* edited by Herbert Kitschelt, Peter Lange, Gary Marks, and John D. Stephens. New York: Cambridge University Press.

McMichael, Philip. 1996. *Development and Social Change: A Global Perspective.* Thousand Oaks, Calif: Pine Forge Press.

McMillan, John. 1992. *Games, Strategies, and Managers.* New York: Oxford University Press.

Metcalfe, J. S. 1995. "Technology Systems and Technology Policy in an Evolutionary Framework." *Cambridge Journal of Economics* 19: 25–46.

Moon, Chung-In, and Rashemi Prasad. 1998. "Networks, Politics and Institutions." In *Beyond the Developmental State: East Asia's Political Economies Reconsidered,* edited by Steve Chan, Cal Clark, and Danny Lam, 9–24. New York: St. Martin's.

Nadvi, Khalid, and Hubert Schmitz. 1994. *Industrial Clusters in Less Developed Countries: Review of Experiences and Research Agenda.* Sussex/IDS Discussion Paper 339.

Piore, Michael J., and Charles F. Sabel. 1984. *The Second Industrial Divide: Possibilities for Prosperity.* New York: Basic.

Pongvutitham Achara. 1999. "Textile Agencies Ready for Progress." *Nation* (Bangkok), 10 May.

Poon, Teresa. 1994. "Comparing the Subcontracting System: Towards a Synthesis in Explaining Development in Hong Kong and Taiwan." Working Paper No. 38. Melbourne, Australia: Asia Research Centre, Murdoch University.

Portes, Alejandro. 1994. "The Informal Economy and Its Paradoxes." In *The Handbook of Economic Sociology*, edited by Neil J. Smelser and Richard Swedberg, 426–449. Princeton: Princeton University Press.

Posthuma, Anne. 1997. "Shifting Policy Regimes and Industrial Renewal in Brazil: Vestiges of Import Substitution and Impacts of Liberalization." Paper presented at the seminar "Flexible Production and New Institutionalities in Latin America" in September, Rio de Janeiro.

Powell, Walter W., and Laurel Smith-Doerr. 1994. "Networks and Economic Life." In *The Handbook of Economic Sociology*, edited by Neil J. Smelser and Richard Swedberg, 368–402. Princeton: Princeton University Press.

Rabellotti, Roberta. 1994. "Is there an 'Industrial District' Model?: Footwear Districts in Italy and Mexico Compared." Unpublished manuscript. Sussex, England: Institute of Development Studies.

Rademakers, Martijn F. L. 1997. "The Institutional Embeddedness of Inter-Firm Relationships in Indonesia." Occasional Paper, Copenhagen Business School, Department of Intercultural Communication and Management.

Romer, Paul M. 1994. "The Origins of Endogenous Growth." *Journal of Economic Perspectives* 8, no. 1: 3–22.

Ruas, Roberto, Leda Gitahy, Flavio Rabelo, and Elaine Di Diego Antunes. 1994. "Inter-firm Relations, Collective Efficiency and Employment in Two Brazilian Clusters." Technology and Employment Programme Working Paper, International Labour Office, Geneva.

Sabel, Charles F. 1986. "Changing Models of Economic Efficiency and Their Implications for Industrialization in the Third World." In *Development, Democracy, and the Art of Trespassing*, edited by Alejandro Foxley, Michael S. McPherson, and Guillermo O'Donnell, 27–55. Notre Dame, Ind.: University of Notre Dame Press.

———. 1994. "Learning by Monitoring: The Institutions of Economic Development." In *The Handbook of Economic Sociology*, edited by Neil Smelser and Richard Swedberg, 137–165. Princeton: Princeton University Press.

Sako, Mari. 1992. *Prices, Quality and Trust: Interfirm Relations in Britain and Japan.* Cambridge: Cambridge University Press.

———. 1994. "Neither Markets nor Hierarchies: A Comparative Study of the Printed Circuit Board Industry in Britain and Japan." In *Governing Capitalist Economies*, edited by J. Rogers Hollingsworth, Philippe Schmitter, and Wolfgang Streeck, 17–42. New York: Oxford University Press.

Schmitz, Hubert. 1992. "Industrial Districts: Model and Reality in Baden-Württemberg." In *Industrial Districts and Local Economic Regeneration*, edited by F. Pyke and W. Sengenberger. Geneva: ILO, International Institute for Labour Studies.

Scott, A. J., and D. P. Angel. 1988. "The Global Assembly-Operations of US Semiconductor Firms: A Geographical Analysis." *Environment and Planning* 20: 1047–1067.

Sirithaveeporn, Wichit. 1999. "Need to Lift Product Quality under Afta Tariff Cuts May Open Market to Attack." *Bangkok Post*, May 12.

Smelser, Neil J., and Richard Swedberg, eds. 1994. *The Handbook of Economic Sociology.* Princeton: Princeton University Press.

Smith, John Maynard. 1974. *Models in Ecology.* Cambridge: Cambridge University Press.

Smitka, Michael J. 1991. *Competitive Ties: Subcontracting in the Japanese Automotive Industry.* New York: Columbia University Press.

Soskice, David. 1994. "Innovation Strategies of Companies: A Comparative Institutional Explanation of Cross-Country Differences." In *Institutionenvergleich und Institutionendynamik*, edited by Wolfgang Zapf and Meinolf Dierkes. WZB Jahrbuch. Berlin: Sigma.

———. 1999. "Divergent Production Regimes: Coordinated and Uncoordinated Market Economies in the 1980s and 1990s." In *Continuity and Change in Contemporary Capitalism*, edited by Herbert Kitschelt, Peter Lange, Gary Marks, and John D. Stephens. New York: Cambridge University Press.

Storper, Michael, and Bennett Harrison. 1991. "Flexibility, Hierarchy and Regional Development: The Changing Structure of Industrial Production Systems and Their Forms of Governance in the 1990s." *Research Policy* 20: 407–422.

Tansathitikorn, Suphat. 1999. "Increasing Thailand's Overall Competitiveness a Big Challenge Now." *Nation* (Bangkok), January.

Thompson, Grahame. 1991. "Networks." In *Markets, Hierarchies and Networks: The Coordination of Social Life*, edited by Grahame Thompson, Jennifer Frances, Rosalind Levacic, and Jeremy Mitchell. Thousand Oaks Calif.: Sage.

Turner, Lowell, and Peter Auer. 1996. "A Diversity of New Work Organization: Human-Centered, Lean, and In-Between." In *Social Reconstructions of the World Automobile Industry*, edited by Frederic C. Deyo, 233–257. Houndsmills, England: Macmillan Press.

Wachter, Michael L., and Oliver E. Williamson. 1978. "Obligational Markets and the Mechanics of Inflation." *The Bell Journal of Economics* 9, no. 2: 549–571.

Wade, Robert. 1990. *Governing the Market: Economic Theory and the Role of Government in East Asian Industrialization*. Princeton: Princeton University Press.

Warren, Mark. 1994. "Exploitation or Cooperation? The Political Basis of Regional Variation in the Italian Informal Economy." *Politics and Society* 22, no. 1: 89–115.

Weiss, Linda, and John M. Hobson. 1995. *States and Economic Development: A Comparative Historical Analysis*. Cambridge, England: Polity Press.

Whitley, Richard. 1992. *Business Systems in East Asia: Firms, Markets and Societies*. London: Sage.

Williamson, Oliver E. 1975. *Markets and Hierarchies, Analysis and Antitrust Implications: A Study in the Economics of Internal Organization*. New York: Free Press.

———. 1991. "Comparative Economic Organization," *Administrative Science Quarterly* 36, no. 2: 269-297.

———. 1994. "Transaction Cost Economics and Organization Theory." In *The Handbook of Economic Sociology*, edited by Neil J. Smelser and Richard Swedberg, 77–107. Princeton: Princeton University Press.

Womack, James P., Daniel T. Jones, and Daniel Roos. 1990. *The Machine That Changed the World*. New York: Rawson Associates.

World Bank. 1993. *The East Asian Miracle: Economic Growth and Public Policy*. Washington, D.C: World Bank and Oxford University Press.

Zeitlin, Jonathan. 1992. "Industrial Districts and Local Regeneration: Overview and Comment." In *Industrial Districts and Local Regeneration*, edited by F. Pyke and W. Sengenberger. Geneva: International Institute for Labour Studies.

Zysman, John. 1983. *Governments, Markets, and Growth: Financial Systems and the Politics of Industrial Change*. Ithaca, N.Y.: Cornell University Press.

———. 1997. "'Wintelism' as an Optic on Society and Economy." *BRIE*, February.

1

Sources of Success in Uncertain Markets: The Taiwanese Footwear Industry

Lu-lin Cheng

This chapter starts from the core premise of the governance literature—namely, that firms often seek to reduce market uncertainties by establishing deeper and more enduring interfirm relationships than those created by the decentralized price mechanism (Campbell, Hollingsworth, and Lindberg 1991; Storper and Salais 1997). In examining this premise, the analysis here follows Fligstein's suggestion that the conditions of uncertainty associated with particular empirical cases provide an appropriate starting point for understanding the institutional formations of markets (Fligstein 1996).

The empirical focus of this chapter—Taiwan's footwear industry—is especially well suited to address specific sources of uncertainty and related governance arrangements.[1] In one sense, the industry ought to be an easy case for a deinstitutionalized market explanation. The low entry barriers and severe cost competition characterizing the footwear export market would seem to make price-mediated competition and cheap labor the principal sources of industry success. Taiwan began exporting footwear in the early 1960s, when its costs were relatively low. From a global perspective, it replaced Japan as the leading exporter in 1971 and maintained its dominant position as a major production site until the 1980s. This growth made the industry one of the major engines of Taiwan's export growth, accounting for almost half the volume of U.S. non-rubber footwear imports in the mid 1980s (table 1.1) and contributing significantly to the island's foreign exchange earnings before being partially displaced by high-tech industries. By the 1990s the country's footwear export position had declined, while that of China, with its low-cost exports, had grown significantly.

A closer examination of the industry, however, suggests the importance of coordination mechanisms other than price, and of competitive assets other

Table 1.1 Market Share of U.S. Nonrubber Footwear Imports, by Volume

Year	Total (millions of pairs)	Japan	Spain	Italy	S. Korea	Taiwan	Brazil	China	Indonesia	Thailand	Other
1970	242	25	9	33	1	17	1	—	—	—	14
1971	269	19	12	29	1	24	3	—	—	—	12
1972	297	9	13	27	3	31	4	—	—	—	13
1973	307	3	12	25	2	36	6	—	—	—	16
1974	266	2	13	23	3	33	8	—	—	—	18
1975	286	1	13	19	6	36	9	—	—	—	16
1976	370	1	10	13	12	42	7	—	—	—	15
1977	368	1	8	11	16	45	5	—	—	—	14
1978	374	2	10	17	8	31	7	—	—	—	25
1979	405	1	7	24	6	31	8	—	—	—	22
1980	366	1	5	13	10	39	9	1	—	—	21
1981	376	1	5	13	12	32	9	2	—	—	22
1982	480	1	5	12	19	38	11	1	—	—	14
1983	582	1	5	10	20	42	11	1	—	1	9
1984	726	1	5	9	16	42	15	2	—	1	9
1985	843	—	7	9	16	44	13	2	—	1	8
1986	941	—	4	7	19	46	12	3	—	1	8
1987	938	—	3	5	20	46	12	5	—	1	8
1988	903	—	3	5	21	38	13	9	—	2	9
1989	860	—	3	5	20	30	13	17	1	2	9
1990	898	—	2	5	18	19	12	30	4	3	7
1991	937	—	2	4	12	13	10	45	5	3	6
1992	974	—	2	4	7	8	11	52	8	3	5
1993	1,065	—	1	3	3	4	12	58	8	2	9
1994	1,101	—	2	4	2	3	11	62	7	2	7

Note: "—" denotes share of less than 1%.

Source: U.S. Department of Commerce, *Non-rubber Footwear Quarterly*, various issues.

than cheap labor. Taiwan's industry has grown despite a combination of higher initial labor costs in Taiwan than in Korea, strong protectionist pressures from the U.S. during subsequent years, and strong cost cutting and network contraction by international buyers in the wake of the Asian financial crisis. As the crisis has forced global footwear sourcing networks to become ever leaner, Taiwanese firms and the core cluster of footwear production in Taiwan itself have become even more competitive, meeting shifting demand patterns despite increasing labor costs.

The keys to the industry's success have been its capacities for meeting changing demand volumes, for prompt and precise commercialization of new styles and technology, and for fast and timely delivery. Changing forms of governance have been key to these capacities. Association-led and government-backed coordination was key for the industry's initial success in stabilizing prices and securing upstream inputs, and subsequently for the industry's ability to upgrade in the face of U.S. protectionist pressure. By the 1980s, global-sourcing networks in athletic footwear had replaced local associations as the critical form of governance arrangement. But these networks have themselves become differentiated into design- and cost-sensitive product segments. And the core of this industry has remained a geographical cluster with vertically disintegrated firms concentrated in the area around the largest city of central Taiwan—Taichung.

This chapter proceeds as follows: In the first section, I review the performance and evolution of the Taiwanese footwear industry, including its continuing vitality after regional reallocation in the late 1980s. The discussion highlights empirical anomalies in the neoclassical, price-mediated market explanation of the industry's growth. These anomalies in turn suggest the need for an institutional approach that focuses on changing market uncertainties and their governance. In the next three sections, I examine the industry's two principal institutional forms in detail. The first, linked to the industry's evolution prior to the 1980s, is industry wide and often centralized: industry wide in the sense that it involved coordination beyond arms-length, bilateral transactions between firms; centralized in that it involved the creation of public goods that help individual firms to adapt to new environments. In this period, industrial associations were important in facilitating industry growth, reducing the uncertainties endemic to the industry's initial formation and later creating competitive rules that transformed the uncertainties entailed by loss of trade protection into impulses for upgrading. The state was important in this process, but more as a mediator and legitimator than as a leader.

Under this institutional umbrella, and in response to some dramatic changes in the retail market, the industry evolved into a different institutional form serving two different global niches after the 1980s. In the third and fourth sections, I explore each niche's specific sources of uncertainty and the governance arrangements rooted in different logics of organizational flexibility: The design-sensitive market (DSM) is characterized by what I call *market closure*; in contrast, the cost-sensitive market (CSM) is structured in the form of *cross-cutting networks*. The fifth section of this chapter examines the industry's ability to maintain its position during the region's economic crisis. The conclusion reviews key findings.

ANOMALIES OF THE TAIWANESE FOOTWEAR INDUSTRY

The price-mediated equilibrium model of mainstream economics no longer defines the only approach for understanding market phenomena (Hirsch et al. 1990; Smelser and Swedberg 1994). The weaknesses of this approach are revealed through an examination of an industry—footwear—whose labor intensity and low entry barriers make it a most likely case for explanation by price and factor endowments. In fact, several empirical anomalies to the price-mediated model suggest the need for attention to intervening institutional factors.

First, why did footwear exports expand earlier in Taiwan than in Korea? While Taiwan was already enjoying 17 percent of the U.S. market share in 1970, Korea was still at about 1 percent. And when Korea climbed to 12 percent in 1976, Taiwan's share was 42 percent. Since Taiwan initially emphasized low-end shoes (e.g., plastic slippers) with lower labor costs, differences in labor costs might account for Taiwan's earlier success. However, Taiwan's GNP per capita was U.S.$140 in 1955, more than 70 percent above Korea's. When Korean GNP per capita reached U.S.$150 in 1970, Taiwan's stood at U.S.$312 (Levy 1991).

Second, in 1977, the U.S. led bilateral quota protectionism against Taiwan to curtail the massive imports of Taiwanese footwear (which had reached 45 percent of the U.S. market—table 1.1). This was a potentially serious blow to an industry relying so extensively on exports. Moreover, Taiwan's existing cost advantages had deteriorated in this period, and government support had shifted to high-tech or capital-intensive industries. Under these conditions, one might have expected other countries to replace Taiwan as key producers of footwear for the U.S. market. In fact, Taiwanese firms responded to the protectionist measures by becoming more competitive. Relocation of production out of Taiwan did not begin for another ten years. Other developing countries with bountiful cheap labor did not capture Taiwan's market share, which reached 46 percent of U.S. non-rubber footwear imports in 1987 (table 1.1). Indeed, three years after predictions of a "Mexican Footwear Revolution" (Kjelleren 1992), a survey of the Mexican footwear industry concluded that "the export performance of the Mexican shoe industry must be judged as disappointing in that less than ten percent of the output (22 million pairs) finds it way on to foreign markets" (*World Footwear 1995*).

The cheap labor and low transportation costs emphasized by neoclassical models thus accord poorly with key developments in the Taiwan footwear industry. Indeed, the footwear industry is not the easy stepping stone anticipated

by factor endowment models for low-labor-cost countries. This is not to minimize the impact of cost pressures at specific times. Primarily due to an abrupt
appreciation of Taiwanese currency, the footwear industry ceased to be a significant Taiwanese export industry by the early 1990s, when it was replaced by
new, capital- or technology-intensive industries.

Yet Taiwanese footwear firms have not followed the Japanese pattern of shifting production overseas and subsequently disappearing from the international
footwear industry. Taiwanese producers continue to exert an important influence
on the sourcing operations of multinational buyers in two ways. First, in response
to currency shifts, Taiwanese footwear producers have invested massively in
neighboring countries. These operations control a major share of the international market. Second, Taichung remains a coordination center for now regional-
ized footwear transactions. And the Asian economic crisis only strengthened the
pivotal role of Taiwanese producers. As sourcing networks have become leaner,
Taiwanese firms and central Taiwan have become more crucial for meeting buyer
demand for low-cost, quick-response deliveries to ever more competitive markets.
The anomalies reviewed above do not exclude the weight of factor endowments
and the presence of atomistic firms driven by price signals. But they do suggest the
operation of more "visible hands" and the benefits of a sociological perspective
which understands markets as socially constructed institutions which reduce uncertainties (Granovetter 1985, 1992).

EARLY INSTITUTIONALIZATION:
TURNING UNCERTAINTY INTO OPPORTUNITY

Institutionalization can be understood as a social force that facilitates interactions
among a large number of actors by providing commonly accepted codes of behavior. Such codes can take the form of legitimated practices which encourage
market expansion by bringing predictability into a volatile transaction environment. A legitimated practice, which includes a cognitive system of classification,
rules of exchanges and competition, and symbols of identification, exerts its influence by offering institutionalized resources for firms in their instrumental interactions. In this section, we focus on how the Taiwanese footwear industrial association, here viewed as a typical institutional entrepreneur, contributed to
overcoming uncertainties associated first with the industry's initial formation and
subsequently with the protectionist shock.

Taiwan's footwear industry originated in the eighteenth-century Ching dynasty
peasant economy of straw hat weaving. Straw hat production reached its apex in
1934, under Japanese colonialism, with most exports going to Japan (Hsieh 1964:
335–336). Production was based in households throughout central Taiwan. After
the devastation of World War II, the straw hat weaving industry reemerged, again
relying on female household labor. In the early 1960s, some businessmen started

to experiment by exporting slippers made with straw-weave uppers and plastic soles supplied by the newly founded plastics industry. Two institutional factors facilitated this initial production. First, building on existing linkages, early entrepreneurs shared market opportunities and technological know-how through informal networks (TFMA 1989). Second, Japanese trading companies, which shifted their orders from Japan to Taiwan, provided initial demand. But the direct contribution of Japanese capital should not be exaggerated.[2] The intermediate role of the Japanese trading companies diminished rather quickly. The majority of footwear exports were conducted by local Taiwanese firms which, by the early 1960s, had developed direct connections with American buyers. A more important legacy of the Japanese trading companies lies in the extensive networks their local employees developed between Taiwanese producers and American importers. These networks helped sustain the industry's expansion even after the withdrawal of the Japanese employers.

The industry only gradually developed a clear identity and strategy. Its main products in the early years, slippers, were seen more as a by-product of the straw weaving industry than as the basis of a new industry. The industry's first association, the Taiwanese Plastic Shoes Exporters' Association (TPSEA), was not established until 1968. Even then, the association's executive director held the same position at the Taiwanese Hat Exporter's Association (THEA), while TPSEA's counseling committee was composed of the chairman of THEA and owners of the five major plastic companies (TFMA 1989). This institutional fuzziness had important benefits, however. The new footwear producers had close ties with the hat industries; retaining these connections assured access to export experience. Equally important, the pioneer footwear producers knew that the industry's development depended largely on moving from exporting plastic slippers to exporting other types of plastic shoes. For the newly established upstream suppliers of plastic materials, the establishment of TPSEA provided an institutional channel to acquire information about (and also to influence) the development of an important downstream industry. These personnel and institutional linkages were key to the industry's early collective efforts at assuring stability in an uncertain environment. Equally important was TPSEA's initiation and implementation of a "minimum price agreement."

The association first presented this concept to the Minister of Economic Affairs (MOEA). The objective was to enforce a minimum price agreement by linking this criterion to the issuance of export permits. Until then, these permits had been subject to the discretion of the government's International Trade Bureau (ITB). In the association's view, the measure was justified by the immaturity of the industry, reflected in firms' lack of basic information about supply and demand. According to the former chair of TPSEA, the agreement was intended to "help firms share minimum understanding of the common costs structure, and therefore, prevent unnecessary pricing that would damage the very survival of the industry."

The government responded cautiously to the proposal. It agreed to link export licensing with private pricing only if written agreements were reached among all association members. In addition, the MOEA refused to enforce the rules on its own. It agreed to block export permits only on the basis of prior decisions by the association. The Taiwanese government thus largely reacted to the association's initiative. Yet even this relatively passive role was important in establishing *de facto* government support and in encouraging intra-industry coordination sufficient to allow the association to implement this initiative.

The process of implementing the minimum price agreement went beyond simple pricing regulation and proved to be an important component of industry institutionalization. After reaching a consensus with the MOEA, TPSEA organized numerous meetings among its members to classify shoes into distinct categories with regard to type, rank, and minimum cost. Although these efforts were not documented, we can assume that the upstream material suppliers were involved in the communication processes to which they were assigned as association counselors. After a series of discussions about materials, designs, specifications, and production methods, TPSEA developed a scheme of seven shoe categories, each with minimum export prices. The project was completed at the end of 1969, with support from the ITB.[3]

The implementation of the agreement reflected industry-wide coordination. It not only strengthened the role of the industry association but also forged an industry identity and facilitated the transparent circulation of information about products and production. Although causal connections are difficult to establish conclusively, there clearly was a relationship between the policy and industry performance. Both export volume and value doubled in 1970. From 1969 to 1976, the eve of the Orderly Marketing Agreement, the average annual volume increase rate was 64 percent.

In fact, from 1968 to 1986, export volumes jumped from 20 million pairs to 842 million pairs, a more than forty-fold increase. Total export value rose from U.S.$19 million to U.S.$3.7 billion for the same period. In 1977, facing mounting pressures from domestic footwear producers, the U.S. government decided to negotiate a four-year Orderly Marketing Agreement (OMA) with the Taiwanese and Korean governments. This challenge turned out to be an opportunity for Taiwan's footwear industry to restructure into higher value-added exports. Increased coordination throughout the footwear value chain was key to this successful response.

This coordination was in fact stimulated by protectionist pressure itself. Prior to the final implementation of the OMA, Taiwanese footwear producers, the Taiwanese government, and U.S. footwear importers had developed strong networks of cooperation through a series of antiprotectionist lobbying efforts. When the quota restrictions were imposed, these networks facilitated mutual adjustments between Taiwanese producers and their foreign buyers. But the key impact of the OMA was the birth of a new and more integrated industrial association, the Taiwanese Footwear Manufacturer's Association (TFMA), and the new organization's institutionalization through quota management. The TFMA emerged in response to the U.S. International Trade Commission's insistence that the OMA should cover all footwear categories except rubber shoes. This created immediate problems for TPSEA, which represented only plastic shoe manufacturers. The association did not cover the new product niches into which local firms had expanded. For example, leather and rubber footwear manufacturers belonged to the Taiwanese Leather Product Industrial Association and the Taiwanese Rubber Products Industrial Association, respectively. These associations represented producers of all kinds of leather and rubber products far beyond footwear. In addition, TPSEA was unable to contend with the expanding number of bilateral negotiations with major European countries concerned about potential dumping of Taiwanese footwear rejected by the U.S. market.

Stimulated by OMA pressures, the TFMA was created in April 1978 to replace the TPSEA. The TFMA immediately moved to address the needs of export-related upgrading. A Quota Research Committee (QRC), including government officials, academics, and representatives of related industries, was formed inside TFMA to design an institution for quota management.[4] The total quota was divided into a basic quota (85 percent) and a free quota (15 percent), with the 3 percent annual increase added to the latter. In the first year, firms' export capabilities were calculated by their average export volume for the three previous years (1974–1976) and the basic quota was distributed accordingly. Following the monitoring system developed during the TPSEA era, firms were granted customs approval only with a stamp from the TFMA. The TFMA was further empowered to keep detailed records of every transaction of its members.

While the basic quota would revert to the free quota if firms failed to exhaust it by the year's end, the free quota was subject to open bidding: those firms holding higher unit-priced orders received the quota. Since daily bidding was not practical, but seasonal market demand required exact timing, the QRC was involved in ongoing consultation with member firms to coordinate periodic bidding based on dates of order receipts and product delivery. To avoid discrimination against new firms and to ensure competition, only new firms or those that used up their basic quota were allowed to enter the bidding. The uncertainty of quota availability created a certain instability in the market, but it also facilitated order-screening, which in turn reduced the tendency of firms to seek as many orders as possible.

The impact of the quota-mediated competition was important. Some firms withdrew from the quota-protected American market and concentrated on other markets, such as Europe. As a result, market diversification occurred simultaneously with the specialization of firms. Small firms were in a difficult situation because they had to collect free quotas to fill orders above a certain quantity. Larger firms grew through somewhat different strategies. A typical large-firm strategy was to set up new firms, concentrating higher-valued orders in them to compete for free quotas, while keeping lower-valued orders in the original firms. As the higher-valued orders stabilized, they were transferred to the older firms to fill up the basic quota.

In sum, when booming exports had just begun to generate cutthroat competition, OMA and the quota allocation system in 1977 reshaped market competition, which thereafter focused on upgrading to higher value-added exports. The institution turned anxiety and likely chaos into new orders of competition. The small guerrilla firms who tried to get orders at any price were pushed out of the game, thereby reducing a source of market uncertainty.[5] Quota flowed to manufacturers who were driven by quality improvement. The periodic bidding held at TFMA created an atmosphere of competition and the competitors' ability to win higher-valued orders constantly set new benchmarks for organizational learning.

To encourage this process, the TFMA organized a team of quality control (QC) experts. The teams were financed by a 0.06 percent quota value levy and were supported by a newly created, semiofficial institute—the China Productivity Center—that conducted on-site factory visits to evaluate firms' QC capability according to a four-grade scale. The QC level of firms was indicated on the TFMA quota export-permit stamp. The frequency of inspection ranged from once a year for the highest-graded firms to once a month for the lowest. At the same time, the TFMA set up a special division to provide training programs and QC assistance for firms that requested help. During the OMA period, TFMA developed into a model association that carried multiple functions, including trade negotiation, training service, quota management, and quality promotion.

Following the imposition of the OMA, mass production of wet-processed PU leather[6] provided further encouragement for Taiwanese footwear manufacturers to move into higher value-added niches. This upgrading was facilitated by the growth of a local footwear machinery industry in the late 1970s. By the mid-1980s, local firms were successfully commercializing new equipment requiring more research investment (hydraulic injection machines, computerized stitching machines, and automatic cementing machines). The result was a well-integrated industrial cluster around Taichung City. As a buyer said, "you can basically have everything [for footwear development and manufacturing] done in just a small area of twenty-five kilometers in diameter." The result was not only continued growth, but also the addition of footwear companies like Florsheim, Survivors, Gilbort, Rockport, and Bass to the list of Taiwanese OEM (original equipment manufacturing) buyers.[7] By 1986, all the major athletic shoe brand names (e.g., Nike, Reebok, Converse, Adidas) had well-established supply lines in Taiwan. Central Taiwan became an indispensable hub for the densely connected networks linking world footwear suppliers to retail markets in the developed countries. As this hub developed, it was drawn into new types of governance arrangements as the result of dramatic changes in the athletic shoe niches of these markets.

NEW COMPETITION IN THE 1980S

In the 1980s, the Taiwanese footwear industry was well established in world markets on the basis of cost and flexibility.[8] This achievement resulted from the upgrading and institutionalization discussed above. But it also involved intensified exchanges among specialized, local firms and greater degrees of local subcontracting. These local linkages in turn became part of more extensive and more differentiated external sourcing networks.

These developments were responses to dramatic changes in the footwear retail market during the 1980s. The most important transformation related to the stylization and high-tech hype of the athletic shoe retail market. Competition based on these new market pressures raised entry barriers by increasing the necessity for coordination, increasing uncertainty in sourcing transactions, and reducing tolerance for lapses in quality and delivery. Moreover, the athletic shoe retail market split into two contrasting segments: the discount market, dominated by nationwide retail chains with general merchandisers (e.g., Wal-Mart) or specialty stores (e.g., Payless ShoeSource), and the brand market, where competition among international marketers (e.g., Nike and Reebok) emphasized high-tech and stylistic designs for fashion-conscious consumers. In this section, I review the competitive pressures in these two segments. In the next section, I explore the corresponding governance arrangements.

Athletic shoes were not a significant sector in the footwear industry prior to convergent waves of technological and marketing innovations in the late 1970s. That period marked the beginning of health consciousness, along with the jogging and fitness craze, in the United States. This trend soon spread globally. Around the same time, Adidas invented a new way of making athletic shoes by cementing nylon textile, EVA, and the plastic outsole, which pushed the athletic shoe industry away from traditional vulcanization production. Riding the fitness craze, Reebok created aerobic shoes using PU "textile leather," which quickly became an enormous success. In 1985 Nike struck back with its Air Force series, firmly establishing athletic shoes as a fashion product. The core of the market now consists of only a handful of national-brand companies that anchor their competitive edge primarily in design and marketing.

The market for these products expanded explosively. In the early 1980s, sports shoes occupied only about 20 percent of the footwear consumer market. By 1992 it reached 50 percent, a huge market estimated at U.S.$12 billion worldwide. As the volume of the market expanded, the number of sports shoe categories also increased. Basketball shoes were the first specialized category, followed by baseball shoes, soccer shoes, jogging shoes, tennis shoes, aerobic shoes, walking shoes, etc.; new categories continue to be added. The sales figures in the 1990s were relatively flat at around U.S.$11.5 billion, indicating a matured stage for the new competition; but new "hot" categories (e.g., hiking boots and sports sandals) are not considered athletic shoes. There now seems to be no finish line for sports shoes.

In this design-sensitive market (DSM) segment, footwear design must complement each new category to show its uniqueness in meeting specific functional demands. Model changes have been especially frequent and rapid for the top performers. Changes in sports shoe product lines used to occur only once a year, but they now occur twice a year, with some shorter backup seasons to fine-tune supply. In 1990, Nike offered three hundred models with nine hundred styles for twenty-four sports categories, while Adidas had about five hundred styles and L.A. Gear over five hundred (Gereffi and Korzeniewicz 1994: 249).[9] The top performers are leading a "tech hype" that promises to bring state-of-the-art technology to the performance of shoes. Every new design also comes with adaptations of the shoe's outer appearance to highlight the technological innovation and convey the value-added image. Nike's dramatic setback during the second half of the 1980s came because it had no replacement when its popular Air Jordan basketball shoes went out of vogue and rival Reebok pushed its stylistic aerobic shoes in the market. Another example of the success of a new design was L.A. Gear, which created a sudden mania when it introduced its flashlight shoes. Shorter product life cycles fueled by constant renewals of technology and models represent the coming of new competition in the athletic footwear market.

These developments are not confined to DSM firms, which represent the clearest emphasis on fashion, quality, and rapid time-to-market. Buyers in the cost-sensitive market (CSM) compete on the basis of offering cheaper products with satisfactory quality and currently popular styles. Two typical buyers in this market are the discount store Wal-Mart and the footwear specialty chain Payless ShoeSource. Wal-Mart's footwear procurement operation outside of the U.S. is concentrated in two places, primarily Taiwan and secondarily Hong Kong. Payless ShoeSource has its Asian headquarters in Taiwan and sources U.S.$900 million worth of shoes each year in East Asia. Cost, however, is not the only factor in competition. A large inventory of unsold shoes can ruin a retailer, no matter how cheaply those shoes are made. Payless ShoeSource, for example, places greater importance on variety of choices and faster model changes than does Wal-Mart, which carries a narrower range of models. Wal-Mart, with relatively fewer models on the shelf and generally larger orders than Payless, also cannot risk developing a wrong line of shoes.

The bottom line in the CSM is getting the *right* product *cheaply* and *quickly* to the consumers in the *right* volume. To reduce the uncertainty involved, buyers in the CSM rely on a follower's strategy by free riding the fashions created by DSM buyers. Firms in the market compete by getting information about major brands' latest models as quickly as possible and then making imitations at a cheaper price. The strategy is adopted so aggressively that almost every point in a transaction flow of the DSM, from early design to final shipment, is subject to possible information leak.[10] Therefore, not only does new competition in the DSM segment create pressure for the CSM, but there is also reciprocal pressure from the CSM that forces the DSM companies to develop new models ever faster and to manage their sourcing networks so as to prevent leakage of valuable information.

DIFFERENT MARKET SEGMENTS/DIFFERENT NETWORKS

The preceding section suggests that athletic footwear producers in both segments must contend with a range of uncertainties from early design and model development, to product manufacturing, and on to final shipment. These uncertainties are found on the demand side, with fluctuating quantity (volume) and quality (style preferences), and on the supply side, with technical, communication, logistic, and administrative uncertainties in the execution of transactions. Yet, because these uncertainties play themselves out differently in the two segments, they involve different sets of governance logics.

Transactions in the DSM developed into what I will call *market closure,* in the sense that the boundaries and identities of firms involved in longer-term transactions become blurred. Those in the CSM rely on what I will call *cross-cutting networks,* where efforts to increase the speed of development and manufacturing involve mobilizing resources through densely interwoven ties.

Flexibility and Market Closure in the DSM

The first and most obvious sign of market closure is the participant firms' preference for direct and often exclusive sourcing. DSM buyers (e.g., Nike, Reebok, and Adidas) and their suppliers avoid doing business through trading companies. This is due to the need to prevent leakage of valuable product development information and to develop trust and cooperation. Buyer preference for exclusivity by suppliers is especially strong. Such relationships vary in degree from one assembly line dedicated to a specific buyer to an entire plant dedicated to production for one buyer. As explained below, suppliers also value exclusivity but often opt to reduce vulnerability by producing for several buyers. Nevertheless, total supplier commitment to one buyer does exist. Feng-Tay, for example, has been Nike's exclusive Taiwanese supplier for over twenty years and their relationship has become an indispensable asset to the competitiveness of both. It has allowed for protection of valuable information subject to theft throughout the long DSM development-manufacturing processes (often lasting over six months). It has also helped both firms to manage orders with greater predictability.

A second feature of the DSM networks—overlapping boundaries—further facilitates reduction of uncertainty. DSM firms typically implement a practice known as an *expatriate program,* in which buyers implant aspects of their own organizations into their supplying firms. This backward penetration involves *de facto* managerial control by buyers beyond inspection to include labor, machinery, materials, training, and production processes. On the other hand, suppliers in the DSM see the chance to participate in the early development or even design stage, which buyers control as a sign of upgrading and securing market position. This synchronization of business operations between buyer and supplier can also be observed in the mutual and intense coordination of regional production reallocations.

Although market closure, in the form of exclusivity and direct linkages, characterizes the DSM firms, it is also clear that not all firms in the same market network have the same strength of ties. For example, firms devoted to several lines differ from those with one exclusive plant. The former stand at the edge of the network while the latter are closer to the core. The scale and scope of overlapped organizational boundaries also differ among different transaction dyads in the same market closure. As a consequence, the market closures of the DSM are internally hierarchical, with tiers of suppliers specialized in their unique functions.

This variation reflects efforts to stabilize orders in volatile markets. As noted earlier, the order stability of DSM is partly supported by the very existence of CSM as a buffer. Similarly, the hierarchical networks of most DSM buyers, composed of suppliers with different degrees of exclusivity, constitute an intrinsic source of order adjustment. Nike's sourcing system shows a two-tier subcontracting network with three types of suppliers (developed partners, developing sources, and volume producers), each designed to carry out certain strategic functions (Donaghu and Barff 1990). Reebok and Adidas have developed similar networks. For example, Reebok's sourcing network is composed mainly of two groups of suppliers: "partner factory" and "preferred factory."

Varying degrees of market closure also constitute opportunities for suppliers to improve their strategic position by becoming increasingly indispensable to buyers. And as these ties intensify, the identities of DSM suppliers become blurred. This occurs not just organizationally, due to increased buyer control over certain functions noted earlier, but also in terms of the symbolic representation of the supplier's identity. A visitor to the supplying factories in the DSM will no doubt notice how the suppliers are concealing their true identity by decorating their factories with symbols, logos, and names of their OEM buyers. Indeed, it would take a visitor considerable effort to find the firm's own sign. Inside the factory, the buyer's symbols are everywhere: on posters, policy announcements, worker IDs, and even uniforms. All the symbolic gestures are aimed at creating a "partnership" context.

And yet, many DSM suppliers typically attempt to diversify their buyers, albeit without losing exclusivity. A successful footwear supplier in the DSM often provides footwear for several buyers at the same time, with exclusive plants and supplementary exclusive lines dispersed regionally for different buyers. This compartmentalization of a single supplier company is thus designed to balance the need to reduce risk through client diversification on the one hand, with the need to court customers through blurring of supplier identity on the other.

The spatial arrangement of the factories of one firm (Bao-Chen) in central Taiwan illustrates this pattern: The firm has four assembly plants making shoes exclusively for specific buyers and one for a variety of buyers. At the center is the company's administrative headquarters, which is the building first seen when entering the main gate. The other five assembly plants are separated by iron fences into four zones, each with its own entrance and facing a different direction. Each plant has become a private compartment for separately dedicated transaction partners. But Bao-Chen is not simply a composition of disintegrated plants. "Our company has a great advantage that Feng-Tay lacks," noted the firm's manager.[11] "At the top of our company we study the new model designs that no buyers in the retail market are able to know from each other months before the products hit the market. Frankly, many designs we offered to our buyers are based on those of the others. The point is not to do it too much so that you irritate any of your buyers. You know trust is very important in the industry."

Market closure has the advantages of accumulating development-manufacturing capability inside the networks. This facilitates speedy and accurate commercialization, encourages flexible adjustment of orders to different types and sizes among suppliers, and reduces the risks of leaking valuable information. It is not, however, the unique creation of powerful international buyers; nor is it the result of the invisible hand of an asocial price mechanism. It is instead a function of numerous interactions between buyers and suppliers, each looking out for its own interests but pursuing close relationships in order to do so.

The Flexibility Embedded in the Cross-Cutting Networks of CSM

While exposed to many of the same sources of uncertainty seen in the DSM, transactions in the CSM are conducted through different organizational principles. Unlike their DSM counterparts, buyers in the CSM have minimal buffering capacities. The result is endemic instability. The uncertainties relate primarily to the buyer's dilemma of picking the right products for making knock-offs versus delivering products to the market as early as possible. Waiting for the best-selling products to emerge can assure the former objective, but by the time knock-offs reach retailers' hands the demand may have already begun to drop owing to a massive inflow of imitative products. In response, transactions in the CSM have developed into what I will call *cross-cutting networks*. These networks provide quick access to product information, fast commercialization, shortened lead time, timely product delivery, flexible adjustment of output volume, and risk absorption when demand shrinks abruptly.

In a clear contrast to the DSM, both buyers and suppliers in the CSM prefer indirect sourcing: trading companies often play an important role in transaction coordination. From the buyers' perspective, trading companies constitute buffers that reduce risk, allow flexibility, and provide timely information (despite the fact that large buyers have their own offices in Taiwan). These considerations are so important that large buyers use trading companies even for large orders that might otherwise justify direct procurement. Most manufacturers also prefer doing business with trading companies. There being no clear difference in profit margins between orders from buyers or trading companies, the key benefit lies in the ability of trading companies to soften the impact of market fluctuations. An order lost to one buyer can be compensated by another buyer's order provided by the trading company. The cross-cutting networks that connect trading companies and footwear producers lie at the core of transaction coordination in the CSM.

Those networks offer a response speed essential to competition in the volatile market. Beginning with the early design stage of a transaction, the line builders of trading companies (the equivalents for the designers of the DSM) must "reinterpret" the original designs for CSM producers in ways that facilitate higher volume production, use readily available materials, and reduce manufacturing costs. Commonly used strategies include substituting original materials like leathers with lesser-grade materials, simplifying manufacturing steps in labor-intensive stages like stitching, reducing the number of upper cuts, and adopting used outsole molds. The trick is to make the adjustments without losing the original flavor, given the very limited latitude of time and cost allowed.

With its well-developed supporting industries, Taiwan has been an excellent place for trading companies not only to produce their orders but, increasingly, to develop their models. The synthetic leather industry of Taiwan, for example, has developed a reputation for constantly developing new products to supply its major downstream industries, like footwear. The ability of many specialized small factories to make footwear accessories like buttons in a few days, even offering many varieties, has amazed the buyers and trading company managers I interviewed. The densely connected networks among numerous material suppliers, component suppliers, footwear producers, and trading companies in a small area are critical for speed in responding to changes in the market. The key is to be able to mobilize readily available materials and components so that the time taken in the development of models is as short as possible.

The development of knock-offs for L.A. Gear's flashlighting shoes in 1995 illustrates these benefits. The original flashlight license belonged to BBC International. Knowing that this little component fit exactly with the DSM's tech-hype, BBC International approached L.A. Gear and struck an exclusive bilateral deal on the product. L.A. Gear was excited about the secret weapon and agreed to the cross-segment cooperation. It proved a tremendous success, lifting L.A. Gear to the number three rank in the DSM, surpassing Adidas. However, just a few months after L.A. Gear launched its flashlighting shoes, trading companies in the CSM developed many varieties of lighting shoes that circumvented L.A. Gear's patent protection. The original lights were placed at the heel and the sensor was designed to respond to an up-and-down movement. Knock-offs, thanks to the well-developed electronics industry in Taiwan, which BBC International also relied on, came up with lights placed at almost every possible position (e.g., toe and upper) with sensors that responded to different directions of movement. L.A. Gear's success stalled within a year, and its shoes subsequently appeared in discount stores.

A similarly flexible response can also be observed in the production stage. The reciprocal exchanges between Taiwanese CSM suppliers, mediated by support from trading companies, hold the key to quick delivery. For example, a pair of outsole molds costs about US$1,800 to a supplier, meaning that a set of five sizes will cost about US$9,000. To save time and money in making outsoles, Taiwanese footwear factories often borrow outsoles from potential competitors whose current production needs do not call for them. The expectation of reciprocity also obliges the borrower to return the favor when asked. The networking of mutual help through the use of substitutable components or materials fits well with the design strategy discussed earlier. Trading companies that travel between suppliers are very active in facilitating this kind of give-and-take relationship when they find that *diau-jie* (dispatch and borrowing) of materials and components is necessary. The ability to *diau-jie* materials from other factories when needed is an indispensable condition for firms in the CSM to "seize orders at the first instance" (*chiun-dun-tz*) when opportunities emerge.

Diau-jie is not only limited to the borrowing of material goods; space in the assembly schedule is also open for reciprocal exchange. There are many contingencies that might interrupt an assembly-line schedule: delay of material preparation in the preproduction stage, push-orders that must wait on hold, rush reorders as part of customer courting, and many technical problems that stall production. Taiwanese production managers commonly move various models of different sizes around the tight production schedule, deciding whether to "let a model flow" or "pull a size out." It is only natural that sometimes a factory fails to provide production space because of overbooked production or a rush reorder. To maintain credibility the factory will need to find space in another factory. In this situation, the factory that gives a favor by subcontracting its production space also gains a "relationship debt" from the space-receiving firm. Although it receives (per unit) monetary compensation, the obligation is not settled through money.

These reciprocal relationships are not based on unconditional trust. They are essentially interest-oriented linkages based on dense networks of information and institutionalized rules of competition. On many occasions I have heard Taiwanese footwear manufacturers gossiping at karaoke bars about which factory might be in trouble with an order from a particular buyer. They monitor other firms closely in order to jump ship if necessary, while they are at the same time struggling to seize orders. Even risk-averting monitoring is based on cross-cutting interpersonal networks built from reciprocal exchanges. It is the mix of cooperation and competition in the networks that have amazed many buyers I interviewed. The Taiwanese-centered CSM is famous for cutthroat competition. Yet these rivals are able to cooperate by defining shared interests on certain occasions within a broader set of rules and relationships. This combination constitutes a critical buffering mechanism for global buyers in the CSM segment.

IMPACT OF THE FINANCIAL CRISIS[12]

The impact of the Asian financial crisis on the Taiwanese footwear industry and its related networks was relatively mild and, if anything, somewhat beneficial. This was partly because the athletic shoe market had been experiencing recession since the early 1990s. The prolonged NBA strikes and Michael Jordan's two re-tirements only deterred the long-awaited recovery. The East Asian crisis further reduced market demand by lowering the value of regional currencies and raising unemployment rates. However, quotations for export orders before the crisis were already near the lowest level possible for a firm with a healthy cash flow to rein-vest in order to survive. To some extent, then, Taiwan's suppliers and their cus-tomers had already adjusted to difficult conditions.

But the recent financial crisis actually helped to strengthen the pivotal role of Taiwanese suppliers in global footwear sourcing networks. A central part of the explanation for this relates to how the institutionalized capacities described in the preceding pages were suited to the increasing competitive pressures brought on by the crisis. Also important were Taiwan's macroeconomic conditions and the modal organization and strategies of Taiwanese firms in general.

After the crisis, the major national brands continued to expand their R&D op-eration in central Taiwan. In the DSM, Reebok and Adidas, following Nike, now rely more on the inner-tier (Taiwanese) suppliers to preserve externalized capaci-ties for quick response, timely delivery, and precise commercialization. In effect, this strategy involves preserving network resources so as to fine-tune sourcing op-erations in anticipation of the next market recovery. CSM buyers like Payless ShoeSource have become keenly alert to the danger of being trapped in price wars. In response, they have reduced their number of suppliers to rationalize over-head costs (to maintain profits under given revenue), reevaluated credibility among suppliers (to reduce risks of credit default), and enhanced quality control (to improve value). These measures have tended to favor established Taiwanese suppliers.

And in both DSM and CSM, the increased uncertainty due to intensified com-petition and financial turbulence has made trust both scarcer and more valuable. With newer suppliers wiped out, relationships with long-term suppliers became even more important.

Taiwan's firms also benefited from several other factors. First, the many Tai-wanese suppliers with dispersed operations were able to garner profits and achieve lower costs by taking advantage of regional currency depreciations. Second, under conditions of economic downturn, labor was both more available and more loyal. Third and perhaps most important, Taiwan itself was much less vulnerable to the broader impacts of the crisis. Part of this had to do with macroeconomic manage-ment: Taiwan had maintained an extensive foreign-exchange reserve, thus allow-ing it more leeway in addressing shocks such as the late 1990s military confronta-tion with the mainland. The island's government-guaranteed foreign debts were almost zero, the private sector's external liabilities were just over 10 percent, well below those of Asian countries harder hit by the crisis, and the private sector's foreign assets actually exceeded its external liabilities.[13] The country did experi-ence an overheated stock-market and real-estate sector, but brought these prob-lems under control well before the outbreak of the crisis. The overall structure and strategy of Taiwanese firms also helped to reduce the island's vulnerability. Taiwanese firms are (relative to, say, their Korean counterparts) smaller in size and risk averse. Their conservative strategy is evidenced by fairly low reliance on bank loans. Some successful firms have gone so far as to insist that they not be listed on the stock market. In the highly diversified and decentralized Taiwanese economy, there are leading firms in each industry but hardly any of them can claim dominance. Finally, the overall strategy of Taiwanese enterprises is, instead of seeking dominance, to be indispensable OEM suppliers to the leading firms in the globalized manufacturing systems. This strategy, which requires market-conforming behavior, is nicely reflected in the country's footwear industry.

CONCLUSION

Much of the current literature on globalized industries attributes flexibility either to the strategic planning of multinational buying companies (Harrison 1994) or to the production capability of local supplying networks (Hsing 1996). In this chapter, I have explored issues of uncertainty, flexibility, and governance arrangements as part of the interorganizational fields of footwear production involving both Taiwanese suppliers and global buyers.

The industry examined in this chapter has been characterized by extensive and diverse sources of uncertainty. As the industry has grown in product volume and diversity, its firms have faced ever-increasing pressures on transactional coordination to achieve the multiple goals of cost efficiency, uncertainty buffering, commercialization speed, volume adjustment, quality assurance, and timely delivery. Successful sourcing relationships are those capable of addressing these pressures simultaneously and smoothly. Even in a labor-intensive industry, such sourcing requires labor beyond the conveyor belt; it requires relationships that cannot only channel market pressures but also facilitate information flows, promote resource sharing, and reconcile divergent interests among industry participants. Taiwan became a key player and remains a coordination center for regional production precisely because of its firms' capacities to develop such arrangements both locally and in conjunction with global buyers.

This chapter has also demonstrated that transaction governance is pervasive but not homogeneous. Temporally, Taiwan's industry benefited from a succession and combination of institutions, ranging from informal networks in central Taiwan, to Japanese and local trading companies, to associational, state-supported coordination, to more diversified global networks. Governance also varies within one product segment—athletic footwear—to achieve flexibility within specific mixes of uncertainties. Although trust-based dynamism was central to both the CSM and DSM, different market pressures resulted in different institutional responses. An OEM transaction in the CSM involves larger numbers of firms both in the production and marketing stages. The kind of direct contacts that breed bilateral expectations and mutual learning in the DSM footwear market are, in the CSM market, spread out in longer chains. In these chains, coordination is achieved through mediating trading companies rather than through an overlapping of organizational boundaries between buyers and suppliers.

This more detailed sectoral perspective thus suggests caution in assuming that organizational flexibility lies within one local-national production system. As emphasized by the global commodity chain literature, the sectoral character of economic governance is both local and global.[14] At the same time, we cannot assume that the simple existence of market pressures will automatically "call forth" an efficient institutional response. The very contrast between Taiwan's continued success in footwear and the more modest and transient performances of other producers, such as Korea and Mexico, suggests the importance of local context. As noted in this volume's introduction, local politics and institutions help to account for cross-national variation in institutional responses to similar pressures for flexibility.

NOTES

1. Unless otherwise noted, information for this chapter is drawn from (1) written documents; (2) in-depth interviews with representative buyers, suppliers, and government officials; and (3) participant observations conducted at Dong-Guang in China, Subic Bay in the Philippines, and the townships of central Taiwan. Specific references are found in Cheng (1996).

2. It is, in my view, an overstatement to attribute the industry's development primarily to the decisions by a handful of Japanese trading companies, especially Mitsubishi, to shift orders to Taiwan (Levy 1991: 155). For a fuller analysis of this issue, see Cheng (1996).

3. To my knowledge, the institution of "price approval for licensed export" has not been established in any other industry in Taiwan.

4. Most of the following analysis is based on interviews with senior government officials and managers of industrial associations.

5. From April 1968 to March 1981, 114 firms left the TFMA (or TPSEA before 1978) and 206 new firms entered. The annual growth rate in numbers of firms was only 4.4 percent, but at least numbers did not decline, as might have been expected.

6. PU textile leather is a synthetic leather designed to imitate NAPA leather (genuine leather). Its characteristics are extra soft hand feeling and stronger physical property (burst strength, tear strength, and tensile strength). The manufacturing process is categorized as wet PU when nonwoven textile is used as backing to enhance its strength and its overall evenness.

7. "In fact, the mark of Taiwan's status as the Far East's number one shoe source, according to one importer, is that 'every nationally advertised brand is involved in some way in Taiwan'" (*Footwear News*, 5 December 1983).

8. For evidence on the industry's reputation, see Cheng (1996: 109–151).

9. It is not at all surprising that, with two major seasons, brand companies are able to come up with three hundred models and nine hundred styles. If we take an average, each category has six to seven models each season (jogging shoes and basketball shoes have

more, while smaller categories like soccer shoes will have fewer models). Different color combinations or upper stitchings create various styles for the same model. The three to one ratio between style and model is about what we observe at retail stores, with some having only two styles and others up to four. There are two other factors to be considered: (1) regional differences, since for example, some models or styles are sold only in the European market and thus are not available in the U.S.; and (2) small backup seasons, which occur two months after regular seasons, when buyers might reduce some orders or add new styles or even new models, after evaluating the market responses during regular seasons.

10. Importers and buyers in the CSM not only imitate the products of companies like Nike and Reebok, but also their differentiation strategy. The exceptional case, in which buyers in the CSM segment enjoy real success, is that of children's shoes, largely ignored by the major national brand companies. The designs of those shoes are mostly based on licensed characters associated with movies or cartoon series, so-called "character brands" like the Little Mermaid or the Lion King. The category has several characteristics that work well with the CSM: the original design is well-established, the fashion is short-lived but large in volume, assembly requires few steps because characteristics are simply printed on the upper, and parents do not require these shoes to be durable, as long as they are safe. It is in a sense still a follower's strategy, except that the original designs are from another industry.

11. Recall that Feng-Tay is devoted exclusively to Nike.

12. Unless otherwise noted, information in this section is drawn from interviews conducted in Taiwan in June and July 1999.

13. Chu (1999: 186). In addition to interviews, this discussion draws on Chu (1999).

14. Gereffi and Korzeniewicz (1994).

BIBLIOGRAPHY

Campbell, J. L., J. R. Hollingsworth, and L. Lindberg. 1991. *Governance of the American Economy.* Cambridge: Cambridge University Press.

Cheng, Lu-Lin. 1996. *Embedded Competitiveness: Taiwan's Shifting Role in the International Footwear Sourcing Networks.* Ph.D. diss., Duke University.

Chu Yun-han. 1999. "Surviving the East Asian Financial Storm: The Political Foundations of Taiwan's Economic Resilience." In *The Politics of the Asian Economic Crisis,* edited by T. J. Pempel, 184–202. Ithaca, N.Y.: Cornell University Press.

Donaghu, M. T., and R. Barff. 1990. "Nike Just Did It: International Subcontracting and Flexibility in Athletic Footwear Production." *Regional Studies* 24, no. 6: 537–552.

Fligstein, N. 1996. "Markets as Politics: A Political-Cultural Approach to Market Institutions." *American Sociological Review* 61, no. 4: 656–673.

Gereffi, Gary, and M. Korzeniewicz, eds. 1994. *Commodity Chains and Global Capitalism.* Westport, Conn.: Praeger.

Gold, T. 1986. *State and Society in the Taiwan Miracle.* Armonk, N.Y.: Sharpe.

Granovetter, M. 1985. "Economic Action and Social Structure: The Problem of Embeddedness." *American Journal of Sociology* 91, no. 3: 481–510.

———. 1992. "Economic Institutions as Social Constructions: A Framework for Analysis." *Acta Sociologica* 35, no. 1: 3–11.

Harrison, B. 1994. *Lean and Mean.* New York: Basic.

Hirsch, P., et al. 1990. "Clean Models vs. Dirty Hands." In *Structures of Capital,* edited by S. Zukin and P., DiMaggio, 9–56. Cambridge: Cambridge University Press.

Hsieh, Chaio-Min. 1964. *Taiwan-Illa Formosa.* London: Butterworths for the Catholic University of America.

Hsing, Y.-T. 1996. "Trader, Manager, and Flexibility of Enterprise Networks: Taiwanese Fashion Shoe Industry in Southern China." Paper presented at the Conference on Economic Governance and Flexible Production in East Asia, Taiwan.

Kjelleren, D. L. 1992. "The Mexican Footwear Revolution." Paper presented at the 16th International Show of the Suppliers and Fashion Preview for the Leather and Shoe Industry.

Levy, B. 1991. "Transaction Costs, the Size of Firms, and Industrial Policy: Lessons from a Comparative Study of the Footwear Industry in Korea and Taiwan." *Journal of Development Economics* 34: 151–178.

Lipietz, A. 1987. *Mirages and Miracles: The Global Crisis of Fordism.* London: Verso.

Piore, Michael J., and Charles F. Sabel. 1984. *The Second Industrial Divide: Possibilities for Prosperity.* New York: Basic.

Porter, M. E. 1990. *The Competitive Advantage of Nations.* New York: Free Press.

Smelser, N. J., and R. Swedberg. 1994. "The Sociological Perspective on the Economy." In *The Handbook of Economic Sociology,* edited by N. J. Smelser and R. Swedberg, 3–26. Princeton: Princeton University Press.

Storper, M., and R. Salais. 1997. *Worlds of Production: The Action Frameworks of the Economy.* Cambridge, Mass.: Harvard University Press.

TFMA. 1989. *30-Year History of Taiwan's Shoe Manufacturing Industry.* Taipei: Taiwanese Footwear Manufacturer's Association.

Wade, R. 1990. *Governing the Market: Economic Theory and the Role of Government in East Asian Industrialization.* Princeton: Princeton University Press.

Winckler, E. A., and S. Greenhalgh, eds. 1988. *Contending Approaches to the Political Economy of Taiwan.* Armonk, N. Y.: Sharpe.

2

Flexibility under Unorganized Industrialism? The Experience of Industrial Restructuring in Hong Kong

Tai Lok Lui and Stephen W. K. Chiu

Rising production costs and the erosion of former competitive advantages have increasingly been recognized as critical challenges for the future development and competitiveness of industries in the newly industrialized economies (NIEs) of East Asia. Accordingly, the agenda for research on the East Asian NIEs has shifted during the 1990s in significant ways. While studies once focused on the structural, institutional, and cultural sources of economic success, today there is more interest in the growing pressures for restructuring in a business environment that is changing due to economic globalization (see, for example, Clark and Kim 1995). Similarly, the search for a single development model has tended to give way to an emphasis on multiple trajectories of development (cf. Humphrey 1995). One key topic at the end of the decade concerns the survival strategies of East Asian manufacturing industries confronting the harsh reality of intensified protectionism, rising production costs, and fierce competition from other industrializing economies. This stimulates a series of interrelated questions: How will crucial actors be integrated in the world economy? How likely are each of the East Asian NIEs to maintain their advantage over other industrializing economies in the region? What new niches and opportunities must be pursued if they are to enjoy continued development?

Like other East Asian NIEs, Hong Kong is undergoing a process of economic restructuring. In this chapter we examine the restructuring process of Hong Kong's industries and relate this to the discussion of flexibility and economic governance in East Asia (also see Chiu and Lui 1995; Chiu, Ho, and Lui 1997; Lui and Chiu 1994). The first section discusses the institutional configuration of the industrial restructuring process in Hong Kong. Briefly, Hong Kong's manufacturing industries failed to upgrade their technology. Nor have they been successful (despite noteworthy exceptions) in moving to the top end of design or marketing activities or in launching their own brand-name products. Essentially, Hong Kong's manufacturing industries remain labor-intensive in character and their main coping strategy has been massive relocation of production to south China. At the same time, capitalizing on its competitive advantages in commercial and trading activities, Hong Kong is becoming a business networking center for manufacturing.

The second section of this chapter reports on our study of the electronics and garment industries and uses these cases to illustrate our arguments put forth in the previous section. In one sense, Hong Kong's industries have demonstrated a remarkable "numerical" flexibility in shifting production to another locality and reducing local production, but they also have exhibited a notable absence of a strategy of constant production innovation or more dynamic forms of flexibility. Lastly, we conclude our discussion of restructuring experiences in Hong Kong by highlighting the impact of societal institutions on the channeling of firms into different restructuring strategies. We argue that Hong Kong's dominant form of institutions of economic governance is primarily based on market transactions with a dearth of public-sector support. Relations among firms are similarly market based and bear little resemblance to the relational and collaborative networks often described in the East Asian development literature.

INDUSTRIAL RESTRUCTURING IN HONG KONG

Elsewhere we have described Hong Kong as a case of industrial restructuring under unorganized industrialism (Chiu and Lui 1995). Hong Kong's manufacturing establishments are mainly run by small local entrepreneurs. With an average of twelve employees in 1995 (Industry Department 1996: 8), in that same year 88.5 percent of all manufacturing establishments employed fewer than twenty persons. Among the 31,114 establishments in the manufacturing sector, only 430 were operated by foreign capital (13). Most of these manufacturing establishments are original equipment manufacturing (OEM) producers oriented toward export markets. They receive their orders through local import-export houses which, in turn, are connected with overseas buyers through global commercial networks (Chu 1988; Yau 1995).

In the language of the commodity-chain literature, Hong Kong is articulated to the global economy through buyer-driven commodity chains (Gereffi 1994). This accounts for both the strength and weaknesses of Hong Kong's manufacturers. On the one hand, it reflects the ability of Hong Kong manufacturers to capitalize on the history of the colony as a port and trading city and highlights the advantage of having been the first of the East Asian NIEs to launch export-oriented industrialization. The experience in trading and commerce and early exposure to foreign markets sharpened the sensitivity of local manufacturers to changes in the global market. Hong Kong manufacturers are renowned for their ability to respond promptly to changes in consumer tastes and fashion, and their commercial sense is widely understood to be among their principal competitive advantages (for an interesting discussion of the attractiveness of sourcing garments from and through Hong Kong, see Birnbaum 1993). However, this very sensitivity also inclines Hong Kong's manufacturers to produce fashionable products with existing labor-intensive production processes, rather than to concentrate on product diversification or on technological upgrading aimed at enhancing competitiveness through a deepening of production sophistication (Lui and Chiu 1993; 1994). In other words, Hong Kong industrialists seem more capable of moving from one fashionable product to another than of carrying out organizational and productive restructuring in order to enhance competitiveness.

Their strength lies in market responsiveness—flexibility in changing from one kind of product to another—which is based on a kind of numerical flexibility in which they can expand and contract production and change products quickly without investing in specialized technologies (Lui and Chiu 1994; also see Ng 1992: chap.7). In this regard, the established subcontracting networks in Hong Kong facilitate a form of flexible production designed to meet the needs of overseas buyers. Hong Kong's manufacturers are flexible OEM producers who know where to find new sources of orders and how to assemble new, trendy products.

It is our argument that the debate about whether the colonial administration pursued a laissez-faire approach to economic governance is essentially misplaced. The colonial administration was always selectively interventionist—or indeed, more correctly put, selectively noninterventionist. It was active in the provision of public housing, education, and medical services, and in building the infrastructure for economic development (Castells, Goh, and Kwok 1990). It assumed an important role in the regulation of matters concerning finance and banking, and at points of crisis it intervened to preserve macroeconomic stability (Jao 1988: 53–4). However, the colonial government eschewed policies that entailed direct assistance to particular industries in production or financial matters (Lui and Chiu, 1996; Chiu and Lui, 1995). While policies such as mass public housing (in the form of a "social wage") were significant as indirect subsidies to manufacturers carrying out labor-intensive production in the 1960s and 1970s, these policies became less relevant with the emergence of a new era of competition that required manufacturers to enhance the sophistication of production processes in order to survive.

Indeed, in contrast to the role of the state in other East Asian NIEs, the colonial administration in Hong Kong was neither developmental nor entrepreneurial. The kinds of support provided by the government were mainly infrastructural and institutional (also see Wong 1991; Lui and Chiu, 1996: 236–241). But such supports were not capable of assisting individual manufacturers in adjusting to the changing business environment. In the eyes of the government bureaucrats, issues of technological upgrading and organizational restructuring were matters best left to the market; these elements formed part of the private domain of challenges to be undertaken by manufacturers on their own initiative. Thus, the government typically maintained its detachment from subsidizing specific industries and from directly favoring any particular industrial activity with regard to R&D or other matters related to technological development or production sophistication. When in the late 1980s the government attempted to launch Hong Kong into high-tech industries and invested more in R&D, it proved too little, too late (Chiu, Ho, and Lui 1997). In fact, the only selective assistance to industries appeared in the area of human resources, in which the state shouldered much of the training needs of industries. Apart from universal basic education, the state invested heavily in publicly funded tertiary institutions and in the Vocational Training Council and its technical institutes. State intervention in training was selective in the sense that it targeted specific industries rather than aiming to instill general basic skills across the workforce. Still, this was the only spot of selective state incentives for manufacturing against the backdrop of universal assistance to all forms of private business.

Elsewhere, we have tried to explain the passive role of the colonial state in industrial development in terms of the historical formation of the state capital alliance (see Chiu 1994; Lui and Chiu 1996: 236–241). Relevant to our present discussion is that existing state policies were unable to assist local manufacturers to cope with the restructuring problem.

Meanwhile, despite the fact that Hong Kong is one of the world's leading financial centers, the local financial sector has maintained an arms-length relationship with industrial capital (Chiu and Lui 1995; Chiu 1994). Most small and medium manufacturers rely on a high degree of self-financing in raising their initial capital (Sit and Wong 1989). As shown in Lui and Chiu (1994: 59), the share of loans and advances to the manufacturing industries accounted for less than 20 percent of the total in the 1960s and declined further in the 1970s and 1980s. Such an institutional separation of finance and industry discourages restructuring strategies that require heavy capital investment and encourages capital-saving options, especially among smaller firms.

While manufacturers in Hong Kong receive little assistance from either the state or the banking sector in restructuring production processes, they are not constrained by a strong labor movement in making decisions about the reorganization of their firms. Local manufacturers are given plenty of leeway for organizing production flexibly—by using homeworkers, internal contractors, and subcontractors, and relocating production plants (on employers' use of informal work, see Lui 1994). Hong Kong's union movement is numerically weak, representing less than 20 percent of all employees. Union membership in the manufacturing sector is even lower—less than 10 percent (on the recent development of unionism, see Levin and Chiu 1993). Union shop-floor organizations are particularly weak. Consequently, in devising restructuring strategies, local manufacturers are almost free of resistance or interference from unions. Particularly relevant here is that unions are unable to resist the relocation of production to China.

It should be noted as well that in Hong Kong neither industrial capital nor labor are organized in such a manner as to encourage the emergence of corporatist arrangements to facilitate negotiation and compromise around joint strategies for shaping industrial restructuring. On the side of capital, local manufacturers have failed to organize to put pressure on the government to support technological upgrading. Similarly, they have failed to reach agreements with local unions on matters relating to a long-term strategy to cope with rising production costs. For its part, labor has also failed to develop its bargaining capability and to negotiate with local manufacturers to deal with massive plant relocations. The absence of some kind of bargaining arrangement makes it difficult to develop concerted action to cope with restructuring. Individual manufacturers are left on their own to devise the least costly strategy to tackle the problem posed by rising production costs.

Given their limited resources, local manufacturers tend to adopt a low-cost, short-term strategy to cope with the mounting pressures of protectionism, fierce competition from other NIEs, and rising production costs. In the mid-1970s they capitalized on the arrival of a new wave of migrants as a source of cheap labor for the continuation of labor-intensive production (Greenwood 1990). Since the 1980s, they have chosen increasingly to relocate production in new plants across the border in south China, where they can take advantage of abundant supplies of cheap land and labor. Indeed, one can argue that Hong Kong's manufacturing has been locked into a particular path of industrial development. The failure of technological upgrading and the absence of greater sophistication in production techniques in the mid-1970s (as noted by the 1979 Report of the Advisory Committee on Diversification) made it even more difficult to restructure industries in the more volatile climate of the 1980s and 1990s. More importantly, the institutional setting has been constitutive of the development trajectory of Hong Kong industries—the continuation of labor-intensive production with a quick response to the changes in the commercial environment of the global economy (for a comparative analysis of the development trajectories of manufacturing industries in Hong Kong and Singapore, see Chiu, Ho, and Lui 1997).

As a result of massive relocation, the number of industrial establishments in Hong Kong has dropped from 50,606 in 1988 to 31,114 in 1995 (on variations in the propensity of relocation, see Lui and Chiu 1994). Manufacturing employment fell correspondingly, from 875,250 in 1987 to 386,106 in 1995. Such restructuring and the concomitant transformation of Hong Kong into a business networking center for manufacturing have differential impacts on the local labor market. Production relocation has brought about a displacement of some 489,000 workers from manufacturing. Workers displaced by industrial restructuring tend to be female, older, and less-educated and less-skilled workers (Census and Statistics Department 1994).

Gender differences in life chances after displacement are significant. A telephone survey of 1,145 workers carried out in early 1995 showed that male production

Table 2.1   Growth of Real Wages (in percentages) by Occupations, 1989–1995

	1989	1990	1991	1992	1993	1994	1995
Craftsmen and operatives	1.4	2.4	–1.1	0.0	1.7	–2.1	–3.6
Nonproduction workers to supervisory level	4.6	2.9	–0.8	0.4	2.6	1.5	–1.3
Middle management and professionals[a]	9.0	4.9	3.8	3.5	4.6	4.1	3.8

Source: Census and Statistics Department 1991, 1996.

[a]Salary index (B) is used for managerial and professional employees. It measures the changes in salaries for middle-level managerial and professional employees who stayed in the same occupation and in the same company in both years. Therefore, it accounts for changes due to general increment, meritorious increase, and gain in seniority. It is a better indicator of the market power of these employees than the alternative, salary index (A), which also reflects changes in salaries, in addition to those measured by the (B) index, resulting from movements across companies and in and out of the occupations.

workers were more likely to keep their jobs in the manufacturing sector (Chiu, Lai, and Lee 1996). Whereas 55.7 percent of the men respondents stayed in manufacturing jobs, only 28.5 percent of women respondents were able to do so. Not only did they have difficulty in keeping their manufacturing jobs, the women respondents also were more likely to exit from full-time employment (29.3 percent compared with 5.6 percent of men respondents).

On the other hand, those who remained in manufacturing experienced only slow improvement, if not deterioration, in their incomes (Chiu and Levin 1993: 20–25). Furthermore, there has been a widening of the income disparity between production workers (i.e., craftsmen and other operatives), middle-level employees (such as supervisors, clerical workers, and technical staff), and managers in many manufacturing industries (for textiles and garment, see Chiu and Levin 1993). While the real wages of lower-level employees remained stagnant, those on top of the income ladder enjoyed hefty increases in wages and salaries (table 2.1). A growing income gap between male and female employees in manufacturing coincided with the internal stratification of the workforce, as women also filled low-level operative positions while supervisory staff or above were often male. Hence, as elsewhere, the impact of restructuring has been dualistic in nature and has widened income inequality based on occupations and credentials.

GARMENT-MAKING

Our survey of garment and electronics manufacturers, carried out in 1992 (Chiu and Lui 1995), found significant differences between the two industries in their restructuring strategies (see table 2.2). While these coping strategies were shaped partially by the existing structure of the two industries, these strategies in turn were constitutive of interfirm linkages and thus shaped the future paths of development of garment and electronics production in Hong Kong. Consideration of the responses of these two leading industries to the changing economic environment illustrates the formation of a particular course of industrial restructuring.

Table 2.2 shows that, compared with electronics, the garment industry is less likely to upgrade its technology, is more restricted to Hong Kong-based production, and has a tendency to rely on various forms of informal work to enhance its production flexibility. The fact that the garment industry has made limited effort in technological upgrading is no surprise. First, the industry itself has made little progress in applying new technology to the assembly process (Mody and Wheeler 1990: 38). Most of the technologically sophisticated and automated processes (such as computer-aided design linked to marking and cutting) are found in the preassembly and postassembly stages. Other than computerization in pattern grading and marker making, "only limited automation of sewing operations has so far taken place" (Industry Department 1992a: 39; also see 1992b: 19).

Second, application of linked automation to garment-making processes must meet the difficult task of matching the needs of volatile markets. In a case reported in the *Report on Industrial Automation Study* commissioned by the Industry Department (1992b: 19), the adoption of an integrated computerized system of pattern grading, marker planning, and cutting was found useful mainly for large batch orders and for production using fabrics not requiring any pattern matching. Those

Table 2.2 Production Strategies of Garment-Making and Electronics Establishments (in percentages)

Production Strategy/Industry	Garment (N = 69)	Electronics (N = 50)
Organization of Production		
Capacity subcontracting	46.4	22.0
Outwork	47.8	10.0
Internal contracting	43.5	0.0
Employment of Flexible Workforce		
Temporary worker	40.6	26.0
Foreign worker	2.9	2.0
Part-time worker	17.4	22.0
Technological Development		
New technology	21.7	48.0
R&D activities	4.3	46.0
Relocation		
Overseas production	30.4	52.0
"Still running own factory production in Hong Kong"	78.3	62.0

Source: 1992 Sample Survey.
Note: Percentages do not all total 100 percent due to rounding errors.

producing fashion garments and working for small batch orders will not find such automation attractive (also see Bailey 1993: 38–39). In short, technological upgrading is not an important strategy for the restructuring of garment production. This is especially so for most Hong Kong garment producers because they are primarily small manufacturers producing for the volatile market for fashion garments.

Although Hong Kong's garment manufacturers are losing their cost advantages, garment production still maintains a local base. Our survey findings show that only 30.4 percent of our respondents use offshore production and 78.3 percent still carry out their factory production in Hong Kong.

However, it is important to note that many garment manufacturers have also moved at least some of their production offshore. Indeed, there are signs that more and more garment manufacturers, in consideration of rising production costs, would adopt the relocation strategy and move their production lines to south China as well. Survey findings reported by the Industry Department in 1990 suggested that only 22 percent of garment manufacturing respondents had production facilities outside Hong Kong (the average for all respondents was 27 percent) (Industry Department 1990: 34). In 1994, survey findings showed that 36 percent of interviewed garment manufacturers had gone offshore (the average figure was 34 percent) (Industry Department 1994: 323). However, despite a trend of moving garment production offshore, the garment industry remains relatively closely tied to its base in Hong Kong (also see Lui and Chiu 1994; Industry Department 1994: 50).

Two major factors explain why garment manufacturing remains relatively Hong Kong-based. First, whereas larger firms with retail outlets in Hong Kong and other Asian cities can rely on their relocated plants in Mainland China for production (Giordano Holdings 1991), other manufacturers produce primarily for the domestic markets. For those small fashion producers for the local market, there is little incentive to relocate. Second, many garment manufacturers decide not to go offshore because of quota restrictions and the rules of origin in effect in Hong Kong. Largely due to such institutional restrictions, unless products are targeted at local consumption or unrestrained markets, garment manufacturers have to continue their production in Hong Kong.

Given the institutional restrictions on relocation and the structural constraints on technological upgrading, garment manufacturers find themselves increasingly locked into a system of flexible production for volatile export markets. Most local manufacturers have to make every effort to increase their production flexibility to keep pace with rapid changes in styles and tastes at the end of fashion and garment retailing. Indeed, the survival of garment-making in Hong Kong hinges upon its success in fighting its battle on two fronts. On the one hand, local manufacturers must maintain their ties with the global sourcing and subcontracting networks. That Hong Kong's garment-making industry has its origins in strong commercial ties is an advantage (Birnbaum 1993; Chu 1988; Kurt Salmon Associates 1992: 72). This shapes local manufacturers' sensitivity to the needs of importing markets, especially at the level of retailing, since in the new consumption environment greater responsiveness to rapidly changing retail markets is the basic requirement for success. On the other hand, given the imperative to respond quickly to changes in consumption, Hong Kong's garment manufacturers have to obtain a high level of flexibility in production. The extensive use of various forms of informal work by local garment manufacturers (see table 2.2) has to be understood in light of such changes in the markets for garment products. Almost half of our garment manufacturer respondents have used capacity subcontracting, outwork, and internal contracting.

Flexible production, of course, can be seen as a game of risk shifting: whereas larger establishments are likely to farm out part of their production to subcontractors, small establishments, relying heavily on such subcontracting activities to maintain their production, shift part of the burden of risk to internal contractors and women homeworkers. Interestingly, the long history of export-oriented, small workshop production has given rise to a network of interdependent producers. The existence of such a network makes various forms of subcontracting activities transaction cost efficient (cf. Levy 1990). This constitutes an industrial structure that suits well the needs of developing flexible, labor-intensive production that can respond to rapid market changes.

The characterization of Hong Kong's garment-makers as "flexible," however, should be qualified by noting the absence of the other indicators of adaptive flexibility in the restructuring process. For example, Hong Kong garment-makers have always had a reputation for high quality and the ability to produce a large variety of products. The restructuring process does not seem to have enhanced capacities for constant quality improvement and product innovation. Garment-manufacturers remaining in Hong Kong are flexible only in the sense that they have been able to capitalize on their long experience in the trade and on the availability of high-quality workers able to move from one type of product to another. The range of product variation remains quite narrow, such as from men's shirts to women's blouses or shirts of different design, for in Hong Kong shifts from one product to another seldom result from a marked improvement in productivity or technological capability. For example, moving from T-shirts to high-quality ski jackets is rare. Rather, because of the versatility of workers and management as well as hefty investment in preassembly and postassembly automation, firms manage to juggle a wide range of different products that nonetheless are technologically comparable. Another indicator of the limitation in the flexibility achieved by local garment firms is that common forms of "flexible" garment-manufacturing technology, like the modular production system, remain rare in Hong Kong (Berger and Lester 1997: 159–160). Instances of reorganization of production to maximize flexibility and quality also appear to be isolated to a few firms rather than diffused across a wide spectrum of enterprises.

Furthermore, the dramatic shrinkage in both local employment and the number of firms and the fact that about 30 percent of all firms have invested overseas reminds us that a large number of Hong Kong enterprises have not been able to shift to high-quality flexible production systems. In terms of product innovation, most Hong Kong manufacturers have failed to move to the higher end of the fashion market in order to offset rising local production costs. As a result, they have to rely on the cheap land and labor across the border to continue producing for mass overseas markets. While we do not have data on production methods after relocation, given the much larger size of most plants in China and the recent migrant status of most workers there, it is difficult to imagine that relocated plants are comparable to local ones in terms of flexibility or versatility. Because of the low costs of production, it also appears that in some cases firms have actually moved downstream in terms of the market segment for which they produce.

Such a strategy of flexible production has significant repercussions on the deployment of human resources in the garment industry. Despite claims among employers about increasing labor scarcity, only about 39 percent of our surveyed garment producers claim to have instituted some kind of employee retention measures. Even among firms that do have employee retention schemes, these do not depart significantly from approaches that are conventional in Hong Kong. The "cash nexus" that permeated employment relations in manufacturing is still evident in our survey. Furthermore, the retention strategy is not tied to a program of human resources development. Our respondents are not enthusiastic about training their current employees. Almost 70 percent of them suggest they have no training program for their employees.

Wage movements in the industry confirm that garment employers are by no means generous in rewarding their workers. Real wages of garment workers consistently lag behind the trend of the overall economy (Chiu and Lui 1994). What is more, garment wages suffered a long-term decline during the 1980s, when labor scarcity was purportedly most severe. For one thing, the small size of garment manufacturers and the competitive pressure they face leave little margin for rewarding their workers handsomely. Furthermore, the relative contraction of local production and the shrinkage of the labor force in the garment industry create a paradoxical situation in which labor scarcity drives up real wages in the whole economy while the reserve army of garment workers enables employers in that industry to put a lid on wage increases. Consequently, adjustments in money wages have lagged behind inflation.

ELECTRONICS

Electronics establishments have followed a different strategy to cope with changes in the business environment. The leading restructuring strategy of the industry has been to relocate production to Mainland China, particularly the Pearl River Delta (Industry Department 1991b: IV–28). Among our surveyed electronics establishments, 52 percent have employed offshore production. More interesting is that 18 percent of our respondents have no production at all in Hong Kong and conduct manufacturing activities exclusively in their plants in Mainland China. A study of investments in the Pearl River Delta conducted by the Federation of Hong Kong industries confirms the trend toward relocation. Of the electronics establishments covered by the study, 69.4 percent had investment in the region (Industry & Research Division, Federation of Hong Kong Industries, 1992: 63), and it is suggested that:

> Such a significant extent of investment can be explained by the labor-intensive nature of the industry. . . . Since full scale automation is still uncommon, a large number of workers, particularly young workers, are needed. Faced with a severe shortage of labor in Hong Kong, which is complicated by the reluctance of the younger generation to enter the industrial workforce, the electronics industry has a strong incentive to take advantage of the abundant supply of labor across the border.

In terms of investment, electronics firms in the Pearl River Delta tend to concentrate in two clusters (67). At the one end, there are small and medium-sized firms with capitalization levels of less than five million Hong Kong dollars (39.2 percent), while at the other extreme there are larger firms with capitalization exceeding HK$20 million (20.8 percent). These findings suggest that the strategy of going offshore is by no means confined to larger firms. Given the geographical proximity between Hong Kong and the Delta, many small and medium-sized firms can "make use of the abundant supply of labor there to reduce production cost" (67).

Our survey findings also show that there is no significant association between the employment size of local establishments and that of offshore plants. In other words, those running larger establishments in Hong Kong do not necessarily have larger plants across the border. Although our survey data do not permit us to conduct a sophisticated statistical analysis of the strategic moves behind relocation, the answers elicited from our open-ended questions do allow us to discern, albeit tentatively, three possible strategic considerations in deciding whether to relocate. First is the strategy of reducing assembly processes in Hong Kong, reorganizing the local plant into an R&D section, and sending the more labor-intensive processes to offshore production. Among our respondents in the electronics industry, there is a significant association between investment overseas and conducting internal R&D. Those manufacturers who have started offshore production are more likely to carry out R&D in their Hong Kong establishments. More sophisticated processes are retained in their Hong Kong premises and assembly is done in their offshore plants. However, the extent to which Hong Kong electronics manufacturers have adopted such a restructuring strategy should not be overestimated, as we found that only about one third (34 percent) of our respondents had adopted this restructuring strategy. Indeed, in terms of technological sophistication, Hong Kong's electronics industry lags behind its East Asian competitors. As pointed out in the review of industrial automation by the Industry Department (1992b: 37), "[o]n the whole, the industry only invests in hard automation equipment if forced to by their buyers, instead of continually seeking out opportunities to add extra value for, and hence extract extra value from, their customers." The R&D activities of these OEM producers consist more of product modifications than of core technology development. In this regard, the progress of technological upgrading achieved by the electronics industry has to be interpreted with caution (see table 2.2; see also Lui and Chiu 1994).

The second strategy is similar to the above except that the local establishment concentrates on trading instead of R&D. Our survey of electronics establishments showed that 36 percent do not have their own factory production in Hong Kong. And among these firms, 50 percent rely solely on their offshore plants for production, while one-third carry out the production through relocated plants and subcontracting out to local or offshore factories, and the rest have all their production finished by subcontractors. While some of these establishments have retained the product development process in their local plants, many have more or less transformed themselves into trading firms. In some cases, these firms assume the role of sourcing agent for transnational corporations. Taking advantage of their business contacts with local subcontractors and manufacturers based in Mainland China, they can become commercial agents facilitating international subcontracting.

Finally, there is the strategy of expanding production capacity by relocation. This strategy is adopted by many medium-sized firms which see the advantages of the abundant supplies of cheap labor and inexpensive land across the border and try to make profits by expanding the scale of production rather than moving toward technological sophistication (Industry Department 1991b: IV–61). For the electronics industry as a whole, this strategy has the danger of further hindering the upgrading of production technology and thus reducing long-run competitiveness. However, for individual manufacturers, this strategy makes it possible to hold on to labor-intensive production and to make lucrative profits through a significant increase in sales volume.

The relocation of electronics production is now in full swing. In this light, it is not difficult to understand why various forms of informal work (like capacity subcontracting and outworking) are insignificant to local electronics manufacturers. If they are looking for production strategies to reduce costs and enhance flexibility, they turn to setting up their own plants in the Pearl River Delta or finding subcontractors across the border. A Hong Kong-based production strategy is losing its attractiveness.

The case of electronics best illustrates the strategy among local manufacturers to pursue one form of flexibility at the expense of another. By capitalizing on the efficient flow of information and resources in the market, both domestic and international, local firms have been able to identify and respond to changing demands quickly. As in the case of garments, the industry's flexibility is manifested largely in its ability to shift from one product to another based on broadly similar technology and production processes. The key component appears to be the industry's "strong capabilities in aesthetic design" (Industry Department 1995: 64), which helps firms make cosmetic changes in products or apply similar technology in different products. For example, electronic watches or radios are being installed on various types of gifts and accessories, such as desktop organizers. Changes in "designs" also often mean only changes in the shape or color of the chassis.

The industry is also flexible in that firms have been able to shed workers and move production abroad virtually at will in response to fluctuating demands and cost conditions. Nevertheless, it is difficult to describe Hong Kong electronics manufacturers as capable of implementing constant process innovation and product development. Most Hong Kong firms remain locked into the lower end of the markets, with their production dependent on the low cost of activity in China rather than improved product quality or innovation. Many of the so-called high-tech or high-end firms in Hong Kong pale in comparison with those of the other East Asian NIEs. Thus, on the one hand, Hong Kong's manufacturers are flexible in shifting production spatially when needed. On the other hand, relatively few firms are following a learning curve and moving "upward" in the technology or value-added ladder. Indeed, Hong Kong firms are flexible in their ability to shift resources from assembly production to other upstream activities like merchandising and headquarter functions, but we believe this only represents a very limited dimension in the adaptive flexibility observed elsewhere. Hong Kong firms have been more flexible in the sense that they have become more focused in their operation and have managed to shed production when necessary, but they have not been capable of generating the momentum for constant process and product innovation. At a time when South Korea, Taiwan, and Singapore are all capitalizing on the boom in computer equipment and producing high-end components like memory chips, optical scanners, monitors, and hard disks, Hong Kong is still strongest in a low-tech niche like subassemblies (e.g., chassis), largely because of the low labor costs in China.

THE EMERGENT INDUSTRIAL STRUCTURE

The impacts of relocation on manufacturing industries are many. What interests us here, first, are the effects of industrial relocation on employment in the manufacturing sector. The drastic reduction of manufacturing employment by almost half a million workers between 1987 and 1995 reflects the character of Hong Kong's manufacturing. It shows that, given the labor-intensive character of manufacturing in Hong Kong, the existing workforce can be easily replaced by cheap labor across the border. Local manufacturers have long been looking for horizontal expansion and numerical flexibility, and thus local workers are displaced.

Meanwhile, in this process of labor-market restructuring, it is interesting to observe that, despite a reduction of the employment of production workers (by 43 percent between 1981 and 1991), most manufacturing industries have experienced an increase in their employment of nonoperative employees, with the level of growth in such employment reaching 11 percent during 1981–1991 (Census and Statistics Department 1993: 119). These nonoperative employees are engaged in "supporting services such as sourcing of raw materials, product design, production management and engineering, marketing and so on" (120). This change in the employment mix shows the general trend of production reorganization in the face of changes in the business environment.

A clearer picture of the impacts of industrial restructuring on manufacturing employment is shown in a review of the changes in workforce composition in the garment and electronics industries (table 2.3). It is evident that there has been a drastic reduction in the proportion of production and related workers in the manufacturing workforce. In 1981, 82.3 percent of the manufacturing workforce was engaged in production and related activities. By 1991, the figure had fallen to 68.2 percent. In the period 1981–1991, the broadly defined white-collar employees increased significantly, reaching 30 percent by the end of the period.

The pattern of reduction in the number of production workers coupled with an increase in white-collar employees is observed in changes in the occupational structure of the garment and electronics industries. In the apparel industry (excluding footwear), the percentage of production and related workers fell from 85 percent in 1981 to 72 percent in 1991. Compared with the relevant statistics of the manufacturing sector, the garment industry still shows its tenacity by maintaining a production base in Hong Kong. However, a trend toward gradually reducing garment production (and thus the employment of production workers) in Hong Kong is also observed.

Unlike garment-making, which has a production base more tightly tied to Hong Kong and, therefore, has experienced less significant changes in the composition of its workforce, electronics manufacturing has undergone a drastic drop in the number of production workers. As a percentage of the entire workforce, production workers declined from 81.5 percent in 1981 to 50.4 percent a decade later.

Table 2.3   The Occupational Structure of the Garment, Electronics, and All Manufacturing Industries, 1981–1991 (in percentages)

	Wearing Apparel			Machinery and Electronics			All Manufacturing		
	1981	1986	1991	1981	1986	1991	1981	1986	1991
PTAMW[a]	1.9	2.7	7.9	5.8	9.6	22.2	3.8	5.5	11.4
Clerical	4.8	6.6	15.9	7.7	9.8	21.7	5.8	8.0	18.6
Prod. and related	85.0	83.1	72.0	81.5	76.0	50.4	82.3	79.8	68.2
Others	8.3	7.6	4.2	5.0	4.6	5.3	8.1	6.7	1.9

Source: Unpublished census data.
Note: Percentages do not all total 100 percent due to rounding errors.
[a]PTAMW = professional, technical, administrative, and managerial workers.

Part of the explanation of the restructuring of the workforce lies in the increase, albeit limited, in the technological sophistication of electronics production itself. But more importantly, this is a consequence of the reorganization of production after relocation. As a result of developing offshore production in China, electronics manufacturers are able to expand production by utilizing the new supply of low-wage labor. That it is possible to relocate parts of or the entire production process to China provides local manufacturers with new options for organizing their business. We have discussed different strategies of production in connection to relocation in the above section and shall not repeat those points here. The increase in the share of professional, technical, administrative, and managerial staff, along with clerical workers (from 13.6 percent in 1981 to 43.9 percent in 1991) in the industry reflects the changing character of electronics production in Hong Kong. Production in Hong Kong and China is increasingly intertwined, and this reinforces the tendency to continue manufacturing fashion goods and to concentrate on the relatively labor-intensive end of electronics production. But as a result of industrial relocation, Hong Kong has become more of a strategic station for maintaining business ties with the world market than a production base for electronics production. A growing proportion of its workforce is engaged in technical, administrative, and clerical duties supporting production that has already gone offshore.

The aforementioned process of industrial restructuring can best be seen in the context of the broader restructuring of the Hong Kong economy since the 1970s. Hong Kong emerged as an industrial colony in the 1960s, and from the 1970s onward quickly developed its tertiary sector. Deindustrialization since the late 1980s is embedded in the economic restructuring process that has shaped Hong Kong into an international financial and commercial center. Indeed, a double restructuring process has taken place.

First, there is the general trend of a sectoral shift toward finance, trading, and services. The increase in employment in finance and business is largely an outcome of the development of Hong Kong into a world city within the global business network. Second, as noted above, within the manufacturing sector itself, the direction of change is toward becoming a more commercially oriented center rather than a production base. Manufacturers and traders are interested in maintaining their controlling headquarters in Hong Kong (Hong Kong Trade Development Council 1991), but the major operations of such headquarters are likely to involve trade and manufacturing-related activities rather than the core production processes. Hong Kong remains "an irreplaceable location for arranging trade financing and documentation" (vi). In this regard, the maturation of Hong Kong as an international financial center gives the colony an edge in strengthening the commercial component of its manufacturing sector. In short, the two processes of restructuring are interrelated. The emergence of Hong Kong as a world city of global financial and commercial activities has come to constitute a positive externality for the future development of its manufacturing sector. The well-developed financial and commercial business structures make it possible for local manufacturers to retain their competitiveness by enhancing their market intelligence and strengthening their ties with the global trading networks, and/or relocating production offshore.

There is, then, a process of restructuring Hong Kong's manufacturing into more of a commercially oriented business networking center (also see Census and Statistics Department 1995). The findings of a survey of manufacturers and traders carried out by the Hong Kong Trade Development Council in 1991 largely confirm our observation. When respondents were asked about their future operations in Hong Kong, 83 percent mentioned "controlling headquarters," 81 percent cited "documentation," 73 percent indicated "business negotiation," and 72 percent noted "trade financing" (Hong Kong Trade Development Council 1991: 13). The council emphasized that

> apparently, operations performed by surveyed companies in Hong Kong in the future would concentrate on trade and manufacturing-related services, including marketing, merchandising, business negotiation, transportation, warehousing and distribution, quality control, testing and certification, product design, R&D, sample making, prototyping, market research and after sale service. (12)

In brief, the strength of the Hong Kong economy lies in its status as a node for business networking.

This can be further illustrated by a government report on the increasing tendency of trading firms to take on manufacturing-related functions (Census and Statistics Department 1996). A growing number of import/export trading firms are now developing subcontract processing arrangements in China (SPAC). The number of such linkages increased by 63 percent, from 12,580 to 20,490, from 1992 to 1994. Many of these (7,280 in 1994) were already established as manufacturing firms. Such subcontracting arrangements include all contractual agreements between a Hong Kong firm and a China counterpart to carry out production processing in China. The report describes the trend as follows:

> In a great number of other cases, essentially all manufacturing processes are moved to China, leaving only such functions as marketing, orders processing, materials sourcing, design, product development, prototype making and quality control with the local firms. That is, the local firms have shifted their operational status from that of manufacturing to that of trading, albeit the fact that they may provide technical support services to the production in China. . . . Besides, many traditional import/export firms have also become engaged in SPAC to take advantage of cheap, abundant resources in China. . . . Furthermore, quite a large number of new . . . [trading] firms are also set up in recent years to serve as a local base for new manufacturing firms in China, operating in a way different from traditional importers/exporters. (Census and Statistics Department 1996: FA3)

The report also outlines the kind of services rendered in connection with SPAC by trading firms with manufacturing-related functions. About 98 percent of the firms are estimated to have provided sourcing of raw materials, 81 percent product design, 79 percent sample and mold making, and 73 percent production planning, management, and control. About 68 percent also offered technical support in quality control. Hence, manufacturing firms in Hong Kong, while shrinking their local production processes, have concentrated on supporting services to manufacturing units in China and elsewhere. Therefore a trend of convergence is observable between manufacturing and trading firms. Nevertheless, it should be recalled that the relocated manufacturing firms or firms with SPAC are essentially producing the same range of products as in the late 1980s, without major enhancements in value-added or technological sophistication.

INTERPRETING THE RESTRUCTURING PROCESS

The experience of Hong Kong's industries shows that economic restructuring is embedded in history and geography. First of all, the trajectory of Hong Kong's manufacturing development has imposed constraints on its own future. The relocation of production to south China has to be seen as a low-cost, short-term strategy in the context of a continuation of labor-intensive production. In this regard, history matters in the sense of path dependency (cf. North 1990: 100). A particular structure of industry functions as a self-reinforcing mechanism for a certain path of industrial development. Massive relocation to south China with an eye on the abundant supplies of cheap land and labor is an outcome of what we have called unorganized industrialism (Chiu and Lui 1995; Chiu, Ho, and Lui 1997).

Second, the effects of history work through preestablished social ties. While it is important to note the diversity in transactional channels for industrial investments in the Pearl River Delta region, ethnic (in terms of place of origin) and kinship ties constitute an important factor in shaping the choice of investment location (Smart and Smart 1991; Leung 1993). And following this point, we can see that relocation is constituted by geopolitical factors, where history and geography interact.

Mainland China is the hinterland for Hong Kong. That Hong Kong was a British colony on the border of communist China did not deter local industrial capitalists from utilizing resources from the mainland for their own profit-making purposes. Prior to its opening to foreign investment, China facilitated industrialization in Hong Kong by supplying food and daily necessities at low cost (Schiffer 1991) and providing industrialists with repeated waves of laborers through legal and illegal migration (Greenwood 1990). When economic reform was carried out after the fall of the Gang of Four, and with the subsequent further opening of the socialist economy for capitalist offshore production, China, especially the region around the Pearl River Delta, became the destination for Hong Kong's relocated plants. Indeed, it is fair to say that south China and Hong Kong, at least in terms of economic connections, were increasingly intertwined (also see Ho and Kueh 1993) well before Hong Kong's reintegration with the mainland. For well over a decade, the development of the Hong Kong economy has been conditioned largely by the course of economic reform in China.

Third, in terms of economic governance, Hong Kong can be put squarely into the category of governance by market mechanism. As stated at the outset, we do not want to deemphasize in any sense the effect of the colonial state on economic activities, but we would stress that one of the most important effects of the state's arms-length industrial policy has been to contribute to the dominance of market considerations in making restructuring decisions. The major institutions in Hong Kong, whether the state, the financial system, or the industrial relations regime, have all operated in the direction of "freeing" industrial production from institutional regulation rather than constraining it. Nor have institutions played a significant role in enabling firms to pursue technological and product upgrading. Elsewhere, our comparative analysis of Hong Kong and Singapore suggests a marked difference in restructuring strategies, demonstrating how different modes of economic governance can shape the course of industrial change (Chiu, Ho, and Lui 1997). In Singapore, economic governance is orchestrated by the state in collaboration with multinational corporations, whereas in Hong Kong a form of "unorganized industrialism" largely leaves this function to individual firms. Vertical linkages, between the state and firms and within multinationals, rather than horizontal interfirm linkages, generally have shaped economic behavior. To be sure, economic or industrial activities are no less embedded or constituted by the institutional framework in Hong Kong than in Singapore, but the effect of the institutional framework on major decisions concerning restructuring has been to accentuate the impact of market signals on the decision-making process of firms.

It is now customary to highlight the importance of relational networks or "trust" in Hong Kong's economic life (Wong 1990). In fact, it is easy to misinterpret our discussion of the presence of a dense network of subcontractors as evidence for the salience of governance by relational network. Zucker (1986) divides trust into three types: process-based, characteristic-based, and institution-based. Institution-based trust in Hong Kong is not uncommon and tends to be generated through the market. This is evident, for example, in the action of banks that issue letters of credit guaranteeing payments by firms, as well as in the proliferation among local firms of ISO 9000 quality assurance programs.

Common conceptions of Hong Kong's economy or manufacturing industries as part of the overseas Chinese business community, however, tend to highlight the "Chineseness" of the relations of trust and networks. The discussion of Shanghainese emigrant entrepreneurs falls squarely into this category (Wong 1988).

Based on the scanty information available, however, it is difficult to generalize this form of trust as permeating networking relations among manufacturing firms in Hong Kong or between contracting and subcontracting firms. Yau's (1995) study highlights, by contrast, the "process-based" character of the "trust" among firms in the manufacturing sector. Apart from a small circle of kin members of personal friends, trust among industrial producers or between them and the trading firms is largely a product of repeated exchanges, in which one party or both parties are willing to forgo short-term, unilateral gains in return for long-term mutual benefits. Yau describes interfirm relations as a "precarious symbiosis," in which the more powerful party often exploits the more vulnerable, with the latter making all of the sacrifices in order to maintain a long-term relationship. The threat of withdrawal from the relationship by the powerful party is also important to preventing cheating and enforcing compliance. Trust, then, is not a generalized commodity permeating the Hong Kong manufacturing sector. Rather, it is cultivated gradually and becomes embedded in personal relations. Relations between firms, although they sometimes can contribute to the mobilization of resources, are often "weak ties" rather than the strong ones observed in such countries as Japan, Taiwan, and Italy.

Furthermore, the generalization of trust in the manner typically associated with Italian industrial districts or the dense networks of firms that dot Silicon Valley is hampered as well by the absence of the mechanisms and institutions which could reinforce collaborative networks. In Hong Kong, familism is strong, but it is confined to members of the immediate kin group (Lau 1982). Neither the state nor the banks have promoted collaboration in production, and business associations are not particularly effective. Nor are entrepreneurs bound together by a strong ethnic identity or professional ethos. In other words, as Doner and Hershberg (1999) point out, spatial proximity in a local area does not necessarily lead to collaboration or trust: "[e]ffective governance institutions are essential in order to bring about successful adaptation to changing environments." Agglomeration of firms in Hong Kong tends to highlight the competitive, rather than the collaborative, aspects of clustering. True, there are countless instances of repeated transactions among firms, but it does not necessarily follow that a "trustful" relationship exists between the relevant actors or that there is a significant exchange of information and resources. Indeed, in another set of interviews conducted for local garment firms, it was found out that interfirm linkages, especially those of a horizontal nature, played little part either in the diffusion of technology or the shaping of decisions for overseas relocation (Lai 1998). While personal relations between Hong Kong manufacturers and individuals (bureaucrats, entrepreneurs) on the mainland fostered the relocation of production there, the absence of a sustained collaborative network among manufacturers in Hong Kong ruled out the possibility for an alternative high road of restructuring. Social relations do play a big part in shaping the restructuring process, but these relations are rooted in noneconomic attributes, such as kinship, local ties, and friendship, and do not necessarily overlap with the preexisting network and linkages among firms.

CONCLUSION

As a result of industrial restructuring, Hong Kong's manufacturing is increasingly embedded in the broader development of the Pearl River region in south China.

However, available information shows that the development of this region bears little resemblance to that associated with the concept of an industrial district (Sabel 1989; Pyke, Becattini, and Sengenberger 1990). Industrial development in Hong Kong-south China exhibits no trend toward specialization. Nor are there signs of a balance between competition and cooperation in facilitating technological and production advancement (Industry & Research Division, Federation of Hong Kong Industries, 1992; 1993). Furthermore, manufacturing activities in the mainland are predominantly connected with buyer-driven commodity chains via Hong Kong. While ethnic and kinship ties contribute to the attraction of Hong Kong industrial capital to the Pearl River Delta, their potential role in helping to reorganize the labor-intensive character of Hong Kong's industries is not clear (but see Tsui-Auch 1999 for an assessment of different forms of production networks).

This question underscores the inadequacy of our understanding of networks and flexible production in Hong Kong. Many researchers recognize the importance of social networks and *guanxi* (personal connections) in handling economic transactions in Hong Kong (Redding 1990; Wong 1990; Yau 1995), and a considerable literature analyzes subcontracting activities and other forms of flexible production (see, for example, Chu 1992; Lui 1994), yet few attempts have been made to unravel the internal dynamics of such networks as they operate in practice. What are the limitations and constraints in the use of social networking in organizing flexible production of Hong Kong (Lui 1998)? Why are the subcontracting networks in Hong Kong not conducive to the formation of cooperative efforts for specialization, technological upgrading, and deepening production sophistication? These are important questions yet to be answered. Indeed, we need to know more about the characteristics of Hong Kong's flexible production in order to grapple with the future positioning of Hong Kong's manufacturing in the broader context of the Hong Kong-Pearl River Delta economic subregion.

Recent attempts by the government of the Hong Kong Special Administrative Region—the new local government created as a result of the transfer of sovereignty—to adopt a more aggressive approach to facilitating and supporting high-tech industries show that, unlike under the former colonial government, issues arising from the industrial restructuring process (particularly the damaging effects of a highly speculative bubble economy and rising unemployment rates) are gradually recognized as problems to be tackled (see Chief Executive's Commission on Innovation and Technology 1999). The slowdown of the Hong Kong economy since early 1998 was not directly an outcome of the Asian financial crisis. The kinds of problems Hong Kong encountered were very different from those that emerged in South Korea, Indonesia, and Thailand. However, the collapse of economic confidence in the region did expose Hong Kong to risks created by its own bubble economy. Attacks by speculators on the Hong Kong currency and the concomitant drastic downturn in the stock and property markets revealed the fragility of the Hong Kong economy. The long-term impacts of the hollowing out of manufacturing in Hong Kong, particularly the difficulties in generating new jobs for local people of different educational attainment and skill levels, came to the forefront in the context of this economic downturn. Unemployment rates rose to 6.3 percent during the summer of 1999. Furthermore, there is little evidence that the Hong Kong economy has been able to regain its competitiveness through cost cutting or enhancing its productive capabilities after the economic slowdown. Indeed, among the Four Dragons, Hong Kong lagged behind Singapore, South Korea, and Taiwan (for growth in GDP in the second season of 1999, Hong Kong had an increase of 0.5 percent while the others scored 6.7, 9.8, and 6.5 percent, respectively) in recovering from the economic downturn (*Hong Kong Economic Times*, 28 August 1999). Whether recent initiatives to launch information technology, such as the project of building a cyberport, can really turn the tide remains to be seen. What is quite clear is that Hong Kong is trapped in a niche of its own creation, and is not likely to find an easy way out.

BIBLIOGRAPHY

Bailey, T. 1993. "Organizational Innovation in the Apparel Industry." *Industrial Relations* 32: 30–48.

Berger, S., and R. Lester., eds. 1997. *Made By Hong Kong*. Hong Kong: Oxford University Press.

Birnbaum, D. 1993. *Importing Garments through Hong Kong*. Hong Kong: Third Horizon Press.

Castells, M., L. Goh, and R. Kwok. 1990. *The Shek Kip Mei Syndrome*. London: Pion.

Census and Statistics Department. 1993. "Structural Changes in Manufacturing Industries: 1981–1991." *Hong Kong Monthly Digest of Statistics: September.*

———. 1994. "Worker Displacement in Hong Kong." In *Social Data Collected by the General Household Survey Special Topics Report No. X*. Hong Kong: Government Printer.

———. 1995. "Trading Firms with Manufacturing-Related Functions." *Hong Kong Monthly Digest of Statistics: August.*

———. 1996. "Trading Firms with Manufacturing-Related Functions." *Hong Kong Monthly Digest of Statistics: August.*

Chief Executive's Commission on Innovation and Technology. 1999. *Second and Final Report*. Hong Kong: Government Printer.

Chiu, S. 1994. "The Politics of Laissez-Faire." Occasional Paper No. 40. Hong Kong Institute of Asia-Pacific Studies, Chinese University of Hong Kong.

Chiu, S., K. C. Ho, and T. L. Lui. 1997. *City-States in the Global Economy: Industrial Restructuring in Hong Kong and Singapore*. Boulder: Westview.

Chiu, S., O. K. Lai, and C. K. Lee. 1996. "Women Workers under Industrial Restructuring: Impacts, Predicaments and Responses." Hong Kong: Hong Kong Federation of Women.

Chiu, S., and D. Levin. 1993. "Labor under Industrial Restructuring in Hong Kong." Occasional Paper No. 21, Hong Kong Institute of Asia-Pacific Studies, Chinese University of Hong Kong.

Chiu, S., and T. L. Lui. 1994. "Sewing for Change: Production and Employment Restructuring of the Clothing Industry in Hong Kong." Paper presented at the Asia Industrial

Relations/Human Resources Research Network Conference in June at the Chung-hua Institute of Economic Research, Taipei.

———. 1995. "Hong Kong: Unorganized Industrialism." In *Asian NIEs and the Global Economy*, edited by G. Clark and W. B. Kim. Baltimore: Johns Hopkins University Press.

Clark, G., and W. B. Kim, eds. 1995. *Asian NIEs and the Global Economy*. Baltimore: Johns Hopkins University Press.

Chu, Y. W. 1988. "Dependent Industrialization: The Case of the Hong Kong Garment Industry." M.Phil. Thesis, Sociology Department, University of Hong Kong.

———. 1992. "Informal Work in Hong Kong." *International Journal of Urban and Regional Research* 16.

Doner, Richard, and Eric Hershberg. 1999. "Flexible Production and Political Decentralization: Elective Affinities in the Pursuit of Competitiveness." *Studies in Comparative International Development* 33, no. 4.

Gereffi, G. 1994. "The Organization of Buyer-Driven Global Commodity Chains." In *Commodity Chains and Global Capitalism*, edited by G. Gereffi and M. Korzeniewicz. Westport: Praeger.

Giordano Holdings. 1991. *Giordano Holdings Limited: New Issue*. Hong Kong: Giordano Holdings.

Greenwood, J. 1990. "Hong Kong: The Changing Structure and Competitiveness of the Hong Kong Economy," *Asian Monetary Monitor* 14: 21–31.

Ho, Y. P., and Y. Y. Kueh. 1993. "Whither Hong Kong in an Open-Door, Reforming Chinese Economy?" *Pacific Review* 6, no. 4: 333–351.

Humphrey, John. 1995. "Industrial Reorganization in Developing Countries: from Models to Trajectories." *World Development* 23, no. 1.

Industry & Research Division, Federation of Hong Kong Industries. 1992. *Hong Kong's Industrial Investment in the Pearl River Delta*. Hong Kong: Federation of Hong Kong Industries.

———. 1993. *Investment in China*. Hong Kong: Federation of Hong Kong Industries.

Industry Department. 1990a, 1991a, 1992a, 1994, 1995, 1996. *Hong Kong's Manufacturing Industries*. Hong Kong: Government Printer.

———. 1990b. *Survey of Hong Kong's Manufacturing Industries: 1990*. Hong Kong: Data and Services Division, Industry Department.

———. 1991b. *Techno-Economic and Market Research Study on Hong Kong's Electronics Industry: 1988–1989*. Hong Kong: Government Printer.

———. 1992b. *Report on Industrial Automation Study*. Hong Kong: Government Printer.

Jao, Y. C. 1988. "Monetary System and Banking Structure." In *The Economic System of Hong Kong*, edited by H. C. Y. Ho and L. C. Lau. Hong Kong: Asian Research Service.

Kurt Salmon Associates. 1992. *Techno-Economic and Market Research Study of Hong Kong's Textiles and Clothing Industries: 1991–1992*. Hong Kong: Government Printer.

Lai, Rebecca. 1998. "The Dynamics of Restructuring and Relocation: The Case of Hong Kong's Garment Industry." M.Phil. thesis, Sociology Department, Chinese University of Hong Kong.

Lau, S. K. 1982. *Society and Politics of Hong Kong*. Hong Kong: Chinese University Press.

Leung, C. K. 1993. "Personal Contacts, Subcontracting Linkages, and Development in Hong Kong-Zhujiang Delta Region." *Annals of the Association of American Geographers* 83, no. 2: 272–302.

Levin, D., and S. Chiu. 1993. "Dependent Capitalism, Colonial State and Marginal Unions: The Case of Hong Kong." In *Organized Labor in the Asia-Pacific Region*, edited by S. Frankel. Ithaca, New York: ILR Press.

Levy, B. 1990. "Transaction Costs, the Size of Firms and Industrial Policy." *Journal of Development Economics* 34: 151–178.

Lui, T. L. 1994. *Waged Work at Home: The Social Organization of Industrial Outwork in Hong Kong.* Aldershot, England: Avebury.

———. 1998. "Trust and Chinese Business Behavior." *Competition and Change* 3.

Lui, T. L., and S. Chiu. 1993. "Industrial Restructuring and Labor Market Adjustment under Positive Non-interventionism." *Environment and Planning A* 25: 63–79.

———. 1994. "A Tale of Two Industries: The Restructuring of Hong Kong's Garment-making and Electronics Industries." *Environment and Planning A* 26: 53–70.

———. 1996. "Merchants, Small Employers and a Non-interventionist State: Hong Kong as a Case of Unorganized Late Industrialization." In *Capital, the State, and Late Industrialization,* edited by J. Borrego, A. Alvarez Bejar, and Jomo K. S. Boulder: Westview.

Mody, A., and D. Wheeler. 1990. *Automation and World Competition.* New York: St. Martin's.

Ng, Irene W. C. 1992. "Flexible Production and the Creation of Competitive Advantage in an Asian Newly Industrializing Economy: Organization and Dynamics in the Hong Kong Electronics Industry." Ph.D. diss., Geography Department, University of California, Los Angeles.

North, D. 1990. *Institutions, Institutional Change and Economic Performance.* Cambridge: Cambridge University Press.

Piore, M., and C. Sabel. 1984. *The Second Industrial Divide.* New York: Basic.

Pyke, F., G. Becattini, and W. Sengenberger, eds. 1990. *Industrial Districts and Inter-firm Cooperation in Italy.* Geneva: International Institute for Labor Studies.

Redding, G. 1990. *The Spirit of Chinese Capitalism.* Berlin: Walter de Gruyter.

Sabel, C. 1989. "Flexible Specialization and the Re-emergence of Regional Economies." In *Reversing Industrial Decline?* edited by P. Hirst and J Zeitlin. Oxford: Berg.

Schiffer, J. 1991. "State Policy and Economic Growth: A Note on the Hong Kong Model." *International Journal of Urban and Regional Research* 15: 180–196.

Sit, V. F. S., and S. L. Wong. 1989. *Small and Medium Industries in an Export-Oriented Economy: The Case of Hong Kong.* Hong Kong: Centre of Asian Studies, University of Hong Kong.

Smart, J., and A. Smart. 1991. "Personal Relations and Divergent Economies." *International Journal of Urban and Regional Research* 15.

Trade Development Council, Hong Kong. 1991. *Survey on Hong Kong Domestic Exports and Re-exports and Triangular Trade.* Hong Kong: HK Trade Development Council.

Tsui-Auch, Lao Si. 1999. "Regional Production Relationships and Developmental Impacts." *International Journal of Urban and Regional Research* 23.

Ward, M. 1991. "Fashioning the Future." *Cultural Studies* 5: 61–76.

Wong, S. L. 1988. *Immigrant Entrepreneurs.* Hong Kong: Oxford University Press.

———. 1996. "Chinese Entrepreneurs and Business Trust." In *Asian Business Networks,* Gary B. Hamilton, ed. New York: Walter de Gruyter.

Wong, T. 1991. "A Comparative Study of the Industrial Policy of Hong Kong and Singapore in the 1980s." In *Industrial and Trade Development in Hong Kong,* edited by E. Chen, M. K. Nyaw, and T. Wong. Hong Kong: Centre of Asian Studies.

Yau, K. C. 1995. "The Precarious Symbiosis: Inter-organizational Relationships Among Domestic Producers in Hong Kong." M.Phil. thesis, Sociology Department, Chinese University of Hong Kong.

Zucker, L. G. 1986. "Production of Trust." *Research in Organizational Behavior* 8: 53–111.

3

Governance and Flexibility: The East Asian Garment Industry

Richard P. Appelbaum and David A. Smith

This chapter examines alternative forms of economic governance in East Asian apparel production. More specifically, we compare the strategies adopted by South Korean and Hong Kong-based overseas Chinese firms to achieve the flexibility necessary to be competitive in the global garment industry. We are particularly interested in understanding how competitive success is achieved in this highly labor-intensive, yet acutely quality- and fashion-sensitive sector, where rapid delivery of small "batch" runs is crucial (Elson 1989; Dicken 1992: chapter 8). Also, we view these factors in light of the recent "East Asian crisis," which created financial volatility in exchange and interest rates, making it imperative for firms to flexibly adapt to a rapidly changing macroeconomic context.

Insofar as flexibility calls for simultaneously minimizing production costs while rapidly responding to frequent market shifts, it has strong appeal in industries that entail tight coordination between design, production, and marketing. Apparel manufacturing is just such a sector (Dicken, 1992)—one that is characterized by ruthless competition, ongoing fashion innovation, and a high need for access to information, suppliers, buyers, production partners, and marketing outlets. Indeed, global garment production is a classic case of what Gereffi (1994) calls "buyer-driven commodity chains," in which "large retailers, brand-named marketers, and trading companies play the pivotal role in setting up decentralized production networks in a wide range of exporting countries" (Appelbaum and Gereffi 1994:44). This form of industrial organization differs from producer-driven commodity chains, in which "large industrial enterprises play the central role in controlling the production system (including its forward and backward linkages . . .)" (ibid.), as are typically found in capital- and technology-intensive industries dominated by transnational corporations (i.e., automobiles, electronics). In buyer-driven commodity chains, profits "derive not from scale, volume, and technological advances as in producer-driven chains, but rather from unique combinations of high-value research, design, sales, after-sales services, marketing, and financial services that allow buyers and branded merchandisers to act as strategic brokers in linking overseas factories and traders with evolving product niches in their main consumer markets" (Gereffi 1994: 99).

In theory, the "core competence" of a decentralized network such as the apparel chain is flexibility. In this chapter we ask whether different governance institutions can facilitate flexibility in the apparel sector, and whether these institutional differences result in different potentials for or kinds of industrial upgrading. Our focus is on the complex coordination of clothing production and marketing by U.S.-based buyers and retailers, the role of regionally based trading companies that serve as "middlemen" between western buyers and Chinese or Southeast Asian factories, and the "on the ground" organization of manufacturing itself. Our emphasis is on the contrasting ways in which Hong Kong and South Korean firms organize to address these challenges. The research for this chapter was carried out prior to the "East Asian crisis" of 1997–1998 (for a general discussion see Lim 1998), and there are now indications that the financial turbulence which struck the region during that period may not have the long-run implications that many feared, as even the relatively hard hit South Korean economy undergoes rapid recovery (WuDunn 1999; Boorman 1999). However, we suggest ways in which the crisis tested the two countries' economic governance structures. While we start from "structural" global political economy assumptions, clearly "local" actors (states, large and small firms, business associations, labor, etc.) can actively shape their situations (via bargaining over investment, contracts, etc.); despite the awesome power of key global corporations everything is not determined solely "from the top down."

From an East Asian perspective, one positive theme of our story is the continued functional importance of large regional firms, in particular the brokerage/mediating role played by Hong Kong- and Seoul-based companies. These institutions continue to be conduits for orders from buyers in the U.S. and Europe, and to play an important and profitable role. Here, social, familial, and personal networks are crucial assets, providing a way to maximize business opportunities. This form of "strategic networking" is far more important than vaguely defined "cultural" traits in explaining East Asia's relative economic success. We address these diverse sources of flexibility in the first two sections of this chapter. The first section lays out the broader context of apparel production in the region and more specifically in Hong Kong and South Korea. Our emphasis is on the maturation of the industry and the contrasting institutional responses of Hong Kong and South Korea to this evolution. Apparel production in Korea led the way toward rapid economic growth in the 1960s and 1970s based on giant vertically integrated companies (*chaebol*), while successful overseas Chinese firms in Hong Kong developed relatively loose, horizontally integrated structures relying on rich social network links.

The second section explores the consequences of these governance arrangements for productive flexibility. The *chaebol* form worked well in the early years and established a Korean reputation as respected "middlemen" in buyer-driven commodity chains; the looser but extensively networked Hong Kong firms seem to have been more successful in concentrating market information and promoting innovation. The third section addresses the implications of these differences for industrial upgrading. While Hong Kong apparel firms greatly benefit from subcontracting to low-wage producers in Mainland China, they also seem to be better suited for industrial upgrading, niche marketing, and diversification; Korean companies are finding it more difficult to adapt and are more prone to opt for "low road" strategies that utilize cheap labor (factories in Southeast Asia or undocumented migrant workers at home). Finally, we include a brief coda on the difficult period in 1997 and 1998 and how the contrasting institutional structures of the two countries fared.

We hold no illusions about the negative and exploitative aspects of "flexible production" at the lower levels of the garment commodity chains. "Flexible accumulation" is often equated with industrial upgrading through training, technological innovation, and reconfigured work organization, and is seen as a key to global competitiveness in a post-Fordist world (see, e.g., Piore and Sabel 1984; Scott and Angel 1988; Storper and Walker 1989). But flexibility can also have a dark underside: it frequently involves large amounts of subcontracting, temporary and casual workers, and aggressive anti-union practices, as Deyo (1995) demonstrates in his research on automobile factories in Thailand (see also Appelbaum 1996). Businessmen running subcontracting factories often are caught in relentless profit squeezes and rely on low wages, casual workers, "homework," and other low road strategies. Under these conditions, the prospects for industrial upgrading and meaningful economic development are poor. In the third section of this chapter, we explore the impact of different governance institutions for upgrading.

THE CONTEXT

The Garment Industry in East Asia

The textile and garment industries were crucial to the rise of industrial capitalism in England over two hundred years ago. They are now a "mature industry" with fairly standardized equipment and technology, relatively low investment requirements, high labor intensity, and the expectation of rapid return on capital (Moon 1987: 106–107). Just as this sector led the historic "Industrial Revolution" in Europe, textiles and apparel are widely seen as "start-up" industries in less-developed countries in the twentieth century. In the 1950s and 1960s, East Asian governments, with financial and technical assistance from U.S. aid programs, encouraged the growth and expansion of textile and garment production. By the

1970s South Korea, Taiwan, and Hong Kong had entered "the stage of massive exports" and were running "huge trade surpluses" in these goods (see, e.g., Moon 1987: 107).

Concurrently, the textile/apparel industry in the core economies of the Pacific—the United States and Japan—was in full decline (Moon 1987: 108). The loss of international competitiveness and falling profit margins prompted U.S. and Japanese capital in this sector to seek alternatives. While trade protectionism represented one response, many companies shifted to overseas sourcing "involving offshore production through direct foreign investment and subcontracting" (Moon 1987: 108). In the 1970s core capitalists looked to the East Asian newly industrialized countries (NICs) as fertile climates for offshore garment and textile production. By 1973 Hong Kong, South Korea, and Taiwan were far ahead of Japan in the total value of clothing exports (GATT data, cited in Dickerson 1991: table 6-12). By the same token, the United States had become the world's leading apparel importer by 1987, taking in $22.1 billion in imports, which represented 27 percent of total world exports in that year (ibid.: tables 6-13 and 6-14). By 1980 just under 75 percent of all U.S. apparel imports came from East Asia (U.S. Department of Commerce Data cited in Gereffi 1998: table 7.1). As Bonacich and Waller (1994) clearly show, the principal feature of the Pacific Rim garment trade is Asian exporting and U.S. importing.

In the most recent years there are signs of further change in the international geography of textile and apparel production. Gereffi (1998: 147) points out that during the 1980s the share of U.S. apparel imports from East Asia dropped from 73.5 percent to 59.6 percent. While the established industries in the East Asian NICs continued high-volume garment production and experienced absolute export growth in the 1980s, in some other Pacific Rim countries newly created apparel industries increased capacity at a much more rapid rate. In 1991 Greater China, which includes Hong Kong, Taiwan, and the People's Republic of China, accounted for 40 percent of U.S. apparel imports (U.S. Department of Commerce 1992), and in 1992, Hong Kong and China alone accounted for 30 percent of world apparel exports (United Nations 1993). In recent years apparel export industries in Thailand and Indonesia have exploded past the three billion dollar mark and India, Sri Lanka, and Malaysia have topped one billion dollars in apparel exports (United Nations 1993). By the early 1990s manufacturers in the garment business in the U.S., Hong Kong, and South Korea made it clear that such far-flung sites as Vietnam, Guatemala, Burma, North Korea, and Mongolia were either targets of planned investment in export-oriented garment factories or had already gone on line.

Our interest here is in the ways in which these industries have sustained competitiveness through their capacity for production flexibility. This refers to the ability to respond to the shifting demand of buyers, in a timely fashion and without sacrificing quality (Gereffi 1991). Industrial flexibility requires some degree of technological sophistication and labor skill, despite apparel manufacturing technology little changed from a century ago. Yet such innovations as electronic networking, fax, and EPOS (electronic point of sales) inventory systems have constituted a virtual revolution in the organization of apparel production, enabling retailers to achieve a high degree of flexibility in responding to changes in market conditions. Technological and organizational innovation may account for some of the continued export growth (or at least the slower decline) of the garment industry in places like South Korea and Taiwan, where wage pressures greatly diminished competitive advantage over the last decade.

The Hong Kong Apparel Industry

Hong Kong's rise as a manufacturing power began with Mao's victories in China in the immediate postwar period. The flight of industrialists from China to the British colony brought capital, technology, and considerable know-how. Shanghainese apparel manufacturers sparked the Hong Kong clothing industry, opening the first cotton spinning mill in 1947 (Lau and Chan 1994: 108). Apparel manufacturing peaked in 1986, with 10,392 firms employing 299,932 workers. By 1990 both the number of firms (9,746) and the number of workers (251,746) had sharply declined. Yet, until very recently, apparel remained Hong Kong's largest manufacturing industry in terms of both export value and employment, accounting for about a third of all manufacturing workers, and roughly the same percentage of total exports (Hong Kong Industry Department 1991; cited in Lau and Chan 1994: table 6.3; see also Lau and Chan 1994: table 6.2).[1] Almost all of Hong Kong's apparel production is destined for export, mostly to the United States, Japan, China, Germany, and the United Kingdom; it is today the world's second-largest garment exporter in the world, and the second-largest importer to the United States, having been surpassed by China only in the early 1990s.[2]

Today Hong Kong has developed into a command center in garment sourcing and production, offering "highly concentrated market information," a particular advantage for manufacturers who must deal in large quantities or require fabric development (Cheng interview, 1991). The city is the preeminent center for the coordination of vast networks of factories spreading across South and Southeast Asia and, particularly, the gateway for European and North American retailers and buyers to China's enormous production capability. According to David G. Birnbaum, owner of Third Horizon Ltd., a Hong Kong-based sourcing company, in Hong Kong,

you are paying for getting exactly what you want, exactly when you want it. People understand the industry here better than anywhere. They understand styles and requests from buyers, are good at quality control, handling samples, logistics (Birnbaum interview, 1993).

The "maturation" of Hong Kong into an internationalized center for garment sourcing concomitant with rapid drops in actual apparel production corresponds to a decline in the importance of manufacturing in general in the Hong Kong economy. Until the 1980s, manufacturing typically accounted for 40–50 percent of total employment in Hong Kong. By 1990, that figure had fallen to 30 percent (Hong Kong Industry Department, 1991: 6; cited in Lau and Chan 1994: 108). In the mid-1990s there were reportedly labor shortages in the apparel industry, with fewer and fewer workers (with the exception of recent immigrants from China) willing to work under industry conditions or for industry wages in those conditions (Lau and Chan 1994).[3] Several recent events make the future hard to predict: possible changes as post-handover Hong Kong is reintegrated into the People's Republic, the phasing out of Multifiber Agreement (MFA) quotas between now and 2005, and the strong possibility that China might gain entry into WTO. But as of this writing, there seems to be little reason to suspect that the division of labor that evolved in the past decade (Hong Kong as crucial corporate "command and control" center over sewing factories in China utilizing plentiful low-wage labor) will change in the near future.

The South Korean Apparel Industry

On the Korean side, the growth of apparel production was a major component to the export-oriented industrialization drive pushed by President Park Chung Hee's development-oriented government in the 1960s and 1970s. In 1967 garments accounted for 18.5 percent of the country's total export revenues (Lee and Song 1994: 147); between 1967 and 1980 the value of apparel exports grew at an annual rate just below 60 percent (Lee, n.d.: 12). Initially, much of this growth, which was an integral part of the country's "economic miracle," no doubt relied on relatively cheap and plentiful labor (Kim interview, 1992). But by the end of this period there had been considerable industrial upgrading, as both garment and fabric production became increasingly specialized and diversified, and internationally known for high-quality goods. Moon (1987) claims that the South Korean garment industry enjoyed a much greater global comparative advantage than most of the country's export industries.

Export data show that the country retained a position as one of the top four suppliers of clothing for the both world and U.S. markets through the late 1980s and into the 1990s (United Nations 1993). Contemporary buyers for major global garment firms continue to look to Seoul and Korean corporations as sources because of their well-established reputation for world–market-quality products and on-time delivery. An American buyer for a U.S. women's fashion wear company (Liz Claiborne), told us that while many "up-and-coming countries" often still fall short, "the Korean garment industry can do things between 99 and 100 percent of the time, because of long experience and excellent technology" (Garwood interview, 1992). But while this view on the future of garment production in South Korea was guardedly optimistic, most insiders were much less sanguine.

Before discussing recent dilemmas facing this industry and the restructuring that is occurring in response, it is important to understand the basic organization of South Korean garment production. The U.S., Japanese, or European retailers and "label" apparel companies provide orders which usually include prototypes and samples of the finished garments. American fashion apparel buyers work through the large trading companies (*chaebols*), including those with familiar names like Daewoo, Samsung, and Lucky-Goldstar (Chang interview, 1992). These giant companies are vertically integrated, centrally controlled, and possess vast financial clout and political influence in Korean society (Kim 1997). Many owe a measure of their success to the apparel export boom in the 1960s and 1970s and still own divisions that produce high-quality textiles used in their clothing; but the actual sewing work is almost always subcontracted out to relatively small-scale factories.[4]

The particular way in which this buyer-driven commodity chain achieves flexibility merits note. The *chaebol* play a pivotal role as brokers connecting the designers and buyers from wealthy core markets with the small Korean businesses that do the actual sewing (Garwood interview, 1992). Although less so than Hong Kong, Seoul continues to mediate garment sourcing. Many North American, European, and Japanese buyers still go through the *chaebol* because of these corporations' reputations for reasonably priced, on-time, good-quality clothes. In addition to brokering the relationship with the buyers, the trading companies provide the financing and administrative support. They often are also involved as suppliers of textiles (a more capital-intensive activity which is much more likely to be under direct *chaebol* ownership and control).[5] Until the mid-1980s or so the trading companies also garnered great clout via control of export quotas set up under the MFA, which set numeric limits on the amount of particular items of clothing that could be shipped from South Korea to the United States. Since the *chaebol* had both the high-level political connections and the financial power, the government allocated them the quota. This forced small producers eager to do export manufacturing to either subcontract or pay (often exorbitant) fees to obtain the quota allotments. This solidified an industrial hierarchy of subcontractors (Lee and Song 1994) that is ideally designed for flexible production. The result is a vertically organized interfirm network that leads to a sort of static flexibility. The giant trading companies dominate in terms of power and profits and are able to "squeeze" small garment subcontractors to make on-time, low-cost deliveries. But, as we argue later in this chapter, if this system works well for the *chaebol*, and plays on an established reputation for expertise, it fosters little impetus toward industrial upgrading. Additionally this highly vertical, top-down governance structure (which pervades the South Korean economy extending well beyond the apparel sector) was ill-suited for dealing with the 1997–1998 economic crisis. This lumbering institutional economic organization and the inherent conservatism of *chaebol* leaders probably made rapid response to the financial and currency fluctuations during the fall of 1997 more difficult, extending the length and depth of the recession that followed (Lee 1998).

Nevertheless, this arrangement flourished for many years and provided a motor for the South Korean "economic miracle." But recently the garment industry shows signs of decline. By the early 1990s escalating general wage rates and rapidly expanding employment opportunities in other sectors of the economy (for instance, construction work for men, service jobs for women) led to severe labor shortages and a serious profit squeeze (Hong interview, 1992). Many garment factories and workers have left the industry, while a few are attempting to specialize and upgrade their existing Korea-based production. One of the most attractive adaptive strategies is to move apparel assembly offshore to sites with cheaper and more compliant labor forces.

Statistical sources confirm declines in indigenous South Korean clothing production. Between 1990 and 1993 there was a nearly 20 percent decline (from 242,400 to 195,000) in the number of employed garment workers (International Apparel Federation Statistics, 1994). Even more dramatically, a study commissioned by the Korea Federation of Textile Industries found that there had been a 13 percent reduction of jobs at 225 surveyed textile, garment, and dyeing firms over a six-month period ending in March 1992; the same report noted a startlingly high quit rate, over 10 percent in September 1991 alone (*Korea Herald*, February 15, 1992). Another indicator of the slide in apparel production is the increasing irrelevance of the MFA export quotas. Although a few items still fill their allotments, most of the quotas are now reportedly unused.

Finally, it is important to note that there have been very clear spatial patterns in the historic and contemporary distribution of the garment and textile industry in South Korea. The industry is clustered into various specialized districts because locating many similar factories in proximity makes technology transfer easier, provides easier access to input materials, and facilitates the recruitment of workers. The South Korean government created special districts where workers could get privileged access to social benefits (like medical care) and businesses could qualify for low-interest loans and tax breaks. In the garment industry, the big cities of Seoul and Pusan have such industrial districts; the central city of Taegu is famous for its textile production; and Pan-wool, an area near the Seoul suburb of Suwon, is a special district for fabric finishing and dyeing (Lee interview, 1992).

STRATEGIES FOR ACHIEVING FLEXIBILITY IN PRODUCTION

The production of garments in Asia and throughout the Pacific Rim is ultimately controlled and directed by U.S.-based firms. Designs and orders are crafted in major cities in North America, like New York or Los Angeles, or in Tokyo. They are transmitted to company representatives (buyers), who either contact local trading companies specializing in apparel manufacturing or use their own offshore offices to identify factories. These companies then outsource production via contracting to the factories. Even in the relatively industrially advanced Asian NICs, these manufacturing facilities conform to the historic image of clothing factories: they seldom employ more than a few hundred low-wage/low-skilled workers, they require limited capital, and they are generally unpleasant places to work. Their lowly position in the organizational network of the commodity chain ensures that little of the surplus is captured at this level. Instead, the real profits seem to be made at the marketing end, especially after the brand name is affixed to articles of apparel.

Within this framework, industrial flexibility is achieved in a variety of ways. In this section we consider several of the more important strategies. We begin with a discussion of Hong Kong-based firms, then turn to a discussion of those based in Korea.

Achieving Industrial Flexibility: The View from Hong Kong

Hong Kong–based firms pursue a number of strategies designed to minimize costs while maximizing flexibility. These include moving production into low-cost countries, the use of offshore buying offices to go "deeper" (and cheaper), subcontracting and homework, achieving factory control, and the role of personal networks.

The Movement to Low-Wage Countries

Arguably, the *most* important strategy for maintaining competitiveness and promoting low road flexibility involves the geographic movement of production to locations that can provide cheaper labor and other cost advantages. Technology plays an important role in facilitating this process (Chan interview, 1993b). And manufacturers often deny that cheap labor is a primary motivation in choosing a factory, since so many other factors come into play (Birnbaum interview, 1993; Cunningham interview, 1993a; Walton interview, 1993a; Kingman interview, 1991). Quota availability and costs, rent, transportation costs and time, quality, productivity, fabric availability, political and social risks, the cost of bribery, and ethical concerns were all stressed as offsetting labor cost considerations (Cunningham interview, 1993b). Nonetheless, it is clear that there is a high premium on cheap factory labor, particularly at the bottom and even middle range of production.

Not surprisingly, much labor-intensive production is shifting to China, where Taiwanese and Hong Kong know-how and capital combine with China's abundant labor and natural resources to form a potent (and highly competitive) synergy. As Jimmy S. T. Leung, general manager of operations for Bugle Boy Express (the Hong Kong buying office for Bugle Boy Industries) put it, "China has uncountable garment factories and uncountable skillful laborers" (Leung interview, 1991a). But in Leung's view, while cheap labor can be gotten anywhere, highly skilled cheap labor cannot. China boasts great flexibility in different kinds of garment production; Chinese factories are willing and able to make complicated styles at low labor costs. In the rapidly industrializing southern part of Guangdong Province, access is further assured by a well-developed highway system, enabling managers to live in Hong Kong while monitoring factories only a few hours away (Wong interview, 1993b). The result is a concentration of five- to ten-story factories extending as far as the eye can see—a vast "industrial district" which has sprung up during the last decade (Cheung interview, 1993). This arrangement allows firms to "change an order, ask for smaller quantities" (Kingman interview, 1991). The advantage is particularly pronounced when it comes to fabrics; the U.S. textile industry only deals in "large, simple orders," with turnaround times reportedly three times faster in China than in the U.S. (Kingman interview, 1991). Without doubt, low labor costs, long working hours, and a relative lack of regulation contribute to making these Chinese factories so flexible.

The Role of Middlemen

Smaller apparel manufacturing companies typically do business through offshore buying offices—agents who receive a 10–15 percent commission for arranging and overseeing production (Chan interview, 1993b).[6] Such buying offices are reportedly encountering difficult times. While it used to be sufficient for buying offices merely to "have a phone book," "everyone today knows the manufacturer—why pay money to know a manufacturer?" (Cunningham interview, 1991). Buying offices may still thrive if they are able to arrange small-scale, specialized production with quick turnaround time; but on large-scale, standardized orders they cannot easily compete with the larger manufacturers who have their own sourcing offices (Ma interviews, 1991).

Larger manufacturing companies, on the other hand, are more likely to maintain their own buying offices for offshore sourcing. When it comes to sourcing "you have to be on site—you can't watch an order by Fax." Even the ability to take a global look at samples through video conferencing does not obviate the need to "feel the fabric" (Cunningham interview, 1991). For example, the Gap Far East is a wholly owned subsidiary of GAP Inc, responsible for offshore sourcing in Asia and India, as well as the Middle East and Europe. Bugle Boy Express is a wholly owned subsidiary of Simi Valley-based Bugle Boy Industries, which sources factories in Hong Kong, China, Macau, Indonesia, Lesotho, and Australia. All expenses are covered by the home office, with no profit-loss calculation: it is simply a Hong Kong outpost of the parent corporation (Leung interview, 1991a).

While Bugle Boy operates as a typical manufacturer, selling its products through established retailers, The Gap is illustrative of a significant trend in apparel manufacturing—bypassing the middleman altogether. The Gap is both retailer and manufacturer: it designs its own clothes, which are then sold in its retail outlets around the world.[7] Indeed, it was striking how large retailer-manufacturers such as The Gap managed to achieve the governance capabilities of the more vertically integrated producer-driven commodity chain, with the flexibility of its more horizontally organized buyer-driven form. This suggests that at least in the case of large retailer-manufacturers, the distinction between the two may not be as large as theory suggests.

EPOS inventorying enables The Gap's San Francisco headquarters to handle orders much like a military deployment. While most orders are placed with The Gap's group of "core factories," The Gap's sourcing offices are constantly researching other options, developing a waiting list of tested potential sites, enabling them to "pull the trigger when we're ready" (Cunningham interview, 1991). Orders from their retail outlet stores initially flow into San Francisco, where they are collated and analyzed, and then sent on to Hong Kong. The Hong Kong office then either deploys The Gap's traditional core factories, or sends the orders to their Singapore Office, which since 1992 has been responsible for "bring[ing] new people to the party," going farther and cheaper to "have a better value and maintain our margin"—specifically, to Malaysia, Indonesia, Brunei, Fiji, and perhaps eventually Vietnam.

Subcontracting and Homework

Subcontracting all or part of the garment fabrication is a common way of reducing labor costs or alleviating labor shortages, particularly in places such as Hong Kong or Singapore, where rising rents and growing wages in the service sector have turned low-wage apparel manufacturing into a sunset industry (Tsang interview, 1991). Many lower-quality factories that lack production capacity today engage in subcontracting; subcontractors provide a highly flexible cottage industry at the low-volume end of the industry (Walton interview, 1993a). Much subcontracting is based on friendship relations. It is clan-like, which blurs the worker's sense of the need for an explicit contract. Homework is widespread in Hong Kong and China, and almost all homeworkers are female (Leung interview, 1991b). Tai Lok Lui concludes that both manufacturers and workers see benefit to homework arrangements: the former get the flexibility they need, while the latter get extra cash (which they typically use for personal and family expenses, rather than turning it over to their husbands). Hong Kong's low-rent, high-rise resettlement estates, filled with recent immigrants from China, provide densely populated industrial districts for garment manufacturers—"dispersed factories" with different sewing operations occurring in different flats. Subcontracted sewing can range from specialized operations (pockets, cuffs, attached belts, collars) to an entire garment, with trucks coming by twice daily to pick up and drop off work. With the exception of machines that do interlock and other complicated stitching (which are likely to be provided by the manufacturer), homeworkers buy secondhand sewing machines; thread and cut goods are provided by their employers. Supervision and quality control are the responsibility of a local resident-supervisor who allocates sewing on the basis of her personal networks. If the operation grows, the middle person may actually become a subcontractor, and the resettlement estate can become virtually a regular subcontracting operation, even to the extent of having to pay for air freight if the lot is late (Lui interview, 1991; see also Yeung interview 1991).

Such arrangements are generally no substitute for routine factory work, since it is difficult to exert control over quality and production. Yet Lui reports having seen a "factory" that consisted exclusively of a truck. Moreover, considerable cost savings result from homework, since factory managers need not worry about paid holidays, overtime compensation, providing ordinary sewing machines, or paying rent. Although this creates a situation that invites labor exploitation, even homework frequently entails long-term commitments between employer and worker: in Hong Kong's tight labor market, according to Lui, women who are not treated well simply switch their loyalties to other factories (Lui interview, 1991).

Since 1990, Hong Kong's Offshore Processing Arrangement has enabled subcontracting to occur across the Chinese border, so long as specified operations (which define the provenance of the garment for quota purposes) remain in Hong Kong. Subcontracting need not be limited to intermediate sewing; ironing, buttoning, packaging, and other forms of finishing work are also possible. According to Lawrence Ma Men Kee, owner of Ridewell Fashion and Sportswear, rents across the Chinese border are a fifth those of Hong Kong; he is able to reduce costs by as much as 10 percent by doing some operations in China (Ma, 1991).

Strategies for Achieving Factory Control: The Dynamism of Leverage

The global dispersion of contracted labor cuts two ways: while it provides manufacturers with a strong take-it-or-leave-it negotiating position in terms of individual factories, it also enables factory owners to choose among competing manufacturers for clients. Manufacturers, however, are eager to impose interfirm dominance and control. One way they achieve this is by becoming a factory's dominant client, thereby assuring that their orders receive preferential treatment in terms of priority, turnaround, and even price (Tsang interview, 1993; Cheng interview, 1993; Hsu interview, 1993). Most factories also prefer to have a few primary clients, in order to assure a steady stream of work, although this renders the factory vulnerable to fluctuations in the manufacturer's business (Chan interview, 1993c). Such vulnerability can compromise the trust that is important to long-term relationships (Walton interview, 1993a), leading the factory to seek other clients. Conversely, manufacturers ordinarily do not want to rely too heavily on a single factory, since such reliance would make them dependent on that factory's performance (Tsang interview, 1993).

How much dominance is too much dominance? According to Joseph Chan, Innova's general manager, when factories producing for The Gap are late with an order, they may be faced with a demand to cover lost expenses or an outright cancellation—terms less likely to be exacted by manufacturers or agents with less buying power (Chan interview, 1993b). Innova managing director Steve Walton offered a figure of 30 percent as an optimal amount of business he would like to have with his key factories (Walton interview, 1993a).[8]

Establishing long-term relationships with at least a core group of factories was seen as extremely important by all of the manufacturers and buyers who addressed this topic. Manhattan Industries (owned by the Atlanta-based Salant Corporation), which specializes in men's dress shirts, in 1993 reportedly sourced from thirty to thirty-five factories in ten countries; yet half of their total production occurred in only five factories.[9] To ensure reliability in terms of quality and delivery, Manhattan placed 60 percent of their production in factories with which they had a long-term (two- to eight-year) relationship. The Gap's Jim Cunningham also reported long-term (five or more years) relationships with 60 percent of their factories: "the longer you know them, the more you have a chance of being successful. . . . [T]here is a learning curve of efficiency and flexibility." Long-term relationships frequently contribute to lower costs as a result (Cunningham interview, 1993b). Switching factories means time spent training, establishing quality standards, and getting the new employees to work to specification, all of which are costly (Wong interview, 1993b; Lee interview, 1993).

At the same time, it is important that a certain percentage of orders go to new factories, whether it be to develop new styles, to find cheaper prices (Ng interview, 1993), or "just to get market information—to find out what other people can produce for what price" (Cunningham interview, 1993b). As noted above, The Gap recently dedicated a new office in Singapore for the purpose of identifying new factories in Southeast Asia. Developing new sources of production is not without its hazards; it is not uncommon, for example, for a smaller manufacturer to groom a new factory, only to lose it to a larger company once it is up to their standards (Walton interview, 1993a). The type of economic dislocation and disruption that swept the region in 1997–1998 (especially currency fluctuations that made production suddenly much cheaper or more expensive in certain countries), illustrates the advantages possessed by knowledgeable buyers open to shifting sourcing strategies.

The Importance of Personal Networks

The role of the Chinese diaspora in Asian industrial development has been well studied. Family and ethnic networks can be crucial in an industry in which orders are often based on little more than a handshake: "In this business, things take place on trust" (Cunningham interview, 1991). In the apparel industry in particular, with the obvious exceptions of Korea and Japan, every country's industry is dominated by ethnic Chinese (Cunningham interview, 1991).

Personal connections are especially important if a manufacturer wants to produce in China. Having a relationship does not mean that one can demand lower prices; it means getting what one wants when one wants it (Birnbaum interview, 1993). Many visits are required to earn a reputation, establish relationships, and ascertain which government officials are the important ones to cultivate (Ng interview, 1991). The person with the most connections, not necessarily the highest-ranking official, is the person with whom one must establish contact (Wong interview,

1993b). For example, in order to get quota, favor must be curried with officials from Chinatex, the only government agency authorized to allocate quota (Lee interview, 1993). County-level government officials are also important, since they have the official right to issue the licenses and rubber-stamp all decisions, as well as to assign land and local government resources like construction, materials, and workers (Tsang interview, 1993). Cultivating relationships with important officials in smaller towns close to Hong Kong (such as Dongguan, less than one hundred kilometers distant) is reportedly easier than doing so in larger cities (Chan interview, 1993c; see also Walton interview, 1993a).

Ordinarily, even the largest European or North American retailers and manufacturers cannot directly access Chinese factories: typically they must work through Hong Kong or Taiwanese intermediaries (Walton interview, 1993a). Partly this has to do with Chinese restrictions on profit repatriation or joint-venture foreign ownership,[10] although requirements can occasionally be circumvented (Walton interview, 1993b). If a person has a family history in a particular locale, they are treated as kin, as sharing a "common language." While it does not guarantee a business relationship, it does provide a "starting point for conversation" (Cheng interview, 1993).

This does not imply that non-Chinese cannot do business with Chinese factories (Birnbaum interview, 1993). Rather, we were repeatedly told, few Europeans or North Americans have the patience to sit down, drink some tea, and cultivate the necessary relationships to get access to raw materials, quotas, transport connections, etc. (Walton interview, 1993b; Birnbaum interview, 1993). Thus, the vice president and general manager of Manhattan Industries describes why he prefers not to source in China:

> You have to have connections with every official from the top to the bottom. If there is a break in the chain—if there is one official with which you have no *guanxi*—you get killed. If you are a large and famous company, relationships can be built fairly quickly. You can make a few trips to China, have some large fancy banquet for all the officials, and give them gifts. A couple of these banquets and you can begin to work. If you are a small firm, however, it is more difficult. You have to have personal connections (Ng interview, 1993).

Achieving Industrial Flexibility: The View from Korea

Although the South Korean economy is generally more vertically and corporately organized, like Hong Kong firms, Korean apparel manufacturers have pursued a number of strategies designed to minimize costs while maximizing flexibility. Primary among these is moving production into low-cost countries.

The Movement to Low-Wage Countries

Many industrialists formerly in the apparel business have simply taken their capital and exited this sector in the past decade or so. But it is also clear that many

Korean firms and garment-makers have decided to take advantage of their own knowledge and experience in the apparel business by moving their investment capital, their equipment, and in some instances their entire factories and themselves to offshore locations where they believe running sewing factories can still be profitable. Over and over it was reported that wage costs and labor shortages in South Korea were pushing Korean firms to invest in Southeast Asia and Central America.

Yet, as with Hong Kong-based firms, labor costs are not the whole story. South Korean offshore production also is a strategy to take advantage of more favorable trade policies, like lack of garment quotas and low tariffs to major markets (this is particularly true for factories in Central America and post-NAFTA Mexico exporting to the U.S.). Industry informants were aware of the difficulties of offshore production, with language and cultural barriers cited as potential pitfalls (Hanil interview, 1992). The tendency of Korean-run factories to cluster together in industrial districts and export processing zones attempts to confront these problems via a sort of "expatriate solidarity."

Korean apparel manufacturers uniformly agreed on the major advantages and rising importance of China as a site for clothing production. Not surprisingly, they have been much less successful building factories there than have Hong Kong's overseas Chinese, though entry into ethnically Korean areas in Manchuria may provide favorable, if limited, access to Chinese production (Park, 1998).

The Role of Middlemen

There is some evidence that Korean firms are able to play a middleman role in low-wage Asian countries. For example, in Vietnam we were told that Korean companies sometimes "work for big Japanese firms that have no Vietnamese experience or are skeptical of Vietnam products" (Nguyen interview, 1994a). While the reasons Koreans might play such a role remain to be explored, our interviews suggested two explanations. First, approximately thirty-five thousand Koreans fought with U.S. forces during the Vietnam War, affording them some long-standing ties that have subsequently developed into business networks. Second, Koreans—unlike the Japanese—historically have not worked especially well in Chinese countries; Vietnam thus represents a potentially important new venue in which Korean firms will be able to operate (Park interview, 1993). Ironically, by 1998 some Korean producers in Vietnam were complaining about relatively *high* labor costs—the indirect effect of the drastic devaluation of currency in Thailand and Indonesia had made Vietnam's relatively stable low wages less competitive.

While Koreans have prospered in this role in the past few years, it seems likely that there is a tendency for both the Western buyers and local garment producers to eliminate the Korean middlemen. The American buyer in Seoul for a U.S.-based high-fashion company admitted that there was a trend toward more direct sourcing. He gave an example in which his company "started buying from Burma through Daewoo, but now buys directly from Burma through an office in

Thailand. This is simpler and cuts out an unnecessary and inconvenient middleman" (Garwood interview, 1992). But for both the Korean-run factories that one of us (Smith) visited in Vietnam in 1994, all orders still go through Seoul.[11] When asked why this was so, we were informed that it was because of "confidence" in Korean clothing makers and "a reluctance to go direct because they think Vietnam is risky" (Seoung interview, 1994). But the same pattern held in the two Korean-operated factories one of us (Smith) visited in the Jakarta EPZ (export processing zone), as well. It is doubtful that Indonesia appears as "risky" as Vietnam. The Jakarta-based Korean factory men implied that the big issue in Indonesia was the lack of worker productivity and skill. Both factories had several Korean technicians in residence to train workers and maintain equipment (as did the factories in Vietnam). This suggests that indigenous entrepreneurs and companies in both places might still face a learning curve before they will be able to work without middlemen.

Subcontracting and Homework

Although subcontracting has historically played a pivotal role in *chaebol*-based Korean garment manufacturing, *chaebols* such as Daewoo or Samsung seem to have directly invested in factories in both Vietnam and Indonesia. This suggests a more direct stake than the contracting role associated with U.S. manufacturers, one perhaps driven by Korea's desire to develop textile industries within these countries (and related to the vertically integrated governance structure of the Korean trading companies). Moreover, unlike Hong Kong, none of our informants emphasized the importance of homework for Korean manufacturers operating in Korea—nor, for that matter, in Indonesia. While extremely low wages in the latter country undoubtedly make homework unnecessary as a cost-saving strategy, the same is clearly not true in Korea.

ECONOMIC GOVERNANCE AND THE PROSPECTS FOR "MOVING UP"

As previously discussed, Hong Kong and Korea are moving from manufacturing apparel into higher-end activities. Partly, this entails upgrading production into higher value-added products, "moving up into higher and higher floors of the department store" (Tsang interview, 1991). In this section we consider strategies in both countries, with an eye toward the way in which distinct forms of economic governance and business organization in different national garment sectors lead to alternative outcomes. Our analysis suggests that while the older *chaebol*-oriented pattern that predominates in Korea may have been adaptive at early stages of industrialization, the horizontally networked flexibility of Hong Kong-based firms has certain advantages today in terms of product and process innovation, steady quality improvement, and integration with activities like design and marketing. As previously noted, the Korean governance mode also seemed to have been a liability during the regional downturn in 1997–1998.

Upgrading in the Hong Kong Apparel Industry

With the growth of the East Asian manufacturing and service economies, garment companies that once specialized in sourcing production for core country capital have diversified into a range of economic activities, including clothing manufacturing and design. This is particularly true of a number of the most successful Hong Kong-based apparel firms. These tend to be loose-knit, horizontally integrated, family-held firms. This form of economic governance is conducive to the sort of "dynamic flexibility" associated with innovation, design, and risk taking. An illustrative case is Wing-Tai, whose founder, Cheng Yik Hung, had fled China and started the company in Hong Kong in 1955 to make jeans, largely for the U.K. market (Kingman interview, 1992). The Singapore office was opened in 1962, when quota was imposed on Hong Kong; the Malaysia office opened in 1985. The 1960s–1970s saw an enormous growth in apparel demand, exceeding Hong Kong's capacity to produce. Wing-Tai saw its next step as getting into wholesaling and distribution as well as manufacturing. Today, Wing-Tai is owned and managed by the Cheng family; the sons of the founder hold M.B.A.s from Columbia, Wisconsin, and Chicago (Cheng interview, 1991).

By 1993 Wing-Tai had acquired controlling ownership of a number of apparel manufacturing companies, including Polly Peck in London, Baxter International in New York City, and Styl-land in Orange County, California. With its holdings encompassing apparel manufacturing, design and wholesaling, sourcing, and even real-estate development, Wing-Tai aptly describes itself as "a diversified multinational corporation with the confidence, ability, and determination to broaden the scope of its operations still further." In the Southeast Asian garment industry alone it has over eight thousand employees and produces "over 13 million pieces of quality fashion garment every year" (Wing-Tai interview, 1991). Wing-Tai factories make clothing for such retailers as Macy's and The Gap, as well as its own offshoot manufacturers such as Styl-land/PCH (Kingman interview, 1991). Wing-Tai employs some seventeen thousand people worldwide (Cheng interview, 1991).

Wing-Tai and its holdings are able to respond rapidly to a variety of market opportunities and spin off new ventures to a large degree because of the dynamic flexibility that characterizes economic governance in Hong Kong among "overseas Chinese" businesses. The fact that Innova is moving into retailing reinforces the importance of understanding production using a commodity chain model that stretches from raw material extraction to marketing. As ironic as it may seem, industrial upgrading in the garment trade may involve moving out of production altogether (like U.S.-based clothing "manufacturers" whose activities are limited to designing, financing, and marketing/advertising). The types of economic governance and flexibility that promote following this route (which leads to profit and power) may *not* lead to more efficient manufacturing or improved products. But this sort of diversified organizational adaptation probably is better suited to weather financial storms like the recent Asian financial crisis.

Upgrading in the Korean Apparel Industry

The distinctive form of economic governance in South Korea, with the giant *chaebol* playing a commanding role, leads to a different set of adaptive strategies. The main thrust, driven by the corporate policies of vertically integrated trading companies, has been gradually to phase out garment sewing, while expanding textile fabrication.

Fabric production, because of its highly automated, capital- and technology-intensive nature, remained highly competitive for Korean firms. Along with low-cost labor, the increased emphasis on textiles partially accounts for Korea's growing interest in manufacturing in China. Since a strong textile industry remains an integral part of the large Korean *chaebols*, securing markets for fabric is an important component of corporate strategies for offshore investment in garment manufacturing. The buyer for a U.S. department store chain in Seoul reported that the Korean textile industry was relatively healthy and "exporting a lot to China and other new garment producing countries" (Chang interview, 1992). Nor is this strategy limited to China. Interviews in both Indonesia and Vietnam strongly suggest that Korean companies operating in those countries are likely to be very dependent on textiles produced in their country of origin. Thus, despite a move toward local fabric in the Indonesian garment industry as a whole, Korean firms rely heavily on materials imported from Korea (Chuan interview, 1994). Such firms are often located in EPZs due to the lack of any duties on materials and very simple customs procedures. They are also linked to large corporate buyers and retailers exclusively through the main *chaebol* offices in Seoul (Jin interview, 1994; Lee interview, 1994). Korean-run factories in Vietnam, such as the Daewoo-affiliated plant in Ho Chi Minh City, operate under similar arrangements. This plant imports all its material (not just fabrics, but even buttons and sewing thread) from Korea, with purchases arranged at headquarters in Seoul (Seong 1994; Park 1994).

While *chaebol* strategies go some distance in explaining the rapid decline of garment factories within South Korea, it is interesting to note that some owners of Korean factories (who have been the subcontractors at the bottom of the industrial hierarchy) are struggling to maintain local apparel manufacturing. Operating almost in the interstices of an economy dominated by giant firms, these entrepreneurs have pursued both high road and low road routes to flexibility and competitiveness. One strategy combines technological upgrading with a more flexible marketing strategy that mimics the more horizontal network governance style characteristic of Hong Kong firms.[12] A second dynamic strategy is niche marketing. One fairly small company which previously produced mostly for the North American market had switched to making coats and jackets for the European

Community and was planning to reorient itself to "small lot, high fashion, quick delivery" production to ship to Japan (Hong interview, 1992). Arguably, this is an "exception that proves the rule," since the lumbering *chaebol* governance structure makes this sort of niche targeting strategy impossible for most of the Korean industry.

One final strategy—already common in the United States, but still relatively novel in Korea—involves employing illegal immigrants in apparel manufacturing to keep labor costs low. Three informants told us in confidence that this was becoming increasingly widespread, and followed two distinct patterns. Some factories recruited undocumented Southeast Asian workers, primarily male and female Filipino workers. These laborers were willing to accept wages as low as $300 per month, about half the average wage for Korean garment workers. Estimates of the extent of this practice varied from as many as a third of the factories (Garwood interview, 1992) to less than 5 percent of the workforce (Hong interview, 1992). The second pattern involved hiring ethnic Koreans from China who were undocumented immigrants, a strategy which had the added advantage of avoiding the appearance of bringing foreigners into an ethnically homogenous country. Chinese Koreans look and dress like Koreans, speak the Korean language, and eat *kimchi* and other traditional foods—but still cost less and reportedly work harder than South Korean citizens, and are considerably easier to discipline. The hiring of illegal immigrants, whether Southeast Asian or ethnic Koreans, is an instance where the competitive pressures of global restructuring promote a form of flexibility that clearly results in the exploitation of labor.

In response to their declining competitiveness, Korean firms have not sought to move up the apparel commodity chain by designing and retailing clothes for the North American and European markets they have traditionally served. Often the explanations informants gave were "cultural" (i.e., East Asian designers cannot understand U.S. fashions [Chung interview, 1992], "Western and Oriental tastes and body shapes" are distinct [Hong interview, 1992]). The story was much the same with marketing. Contrary to what we were told in Hong Kong, our Korean informants placed little importance on developing markets in East Asia, with the obvious exception of Japan. There was even some skepticism about the Korean market, which several informants viewed as too small; at least one reported that Koreans were more eager to buy products with western labels than Korean ones.[13] Where textile *chaebol* do manufacture brand names (Jenova, Windy, and Cezanne were all mentioned), the exporting was all OEM, with no Korean overseas marketing (Hanil interview, 1992).

A NOTE ON THE "EAST ASIAN CRISIS"

The financial meltdown that struck the region in 1997–1998 generated enormous worldwide attention. Within a relatively short time-span the East Asian NICs—and especially South Korea—went from admiration and emulation of their "economic miracles" to concern about the danger of their "Asian flu." In Western nations, economic experts and pundits delivered post hoc analyses of how tenuous the East Asian model had been all along (based supposedly on "crony capitalism" and state-led development) and how urgent it was to move rapidly toward neoliberal reforms (for a very recent critique, see Johnson 1999). Yet less than two years after the early signs of trouble began rippling through currency markets, even IMF spokesmen classified the events of 1997–1998 as a "fading" crisis (Boorman 1999).

There is no doubt that the financial crisis was very real and exacted a terrible price. South Korea (along with the second-rung NICs in Southeast Asia) was particularly hard hit as the won was dramatically devalued, corporate and personal bankruptcies cascaded, and massive economic dislocation caused the GDP to plunge from U.S.$10,000 to U.S.$6600 in a single year, with the IMF austerity "cure" causing almost as much pain for the population as had the initial "disease" (Lee 1998). Unemployment skyrocketed to almost unheard of levels (8.1 percent in early 1999; *Korea Times*, April 23, 1999) and the press reported new levels of inequality and the decline of the middle class as persisting legacies of the crisis (*Korea Times*, May 17, 1999; June 15, 1999; July 6, 1999; July 19, 1999). The aftermath of the crisis will be felt by ordinary Koreans for many years. The economic uncertainty has reduced their faith in the government, and personal bankruptcies have undermined traditional bonds of trust and mutual support between neighbors and kinfolk (Su-Hoon Lee, personal communication, November 1998).

Nevertheless, by mid-1999 there was a growing consensus that the "crisis" was over and these economies had rebounded (see Boorman 1999; Sanger and Landler 1999). But some U.S. commentators now almost lament this seemingly good news: "the recovery may have come too fast," derailing economic reforms. There is a certain truth to this. In South Korea, where much was made of a variety of policies to restructure the economy led by a "Big Deal " to dismantle the *chaebol*, this form of economic governance has proven to be deeply entrenched (see Ernst, this volume). At a recent conference in Seoul, economists argued that the IMF pressure helped promote a variety of banking and financial reforms, regulating out-of-control fluctuations in short-term interest rates (*Korea Times*, June 9, 1999), but big business resistance to corporate reform has been so strong that, in terms of concentrated ownership and control of various financial institutions, the *chaebol* dominance has actually *increased* in the past year (*Korea Times*, July 16, 1999). This led one journalist to reluctantly conclude that, "The government's efforts to put an end to the existing corporate governance system under which *chaebol* owners rule their corporations like monarchs have yet to produce any breakthroughs." However functional or dysfunctional, economic governance regimes are resilient and slow to change, even with a shock of the magnitude of the financial meltdown of 1997–1998.

What effect did the recent "East Asian crisis" have on the garment industry and, in particular, Hong Kong and South Korean interests in this sector? Of course, the implications of any series of events that has such significant macro-economic impacts (sudden and dramatic currency devaluations, corporate and financial failure, personal and familial bankruptcy—all followed by efforts to dramatically alter government economic policies) touch virtually all businesses and industries. Undoubtedly, the uncertainty and flux made garment sourcing throughout East Asia much more risky, and it is likely this dampened export apparel production throughout the region. However, for the two cases that we are considering, it is unlikely that the crisis brought about any major change in trajectory. In both Hong Kong and South Korea, competitive garment production is increasingly a thing of the past (even if that history remains well within memory). While the form of corporate governance emerged during this earlier period, today these countries play a different role as intermediaries in the buyer-driven chains that characterize the garment industry. While the economic downturn hit Hong Kong with less force and the Chinese corporate networks were probably better able to cope with this period of flux, it is likely that the *chaebol*-organized and directed Korean webs of overseas sourcing will survive as well. Indeed, one can argue that the Hong Kong and Seoul-based corporate players will end up weathering this storm better than the entrepreneurs and production workers in the factories (particularly those in Southeast Asia) where the actual sewing takes place.

CONCLUSION

The East Asian garment industry provides some vivid illustrations of the impact of global restructuring in an extremely competitive industry where various types of flexibility are critically important. There are a variety of strategies (both high road and low road, dynamic and static) to maximize flexibility: relocation of manufacturing to low-wage countries, eliminating middlemen who mediate between buyers and producers, various types of subcontracting and homework, technical and organization forms of scientific management, and the crucial role of personal networks.

In this chapter, we have focused on the contrasting nature of economic governance in the apparel sectors of Hong Kong and South Korea. *Both* forms of business organization have promoted a degree of flexibility—but they have done so in very distinctive ways, leading to different strategies and trajectories. Successful overseas Chinese firms, with relatively loose, horizontally integrated structures that utilize rich network linkages throughout China and Southeast Asia, have transformed Hong Kong into a command center for garment sourcing which offers "highly concentrated market information." This represents a very dynamic example of moving up the commodity chain, as Hong Kong firms now actively participate in retail and fashion design. On the other hand, South Korea's economic miracle in the 1960s and 1970s to a large degree was driven by the export garment sector. But economic governance in Korea was very different:

giant vertically integrated trading companies, the *chaebol*, dominated the economy. Though they developed a reputation for producing quality clothing, increasingly these firms subcontracted out to small sewing factories and moved
their huge stocks of capital into more dynamic sectors. Today, the Korean garment industry has moved offshore, and even this activity is largely motivated by
a need to continue to guarantee markets for the nation's still competitive textile
industry. Despite all the hype over the "East Asian crisis," the basic dimensions
of these contrasting governance systems remain intact and continuities outweigh
changes.

But if we have emphasized variation between types of economic governance
and their implications for upgrading, we wish also to note a common trait toward
verticality in the apparel chain, despite its qualities as a paradigm case of the more
flexibly organized, buyer-driven commodity chain. Among the largest "footloose"
global firms, apparel manufacturers appear to possess an essential governance feature of the more vertically integrated producer-driven commodity chain: effective
control over all aspects of production, even despite lack of direct ownership (The
Gap is the illustrative case). This leads us to wonder whether flexible accumulation can be achieved without sacrificing the degree of control associated with
older, more bureaucratic forms of industrial organization.

NOTES

This paper was based on research supported by a grant from the Pacific Rim Research Program. We would like to thank the volume editors (particularly Fred Deyo), participants at the
Taiwan conference, Judi Kessler, and Tonya Schuster for comments on versions of this draft.

1. Hong Kong's chief manufacturing industries are textiles, apparel, electronics, household electrical appliances, plastics, and metal products. In 1990 these sectors accounted for
71 percent of manufacturing employment and 73 percent of domestic exports, valued at
U.S.$21 billion (Lau and Chan 1994: 109).

2. With the passage of the North American Free Trade Agreement (NAFTA), this
picture is changing; Mexico has now surpassed Hong Kong and approaches China in
terms of combined textile and apparel exports to the United States. While Mexico
lagged far behind as recently as 1990, by 1996 U.S. apparel and textile exports from
Mexico had grown to $4.2 billion, greater than imports from Hong Kong ($4.0 billion)
and approximating imports from China ($4.9 billion) (U.S. International Trade Com-
mission 1997: 6).

3. According to Leung Wing-yue of the Hong Kong Trade Union Educational Center
and Cheung Lai Ha, president of the Clothing Industry Workers General Union, there is
no labor shortage in Hong Kong; rather, they argue, firms simply prefer to take advantage
of far lower wages and a lack of legal protections in China, and thus are unwilling to hire
Hong Kong workers at even a minimal living wage. They claim that many employers merely
retain a facade of garment manufacturing in Hong Kong in order to avail themselves of the
much higher Hong Kong quota.

4. A recent survey by the Korean Association of Textile Industries showed that nearly 90 percent of the apparel factories employed less than one hundred workers (Lee and Song 1994).These factories are *much* smaller than newer Korean owned or managed factories in Southeast Asia (see below).

5. Indeed, an interview with a group of midlevel managers responsible for apparel production at one medium-sized trading company (Hanil 1992) revealed that the most important product of the division was textiles, with garment production a way to build in a guaranteed market.

6. The Domino/Jefferson Trading Company, headquartered in Los Angeles, is an example: its overseas offices in Hong Kong, Taiwan, and Thailand source Asian factories for such U.S.-based clients as Gotcha, Polydrama, L.A. Gear, Big Dog, and Rusty (Yeung 1991). Ridewell Fashion and Sportswear Ltd. has sourced for such diverse firms as Gotcha, Levi's, Esprit, L.A. Gear, as well as some European companies (Ma interview, 1991).

7. As expressed by The Gap's Jim Cunningham, "the stops between cash register and factory are shorter . . . the best retailers will be the ones who respond the quickest, the best" (Cunningham interview, 1991). Cunningham describes The Gap's method of sourcing as highly "statistical," with codified testing and inspection standards, and contingency plans for accessing a global stable of more than five hundred factories: "When you think Gap, think vertical integration" (Cunningham interview, 1993a).

8. The Gap's Jim Cunningham noted that among their five-hundred-plus factories, The Gap's even more dominant position gives them a great deal of clout: "for a minority of factories we are more than half of their production. But not a small minority. We are not an insignificant percentage of production in any of the factories we work with. We have never had a factory refuse to work with us" (Cunningham interview, 1993b).

9. One each in Hong Kong-China, South Korea, Indonesia, Taiwan, and the Philippines.

10. Under typical contractual joint ventures, China provides the land; foreign investors provide the equipment and sometimes the factory itself (Sung interview, 1991).

11. Although the final buyers do send their own quality-control inspectors directly into the Vietnamese factories, we were told that these people were often from third countries in Southeast Asia. In one factory a Filipina woman and a Sri Lankan man were doing this job.

12. The Sun Trading Company is a very new, modern facility that makes high-quality silk women's fashion wear. Sun is a small company that works directly with a U.S. partner based in New York City. While all the production is original equipment manufacturing (OEM), with no design in Korea, the factory sells directly to buyers rather than going through a trading company (partly because the absence of quotas for silk products eliminates one of the major reasons to work through an intermediary). The owner, Mr. Chung, reported that all of his clothing is shipped to the United States and marketed by top-end retailers (Saks, Neiman-Marcus, Macy's). The factory was new and filled with high-tech equipment. While Mr. Chung was well aware of the "terrible" overall condition of the garment industry in South Korea and, like many informants, saw China as an extremely attractive (and competitive) production site, he put a great deal of stock in upgrading both technology and organization/management. The factory's location an hour's drive from downtown Seoul, next to Kimpo International Airport, was also unusual and chosen to provide a competitive advantage. Workers load boxed merchandise directly into Korean Air containers and virtually all the company's clothes are shipped by air. There is very little "friction of space" here—the company's fashion clothes can be delivered to New York or Los Angeles within a day.

13. We were told that the label, not the origin of the product, was important, hence there was competition to buy licensing rights, especially from high-fashion European companies.

BIBLIOGRAPHY

Appelbaum, Richard P. 1996. "Multiculturalism and Flexibility: Some New Directions in Global Capitalism." In *Mapping Multiculturalism*, edited by Avery Gordon and Chris Newfield. Minneapolis, Minn: University of Minnesota Press.

Appelbaum, Richard, and Gary Gereffi. 1994. "Power and Profits in the Apparel Commodity Chain." In *Global Production: The Apparel Industry in the Pacific Rim*, edited by Edna Bonacich et al., 42–62. Philadelphia: Temple University Press.

Appelbaum, Richard, and David Smith. 1996. "Global Restructuring and Industrial Location: Some Lessons from East Asia." Paper presented at the annual meeting of the American Sociological Association in August, New York City.

Appelbaum, Richard, David Smith, and Brad Christerson. 1994. "Commodity Chains and Industrial Restructuring in the Pacific Rim: Garment Trade and Manufacturing." In *Commodity Chains and Global Capitalism*, edited by Gary Gereffi and Miguel Korzeniewicz, 187–204. Westport, Conn.: Greenwood Press.

Bonacich, Edna, and David Waller. 1994. "Mapping a Global Industry: Apparel Production in the Pacific Rim Triangle." In *Global Production: The Apparel Industry in the Pacific Rim*, edited by Edna Bonacich et al., 21–41. Philadelphia: Temple University Press.

Boorman, Jack. 1999. "The World Financial System Must Work to Prevent Crises." *International Herald Tribune*, 28 June. (Reprinted at www.imf.org)

Deyo, Frederic C. 1995. "Capital, Labor and State in Thai Industrial Restructuring: The Impact of Global Economic Transformations." In *A New World Order? Global Transformations in the Late Twentieth Century*, edited by David A. Smith and Jozsef Borocz, 131–144. Westport, Conn.: Greenwood.

Dicken, Peter. 1992. *Global Shift: The Internationalization of Economic Activity*. 2d ed. New York: Guilford.

Dickerson, Kitty G. 1991. *Textiles and Apparel in the International Economy*. New York: Macmillan.

Elson, D. 1989. "Bound by One Thread: The Restructuring of UK Clothing and Textile Multinationals." In *Instability and Change in the World Economy*, edited by A. MacEwan and W. K. Tabb, 187–204. New York: Monthly Review Press.

Gereffi, Gary. 1998. "Global Sourcing and Regional Divisions of Labor in the Pacific Rim." In *What is in a Rim? Critical Perspectives on the Pacific Region Idea*, edited by Arif Dirlik, 143–61. Lanham, Md.: Rowman & Littlefield.

———. 1994. "The Organization of Buyer-Driven Global Commodity Chains: How U.S. Retailers Shape Global Production Networks." In *Commodity Chains and Global Capitalism*, edited by Gary Gereffi and Miguel Korzeniewicz, 95–122. Westport, Conn.: Greenwood.

Hong Kong Industry Department. 1991. *Hong Kong's Manufacturing Industries, 1990*. Hong Kong: Government Printer.

Kim, Eun Mee. 1997. *Big Business, Strong State: Collusion and Conflict in South Korean Development, 1960–1990*. Albany, N.Y.: SUNY Press.

Korea Herald (Seoul). 1992. "Number of Workers at Garment, Textile Factories Declining." 15 February.

Korea Times. Various. English-language newspaper printed in Seoul, available in digest form from electronic *Korea Letter* listserv.

Lau, Ho-Fuk, and Chi-Fai Chan. 1994. "The Development Process of the Hong Kong Garment Industry: A Mature Industry in a Newly Industrialized Economy." In *Global Production: The Apparel Industry in the Pacific Rim,* edited by Edna Bonacich et al. Philadelphia: Temple University Press.

Lee, Chung H. n.d. "Korea's Direct Foreign Investment in Southeast Asia." Unpublished paper. Honolulu, Hawaii: East-West Center.

Lee, Seung Hoon, and Ho Keun Song. 1994. "The Korean Garment Industry: From Authoritarianism to Patriarchism to Industrial Paternalism." In *Global Production: The Apparel Industry in the Pacific Rim,* edited by Edna Bonacich et al., 147–161. Philadelphia: Temple University Press.

Lee, Su-Hoon. 1998. "Crisis in Korea and the IMF Control." In *The Four Asian Tigers: Economic Development and the Global Political Economy,* edited by Eun-Mee Kim, 209–228. New York: Academic.

Moon, Chung-In. 1987. "Trade Frictions and Industrial Adjustment: The Textiles and Apparel Industry in the Pacific Basin." *Pacific Focus* 2, no. 1: 105–133.

Park, Hyun Ok. "South Korea's Morning After the Economic Miracle: State Nationalism and Small-and-Medium-Sized Factories in the 1990s." Paper presented at the Annual Meeting of the American Sociological Association in August, San Francisco.

Piore, Michael J. and Charles F. Sabel. 1984. *The Second Industrial Divide: Possibilities for Prosperity.* New York: Basic.

Sanger, David, and Mark Landler. 1999. "Asian Rebound Derails Reform as Many Suffer." *New York Times,* 12 July. (Printed from www.nytimes.com)

Scott, A. J., and D. P. Angel. 1988. "The Global Assembly-Operations of US Semiconductor Firms: A Geographical Analysis." *Environment and Planning* 20: 1047–1067.

Storper, Michael, and Richard Walker. 1989. *The Capitalist Imperative: Territory, Technology and Industrial Growth.* London: Blackwell.

United Nations. 1993. *Demand, Production and Trade in Textiles and Clothing: Statistical Report to the Secretariat.* Prepared by the Textiles Committee, General Agreement on Tariffs and Trade (GATT). New York: United Nations Statistical Division.

U.S. Department of Commerce. 1992. *U.S. General Imports.* Washington, D.C.: Bureau of the Census.

U.S. International Trade Commission. 1997. *U.S. Imports of Textiles and Apparel under the Multifiber Agreement: Annual Report for 1996.* Washington, D.C.: USITC Publication 2947.

WuDunn, Sheryl. 1999. "South Korea's Mood Swings from Bleak to Bullish." *New York Times,* 24 January. (Printed from www.nytimes.com)

INTERVIEWS

Birnbaum, David G. 1993. President, Third Horizon Ltd., Hong Kong (Christerson interview, July 1).

Chan, Jan. 1993c. Managing director, David and David Fashion Wholesale and Retail Ltd., Hong Kong (Christerson interview, July 29).

Chan, Joseph. 1993a. General manager, Innova Ltd., Hong Kong (Appelbaum interviews, April 22 and May 2).
———. 1993b. (Christerson interview, June 30).
Chang, Bob. 1992. Vice president and managing director for Korea-Japan, May Department Stores International, Inc., Seoul (February 18).
Cheng, Francis Man-Piu. 1991. Assistant managing director, Wing-Tai Exporters, Ltd., Hong Kong (Appelbaum interview, November 25).
———. 1993. (Christerson interview, July 19).
Cheung, Rio. 1993. Assistant merchandiser, Innova Ltd., Hong Kong (Christerson interview, June 30).
Chuan, A. T. 1994. General merchandising manager, Indonesian Textile Association (Asosiasi Pertekstilan Indonesia), Jakarta (Smith interview, September 22).
Chung, B. S. 1992. President, Sun Trading Company, Ltd., Seoul (Smith interview, February 17).
Cunningham, James P. 1991. Vice president, Offshore Sourcing, The Gap (Far East) Ltd., Hong Kong (Appelbaum interview, November 28).
———. (1993a). (Appelbaum interview, May 5).
———. 1993b. (Christerson interview, July 12).
Garwood, Lon. 1992. Director, Seoul Branch Office, Liz Claiborne Inc. (Smith interview, February 11).
Hanil Synthetic Fiber Industrial Co., Ltd. 1992. Chang Ho Park, manager, Export Garment Department; J. W. Lee, assistant manager, Sweater Export Department; and two other employees, Seoul (Smith interview, February 25).
Hong, Jin S. 1992. President, Namyang International Co. Ltd., Seoul (Smith interview, February 18).
Hsu, Norman. 1993. Managing director, Newton Enterprises, Hong Kong (Christerson interview).
Jin, Chung Dong. 1994. President-director, Pt. Bintang Adibusana, Jakarta (affiliated with Samsung Corporation, Seoul) and director, Korean Industrial Garment Association of Indonesia (September 21).
Kim, D. Y. 1992. Chairman, E. G. Ltd., Seoul (Smith interview, February 19).
Kingman, Matt. 1991. Senior Vice President of Styl-land, PCH-Innova, Hong Kong (Appelbaum interview, November 25).
———. 1992. (Christerson interview, August 26).
Lee, Bum Woo. 1992. Principal, Korea Sewing Science Research Institute, Seoul (Smith interview, February 11).
Lee, Dennis. 1993. General manager, Domino and Jefferson Trading Company, Hong Kong (Christerson interview, June 29).
Lee, Jong-In. 1994. President-director, Pt. Rismar, Jakarta (a subsidiary of Daewoo Apparel, Seoul) (Smith interview, September 21).
Leung, Jimmy S. T. 1991a. General manager of operations, Bugle Boy Express, Ltd., Hong Kong buying office for Bugle Boy (Appelbaum interview, November 28).
Leung, Wing-yue, and Trini Leung. 1991b. Hong Kong Trade Union Educational Center (Appelbaum interview, December 3).
Leung, Wing-yue, Trini Leung, and Cheung Lai Ha. 1993. Hong Kong Trade Union Educational Center (Leung) and president, Clothing Industry Workers General Union (Cheung) (Appelbaum interview, May 4, 1993).

Lui, Tai Lok. 1991. Lecturer, Department of Sociology, Chinese University of Hong Kong, Shatin, N. T., Hong Kong (Appelbaum interview, November 4).

Ma Men Kee, Lawrence. 1991. Ridewell Fashion and Sportswear Ltd., Hong Kong (Appelbaum interview, December 5).

Ng, Ringo. 1991. Vice president and general manager, Manhattan Industries (Far East) Ltd., a division of Salant Corporation, Hong Kong (Appelbaum interview, December 3).
———. 1993. (Christerson interview, July 9).

Nguyen Xuan Mien. 1994b. Director, Tienlong Company, Ltd., Ho Chi Minh City, Vietnam (Smith interview, September 17).

Park, Dong-Hyun. 1993. Representative, Shinsung Tongsang Company Ltd., Ho Chi Minh City, Vietnam (subsidiary of Daewoo Corporation, Seoul, Korea) (Appelbaum interview, April 19).
———. 1994. Shinsung Tongsang Co. Ltd., Ho Chi Minh City, Vietnam (subsidiary of Daewoo Corporation, Seoul) (Smith interview, September 13).

Seong, Jung Kyung. 1994. General director, Han Joo–Viet Than Co. Ltd, Ho Chi Minh City (Smith interview, September 15).

Sung, Yun-wing. 1991. Senior lecturer in economics, Chinese University of Hong Kong (Appelbaum interview, November 4).

Szetoh, K. L. 1993. General manager, The Gap Singapore Pte. Ltd., Singapore (Appelbaum interview, April 28).

Tsang, Paul C. M. 1991. General manager, Unimix Limited, Hong Kong (Appelbaum interview, November 28).
———. 1993. (Christerson interview, July 17).

Walton, Steven R. 1993a. Managing director, Innova Ltd., Hong Kong (Appelbaum interview, May 2).
———. 1993b. (Christerson interview, June 30).

Wing-Tai. 1991. Wing-Tai's *Brochure.*

Wong, Victor Witt H. 1993a. Assistant production manager, Production Planning Department, Wing-Tai Garment International, Ltd., Hong Kong (Appelbaum interview, April 24).
———. 1993b. (Christerson interview, July 4).

Yeung, Raymond. 1991. General manager, Domino and Jefferson Trading Company, Hong Kong (Appelbaum interview, November 26).

4

Dynamic Flexibility and Sectoral Governance in the Thai Auto Industry: The Enclave Problem

Frederic C. Deyo and Richard F. Doner

Since the early 1980s, arguments on the sources of economic growth have emphasized two types of economy-wide systems of governance. The first and most prominent stress the virtues of systems with deregulated product, labor, and financial markets. The second and more recent approach is skeptical as to the benefits of pure deregulation and stresses the virtues of coordination among firms and other key economic actors. Although similar to corporatism in its general emphasis on the benefits of coordination, this approach does not share corporatism's emphasis on macro-tripartite bargaining. Instead, the focus is on industry- (meso) or firm- (micro) level coordination. Advocates of this approach stress the significance of financial systems, industrial relations, education and training systems, and intercompany relations (reflected in business associations). These national and sectoral institutional systems, labeled "production regimes" or "social systems of production," can be distinguished by the degree to which they promote long-term financing, cooperative industrial relations, serious vocational training, and technology and standard-setting cooperation among companies (Soskice 1991; Hollingsworth and Boyer 1997; Soskice 1999).

More than simply a descriptive device, this distinction also constitutes an effort to understand the consequences of different "national systems of innovation" (Lundvall 1992; Nelson 1993). Those systems promoting greater collective learning and resource sharing among economic actors within and across firms are presumed better suited for dealing with changing product markets and technology than are their "liberal" or "uncoordinated" counterparts. Hollingsworth explicitly extends the argument to the flexibility question, arguing that more coordinated governance structures support flexible rather than mass standardized production (Hollingsworth 1997). Following the discussion in the introduction

107

to this volume, our working definition of production flexibility encompasses performance capabilities enabling firms to respond effectively to a variety of market pressures and technological opportunities. In particular, successful firms in increasingly open economies must now adapt to demands for product diversification, high quality, small-batch production, and quick time to market. And where firms seek to upgrade to higher value niches, there is need for even more dynamic flexibility[1] capabilities, including constant quality and process improvements, process engineering capabilities to cope with ever shorter product life cycles, an ability to procure and utilize changing technologies, and new capacities for product design, development, and even innovation. Our working assumption is that the organizational, informational, and resource requirements of flexible production are considerable and depend on heightened information flows and collaboration, as well as on the timely provision of goods and of services such as market information, skilled labor, new technologies, finance, and material inputs. Achievement of these informational, institutional, and resource requisites is in turn a function of the governance structures emphasized by the idea of "coordinated production regimes" and "flexible social systems of production." Of particular importance here are close, network-like, interfirm relations that enhance flexible production capabilities through bilateral and collective provision of resources on the one hand, and the binding of firms into tightly integrated and thus adaptive production systems on the other.

In this chapter we explore the validity of this presumed link between coordination-enhancing institutions and flexible production. Following the discussion in the introduction to this volume, we further elaborate the "social systems of production" framework by distinguishing between meso- and microlevel institutions, asking how national and sectoral institutions influence microlevel economic governance, here pertaining especially to the nature of the inter- (and intra-) firm relations in which a firm's economic transactions are socially embedded. Our central questions are: (a) how can firms achieve high-quality flexible production in the context of weak meso-institutional provision of essential collective goods or support for interfirm cooperation; (b) how important are interfirm network relations for the achievement of flexible production; and, if network relations are important, (c) how can firms develop and utilize such relations in meso-institutional environments which discourage their development?

We explore this question by focusing on Aapico, a successful Thai-based auto parts firm. This choice is based on the firm's performance and the national context in which it operates. Cited by the *Economist* (1996) as "one of the biggest local component companies in Thailand," Aapico is not only an original equipment manufacturer (OEM) supplier of dies[2] and press parts to many Japanese auto assemblers operating in Thailand, it is also a successful exporter of automotive jigs to multinational operations across and even outside East Asia. Indeed, the firm is Southeast Asia's largest automotive jig manufacturer (Fairclough 1995: 120–122). Aapico is also an interesting case because its operations reflect different kinds of flexible production. In its jig business, the firm has moved from something akin to craft production toward higher-volume production with greater emphasis on changing technology and time to market. In press parts, Aapico has been pushed from medium-quality, low-volume production toward a capacity for both high- and low-volume production of export-quality goods.

Aapico operates in a country—Thailand—that until the recent economic crisis was known as Southeast Asia's regional hub for automotive production (*Economist* 1996). With the largest market in Southeast Asia and a significant base of local suppliers, Thailand seemed to be an ideal place for an expanding auto parts firm. However, few Thai auto parts firms have achieved the quality and price levels necessary for export, and this is in no small measure a function of the country's failure to provide either the collective goods and services or the incentives to collaboration necessary for continuous upgrading. As argued below, Thailand's manufacturing-oriented institutions are decidedly weak. How, then, do we account for this firm's achievements? We shall argue that while Aapico's success owes much to Thailand's open and competitive auto market, the creation of network-like interfirm governance relations has been quite important in its movement into more complex and higher-quality products. But these network relations have developed outside Thailand's core institutional structures. This then raises a second question: How long can a firm sustain its successes when these achievements depend on institutional arrangements which fail to correspond to or find support in the larger institutional context (Hollingsworth and Boyer 1997: 25)? This question is especially pressing for two reasons. First, since the mid-1990s, multinational auto producers have intensified their presence in Thailand, their rivalry in the region, and their pressures on local parts firms for higher quality, faster time-to-market, and higher-volume, customized production. Second, the economic crisis affecting Thailand and the rest of the region has undermined some of the macroeconomic stability and overall automotive demand so important to Aapico's success until 1997.

To address these questions, in the first section we describe the national and sectoral context in which Aapico operates. We argue here that national and sectoral institutions in Thailand are conducive neither to the provision of collective goods nor to the institutionalized coordination within and among firms necessary for the flexible production of quality manufactured goods. These weaknesses became especially critical in the context of growing efforts on the part of multinational assemblers to consolidate Southeast Asian regional operations and because of the increased need to expand exports. In the second section, the paper's empirical core, we examine Aapico's evolution, strategies, and successes prior to Thailand's (and East Asia's) late-1990s financial crisis. The firm's ability to succeed despite Thailand's nonconducive institutional environment is, we argue, in part a function of an expanding national and regional market, but also the result of a range of organizational and managerial innovations initiated by management. The third section demonstrates the importance of strategically initiated network relations, especially with multinational assemblers and other suppliers, for Aapico's flexibility in meeting new competitive challenges up until the 1997 economic crisis. The final section examines Aapico's capacity to contend with an increasingly volatile macroeconomic environment during the economic crisis itself, again noting the importance of network-based production flexibility.

THE PROBLEM OF NON-SUPPORTIVE
SECTORAL INSTITUTIONS

To what extent does Thailand's national and sectoral economic and institutional environment support production flexibility and upgrading through provision of collective goods and encouragement of long-term cooperation among and within firms? In answering this question, we focus here on six institutional arenas commonly stressed in the governance literature: financial institutions, trade regimes, industrial relations, human resource development, public-private sector linkages, and sectoral business associations.[3]

The Thai *financial system* generally discourages long-term financing. Firms in textiles, autos, and electronics typically have had access to the equivalent of medium- and long-term financing through the rollover of short-term debt. But, until the 1990s and the Asian financial crisis, equity rather than debt was the principal source of long-term finance for most manufacturing firms, with retained earnings the main source of equity expansion in Thai industry.[4] Long-term finance for the productive upgrading of local firms has been similarly weak. Government efforts to build up a development bank for industry—the Industrial Finance Corporation of Thailand—have been less than successful. Financing for small- and medium-sized enterprises (SMEs) has, despite government intentions, remained quite weak, with most SMEs lacking access to finance, whether from state or private sources (Changsorn 1997).

The *trade regime* has further discouraged technical upgrading among firms producing for the domestic market. Best characterized as export-oriented protectionism, Thailand's trade regime has involved extensive incentives for mostly foreign-owned exporters grafted onto continued protection for locally owned, import-competing industries. That there has thus been little pressure for the latter to develop export-quality capacities is clear in the case of the auto parts industry. Comprising roughly 225 OEM firms, auto parts is dominated by Japanese joint ventures and technical licensing agreements, with local Japanese-owned or joint-venture firms capturing 77% of local procurement by Japanese assemblers (Buranathanung 1996). Indigenous firms are "fragmented and sub-scale," with auto part exports dominated by a small number of Japanese joint ventures (Brooker Group 1997).

Thai *industrial relations* are fragmented and conflictual. Labor has little influence in politics. Despite the existence of formal tripartite arrangements, little tripartite bargaining has actually taken place (Siengthai 1994: 366). With low-cost competition from neighboring countries increasing, labor-management relations have deteriorated in recent years. Lacking any real influence, workers' organizations revert to wildcat actions such as organized sick leaves and pre-work/post-work rallies. Management in turn frequently reacts with selective lockouts, in which union leaders and supporters are kept out of the workplace while operations continue with non-unionists and new hires. These problems have hit the automotive industry. As recently as 21 January 1998 workers from Thai Summit Autoparts staged a strike/demonstration that turned violent.[5] Conflictual labor-management relations in turn undercut training efforts and intraorganizational collaborative upgrading programs. Similarly, lack of effective labor representation means there is little worker pressure for high-road, skill-based, high-wage competitive strategies within a framework of labor-management cooperation. Thus, Thai firms have generally reacted to foreign competition by moving production out of the country, raising the proportion of work done by lower-cost subcontractors (often in the informal sector), or cutting costs through mechanization (Deyo 1996: 139).

Human resource development has been similarly weak. The country's education is largely geared toward the needs of an agrarian economy with most people (80%) completing only primary education (as of 1996) and a small number of college students focusing largely on traditional liberal arts curricula. Until the recent economic downturn, turnover among Thai employees in technical and managerial positions was quite high (Deyo 1996).

The lack of skilled workers has been especially harmful in the textile, electronics, and automotive industries. Despite Thailand's role as a regional automotive manufacturing center, the country has lacked a significant program in automotive technology. In fact, to attract a major investment from General Motors in 1997, the Thai government committed U.S.$15 million for establishing a GM automotive technology institute ("GM University").[6] In part, this weakness in human resource development flows from a lack of government provision. But it also reflects a corresponding weakness in public-private sector linkages and interfirm cooperation relating to collective provision of industry-relevant skills.

Public-private sector linkages in Thailand have been uneven and increasingly problematic. Sectorally, systematic exchanges between government and business have been most developed in key export sectors such as rice, sugar, and textiles, as well as in banking (prior to the financial sector liberalization of the 1990s). And during the economic crisis of the 1980s, Thai business and government formed a "liberal corporatist" Joint Public-Private Sector Consultative Committee composed of peak business associations and technocrats (Laothamatas 1991). Although this body made important contributions to the country's export regime during the 1980s, it proved fragile and after 1988 met only during Thailand's frequent changes in government. By early 1998, when business and government officials were discussing ways to restructure several Thai sectors, a government official acknowledged the "lack of joint vision among the state, the private sector, academics and investors. Each group walks along on its own without direction, resulting in 'hesitancy' and lost business opportunities when modern business must compete against time"(*Nation* 1998).[7] This lack of coherent government industrial policy making is further exacerbated on the one hand by a lack of coordination between macroeconomic and line agencies, and on the other by the tendency for line agencies to maintain largely clientelist relations with favored businesses.

The resulting lack of coordination, especially as regards technological and managerial upgrading, has been a key contributor to what all observers recognize as Thailand's striking weaknesses in human resource and vendor development. The country lacks public or collective institutions devoted to technology acquisition and diffusion-oriented technical services. A recent report concluded that Thailand's science and technology environment reflects "mismatches in S&T human resource supply, very low levels of R&D activity, a private sector with strong manufacturing capability but weak research, development and engineering capability, and an information technology that is growing but remains insufficient" (Brooker Group 1996: 96; see also Fairclough 1995; Felker 1997). Each of these problems is evident in the Thai auto industry. An Automotive Development Committee, composed of government officials and key private sector officials, has operated under Ministry of Industry supervision for some twenty years. Yet the committee lacks expertise and is frequently circumvented by particularistic linkages between individual firms and officials.[8] Similarly, Dollar et al. (1998: 26) find that there is little utilization of existing government industry-support programs, that utilization of those programs is not associated with high productivity, and that "only 5% of high-productivity firms take advantage of BoI [Board of Investment] R&D programs, and only 3%, of Thai research programs."

A source and a consequence of Thailand's problematic public-private sector linkages is the general weakness of sectoral coordination, especially as reflected in the country's *business associations*. Associational strength can be assessed on the basis of cohesion and density (i.e., the percentage of firms in the industry). On this basis, Thailand's peak manufacturing group, the Federation of Thai Industries (FTI), has been fairly weak. The FTI has been fragmented by divisions between upstream and downstream firms and by the tendency of larger firms to deal directly with particular officials rather than work for a consensus among the industry's members. The strongest sectoral associations have been those considered key to the country's export growth and thus supported by state officials, e.g., rice, sugar, garments, tourism, and jewelry.[9] The principal emphasis of these groups has been on market access through quota management, information dissemination, tariff protection, and capacity control. While some have also addressed standard and quality issues, as well as administrative reform for improved export performance, these efforts have not generally involved technological upgrading. Indeed, it took over ten years for the textile industry associations to agree on the creation of a textile technology institute, despite widespread recognition that such an institution was necessary given Thailand's loss of wage competitiveness. Similar problems have characterized associations of domestic electronics producers and, key to the present chapter, domestic auto parts firms.

There are four automotive associations, two each for assemblers and parts firms. Although there is significant overlap in membership among these, the organizational differences reflect a general lack of cohesion due to splits between assemblers and parts producers, and between local and foreign parts firms. During the industry's early years (the mid-1970s to late 1980s), the auto parts associations were quite successful in ensuring that locally based firms would have the opportunity to supply the domestic market. The key was a series of local content regulations that compelled auto assemblers gradually to increase the percentage of the vehicle sourced locally to roughly 61 percent for pickup trucks and 54 percent for passenger vehicles (Doner 1991). In many cases the assemblers have been able to circumvent these regulations; according to one estimate, true local content of cars is much lower than official figures. Nevertheless, local content has provided the basis for significant growth in local parts firms. This supply base, along with a stable macroeconomic environment, cheap labor, openness to new investment, and an expanding domestic market, led to Thailand's becoming Southeast Asia's hub for auto production. The country's dominant position was reflected in the 1996–1997 decisions of GM,[10] Ford, and Chrysler to establish operations in Thailand.

But while the country's overall growth led to the Thai market becoming the largest in Southeast Asia (*Bangkok Post* 1998),[11] the parts associations did not address two related objectives: rationalization and technical development. Despite continued efforts, the auto parts associations failed to reduce the numbers of makes and models. The result has been low production runs in Thailand and elsewhere in the region. Assembly lines in Japan and the U.S. may turn out over fifty vehicles per hour, while most plants in Southeast Asia have typically reached no more than ten vehicles per hour. These low-scale economies have undermined the capacity of local parts firms to reduce costs, increase quality, or create more efficient plant layout, problems exacerbated by the generally weak production flexibility of auto parts makers (Brimble 1993: 207). The auto parts associations have also been almost completely silent on such issues as skill shortages, managerial weaknesses, and research and development. The response to shortages of skilled workers, for example, has been mutual poaching rather than concentration on the provision of industry-wide training. Thai parts firms have also been criticized for their "wait and see attitude" toward quality standards such as ISO and QS 9000 (*Bangkok Post* 1997).[12]

In sum, Thai auto parts firms have had to contend with fragmented markets, lack of long-term finance, conflictual industrial relations, little if any provision for collective goods necessary for technological upgrading, weak sectoral representation and cooperation, and lack of encouragement of interfirm collaboration.[13] It is thus not surprising that only seven firms export OEM components in significant quantities, and that these are all foreign (mostly Japanese) joint ventures using relatively few local inputs (Brooker Group 1997). The weakness of local parts producers became all the more alarming by the mid-1990s in light of two developments. First, the Thai government pledged to end local content requirements and to reduce tariffs due to pressures from new entrants such as GM and the requirements of WTO membership.[14] Second, local parts firms had increasingly to contend with ever more stringent requirements by the multinational auto assemblers. Mostly Japanese (with 90 percent of the region's markets), the assemblers are now intent on consolidating operations throughout the region. To increase economies of scale, Japanese subsidiaries in each Southeast Asian country are moving away from self-contained, national operations toward national specialization in particular components and/or vehicles for regional exchange and even extraregional export. Finally, GM and Ford have also entered the Thai market. With the goal of capturing 10 percent of the Asian auto market by the year 2005, GM announced plans for a one-hundred-thousand-units-per-year assembly operation in Thailand, located at the Eastern Seaboard Industrial Estate, aimed at exporting to Japan and neighboring countries. With Mazda, Ford has shifted its Asian pickup truck production from Japan to the same Thai industrial estate and intends to source a significant portion of components from Thailand. Both GM and Ford have signaled their intention to bring many of their key suppliers with them to Thailand.

Thailand's weak institutional context, more stringent demands by multinational clients, and continuing competition from foreign suppliers makes it all the more compelling to explain Aapico's export success. This is especially the case for jigs. Since each jig is designed for a particular vehicle model, this product requires very high quality and extremely low production runs. In the following two sections, we examine the sources of Aapico's success through the mid-1990s. We begin with the firm's overall evolution, then address production changes in jigs and press parts, identify organizational changes, and conclude by examining some institutional explanations for Aapico's success in meeting new competitive challenges and in confronting the recent economic crisis.

FROM SUCCESS IN SMALL VOLUMES TO THE CHALLENGE OF LARGER VOLUMES/HIGHER QUALITY

Background and Evolution

Aapico began operations in September 1985 on the facilities of Auto Parts Industries Co.[15] (APICO), a producer of parts, jigs, and dies that had operated in Thailand for fifteen years. The firm had done well, but the previous owners had funneled profits to another company. The new owners, a group of Malaysians, Singaporeans, and Thais led by the present managing director, decided to set up a new firm with a similar name to benefit from the company's positive image without the responsibilities of its liabilities. In early 1988, Aapico's owners initiated construction of a new factory and purchase of new machinery. The firm completed this project in 1989, and by 1995 had roughly three hundred employees. Annual sales rose sharply, from $3.2 million in 1991 to $5.3 million in 1993, $7 million in 1994, and around $8 million in 1995.

By 1996, Aapico's business consisted of three parts: (1) the design, manufacture, and assembly of auto body jigs (roughly 50 percent of sales by value); (2) the design and manufacture of dies (10 percent of sales, of which around 70 percent have been devoted to in-house use for the manufacture of press parts); and (3) the production of press parts such as fuel tanks, body panels, exhaust systems, and brackets (40 percent of sales). Altogether, the firm produces some three hundred OEM items. Its clients for all three types of products include almost all auto assemblers operating in Thailand and Southeast Asia, as well as some from outside the region. Jigs account for most of Aapico's exports, with around half of its jigs sent overseas. Toyota and Honda have traditionally been Aapico's largest customers, although Ford is slated to become much more important for press parts (see below).

Expanding national and regional markets, along with increasing multinational interest in Thailand as a production base, encouraged Aapico to expand. As of 1997, it planned to begin exporting press parts through linkages with foreign parts firms and participation in the multinationals' regional complementarity schemes. It also moved to expand its tooling development capacity to include a transfer or assembly line in which a series of jigs can be tested before being shipped to clients. In terms of plant capacity, Aapico invested some $12 million (three hundred million Thai baht) to build a new 10,800-square-mile factory in the Hitech Industrial Estate, an industrial park in Ayuthya province north of Bangkok which provides seven years' tax relief under the Board of Investment's industrial decentralization tax incentives program. The plant has four times the stamping capacity of the older factory, as well as space for building and testing multiple jigs on assembly lines. The firm has also established another joint-venture plant close to Ford's new Autoalliance facility in the Eastern Seaboard.

Early Success in Fragmented Markets: Low-Capacity Jigs

Through the mid-1990s, Aapico's competitive position varied across the three product areas. In press parts, the firm has faced a very large number of rivals—probably almost one hundred. The firm's managers estimate that, as of 1996, Aapico was not close to the top with regard to volume and quality, although the firm's product was good enough for Japanese OEM status in the Thai domestic market. With the new stamping line in the Hitech Industrial Estate, the firm has now moved considerably up the ladder to the very top tier. Although Aapico's competitive position in die production is somewhat difficult to assess, since it produces most of its dies for in-house use, the firm has probably been in the upper second tier in the past. But Aapico's managers believe the move to the larger new facility now enables the firm to meet the highest standard.

It is in jig production that the firm has stood out. Aapico is the best jig producer in Thailand and the region in terms of capacity-to-produce, stand-alone projects. The firm began by manufacturing jigs based on Japanese designs. Senior management gradually realized that Japanese designs assumed relatively high volumes and were thus unsuited to Thailand's limited markets and small factories. Most factories were assembling fewer than ten vehicles per hour and often were assembling different models and, in the case of certain general assemblers, different brands during the same day. In addition, Thai facilities often lacked space. With only one set of welding guns, jigs needed to be moved in and out rapidly. Speed was especially important since the Japanese automakers wanted to amortize their costs quickly by launching new vehicles in Thailand simultaneously with or soon after their launch in Japan.

To address this problem, Aapico expanded from jig assembly to jig design and manufacture. Its focus was on what it termed "low capacity jigs"—tooling capable of efficiently assembling five cars an hour. Such jigs were intentionally low technology: on caster wheels and thus easy to move, they also substituted mechanical, manual clamps for electronically controlled, pneumatic clamps. With Aapico capable of producing a main-frame jig for U.S.$100,000 to U.S.$200,000—significantly less than the assemblers could make it for—Japanese clients saved money in tooling and in overall plant size. And while vehicles assembled by such jigs were not at the level of those made in Japan, they were quite acceptable for the Thai market.

Two factors were important for success in this market niche. One was a relatively informal production process run by the shop foreman—a sort of job shop focused on craft-like production. But this job shop benefited from a second factor—the development of in-house design capacity for jigs (the firm had always designed its own dies). As the firm's tooling director noted, most firms can manufacture. Long-term success requires the capacity for total turnkey programs, i.e., the design, manufacture, and testing of tooling. Only such a program can provide sufficient support for the assemblers' own shop-floor operations that the assemblers are willing to vacate the production of local tooling completely. Design capacity also allows the firm to speed up manufacture by beginning production of the jig's base plate before the entire jig is designed. Most recently, Aapico has been especially successful in developing flexible, multimodel jigs, in introducing new supporting technologies, and in greatly improving tooling quality.

The Challenge of High-Capacity Jigs

By the mid-1990s, Thailand's strong supplier base and the region's automotive growth were drawing increased multinational automotive investment. But because this investment was more export-oriented and rationalized, it posed greater challenges to local firms such as Aapico. New markets mean higher volumes, which require investments in new plants and equipment. Even more daunting, these volumes involve more stringent quality cost delivery standards. Trade liberalization and the intensification of interbrand competition in the region, along with assembler pressure for continual cost and quality improvements and just-in-time-delivery increase, all figured heavily in the area of press parts, where the firm evaluated its own quality somewhere around C+/B–. We shall address press parts production below. But there has also been significant pressure for more rapid design and manufacture of higher volume jigs involving more complex technologies. Indeed, to continue its growth, Aapico has had to develop the capacity to produce an entire assembly line. To some degree this pressure reflects the Japanese practice of extensive reliance on subcontractors. But it also probably reflects the deterioration of relevant expertise among the assemblers, along with possible cost advantages.[16]

The firm's success in obtaining new orders for higher-capacity jigs requiring more advanced technology pushed the firm to improve overall workflow control. Until the summer of 1995, workflow monitoring and documentation was relatively loose. The jig foreman managed successive stages, not through an explicit and systematic reporting system, but through an informal process developed by and known only to him. This system worked well for producing relatively small volumes of low-capacity jigs, but was not well suited for the firm's new competitive environment. One experience illustrates the problem: when Honda officials visited the plant to discuss jig sourcing possibilities, Aapico had difficulties providing a formal analysis of each workflow step requested by the Japanese assemblers. Aapico was not operating the kind of systematic, bottom-up information gathering and exchange necessary for *kaizen* or constant improvement.

This began to change in mid-1995, when the tooling director instituted a production control system under the management of the Engineering Department (ED). The ED establishes start and completion dates for the production of each tool. These are then conveyed to the foreman of the jig shop, who, together with the rest of the shop, establishes target dates for more intermediate stages: tooling design, base fabrication, base machining, unit fabrication, unit machining, unit assembly, installation, inspection, pipping, tryout, and buy off. The jig foreman does not run each tooling project. Rather, each project has a specific leader chosen by the foreman. The ED monitors each project's progress through consultation with the foreman and section leaders based on status report forms developed in late 1995. Through this organizational innovation, coordination between design and production has been greatly enhanced, thus reducing time to market.

Nowhere are the pressures for more rapid delivery and technological complexity more evident than in a 1997 Aapico bid for a transfer line for Hyundai vehicles assembled in India. This assembly line incorporates thirty-five jigs linked by transfer stations. It was different from previous projects in several respects. First, Aapico had to deliver the entire line as a turnkey facility. In the past, the firm had provided particular jigs to an assembler. Although Aapico tested the jigs in its own facilities, most of the debugging involved Aapico employees traveling to the assembler's plant for installation and adjustments. In this project, the entire line had to be ready to operate as delivered. To contend with these kinds of demands, Aapico's new factory devotes a large area of its jig shop to the testing of assembly equipment. Second, this Hyundai project forced Aapico to become better acquainted with and more capable of integrating diverse technologies. The very nature of this line requires a combination of pneumatics, robotics, and programmable logic controls. Although they work within broad guidelines provided by Hyundai, Aapico engineers decided on the precise combination of these technologies to meet client guidelines. The firm's technology links with Kawasaki Robotics and Petro Instruments Corporation (PICO, which contributed programming assistance) provided critical technological support for this effort. Third, the project pushed Aapico toward increasing its capacity for standardization. Because the transfer line includes numerous jigs, it involves multiple parts and components, all of which have to be perfect and uniform.

Although jig production is still quite skill-intensive because of the highly customized nature of each tool, the firm's growth in this area involves the acquisition and mastery of more complex equipment. Base plates are all cut and bored by computer numerical controlled (CNC) machines and are of the same quality as those made in the U.S. and Japan. Advanced instruments are required for measurement. Some 10 percent of Aapico's clients now require that the surfaces of various parts of the jig be cut by highly accurate wire cut machines (the firm assumes that the level will reach 90 percent in the not-too-distant future). And computer-assisted design (CAD) is used since Aapico receives lists of jig control points on CAD from several assemblers. However, due to their need to incorporate spot welds and to see all parts of the design, the jig designers work largely from hard-copy drawings.

THE CHALLENGE OF HIGHER-VOLUME/ HIGHER-CAPACITY PRESS PARTS

The pressures for higher volumes, higher quality, lower cost, and quick delivery are most evident in press-part production, especially for the large orders secured from Ford. Indeed, the firm's new press line has been designed specifically with the needs of Ford's new pickup plant in mind, although Aapico expects this line to be a major selling point as the firm supplies parts to other brands as well. The new press line differs from Aapico's old arrangement in three important ways. First it combines high volumes[17] with reduced work-in-progress. A visit to the factory in 1999 revealed a successful program of reduced process inventory, and virtually no accumulation of finished press parts, which were generally shipped out immediately upon completion. Also, the new line permits improved quality and allows for greater flexibility in terms of the capacity to shift among different product types and variations based in part on the introduction of quick-change dies.

Aapico's die production reflects both client pressures and the need to support this expanding press-part operation. Until the new plant came on line, the firm relied principally on two large milling machines. One, a traditional electro-mechanical machine, was used largely for work overflow due to its slowness and relatively wide tolerances. But the primary tool for die production was a much more rapid and close tolerance CNC copy/scan machine linked to the design department through a CAD/CAM (computer-assisted design/computer-assisted manufacturing) system. Aapico's management points to two factors in explaining their use of this newer equipment. One is the shortage of highly skilled workers. While there are few model builders, many people are able to operate CAD/CAM systems. As one manager noted, "the mouse has replaced the artisan." The other factor is simply client pressure for higher quality, greater speed, and closer tolerances. Given the growth of the Thai auto industry, assemblers will no longer contract an order to a supplier without CNC machines.

Client pressures for quality enhancement have reinforced Aapico's efforts to meet industry-wide quality standards—ISO and QS 9000. These standards are significant because they involve not the ability to meet particular production targets, such as volumes or characteristics of output, but rather the capacity for constant self-evaluation and problem solving. This capacity assures clients that a supplier is a competent partner, one that can engage in the kinds of quality assurance and upgrading necessary to respond to changing demand conditions. Most critically, Aapico's managers know the firm must meet these standards because of its changing market. For example, the firm initially produced uniquely configured "one-off" jigs at relatively slow rates; mistakes could be corrected after production. This is no longer possible, with orders for several jigs with shorter deadlines. Similar pressures are evident in press parts. The earliest pressure to meet these standards came from Japanese assemblers such as Toyota and Honda, as well as large Japanese suppliers such as Bridgestone and Nippondenso. In fact, as an Aapico manager noted, neither Toyota nor Honda has itself yet achieved ISO 9000 in Thailand. But they do emphasize *kaizen* or constant improvement, while urging their suppliers to conform with QS 9000 and to try to achieve certification.[18] A more recent and critical source of pressure is the fact that Aapico's contract to supply fifteen press parts for Ford is conditional on the firm's being certified in QS 9000 by the time production starts. But Aapico's managers have also been interested in ISO-type programs simply as a way to get a fuller understanding of what is going on in the plant. In 1997, for example, they acknowledged that because they did not know exactly what was going on at each stage of production, they sometimes did not know why they were making money in one operation and losing it in another.

Finally, the ISO process has prompted a greater concern for employee training, an activity that the firm's managing director believes is one of the key components of ISO certification. The firm has only just begun to develop formal training programs for press parts, and has constructed a dedicated training facility in its new plant.

INSTITUTIONAL SOURCES OF FLEXIBILITY AND SUCCESS

Expanding and competitive markets were clearly critical for Aapico's success, at least until 1997. But given Aapico's relatively unique performance as a producer and exporter of automotive tooling, we need to look at the factors that distinguish this firm from others. One is that Aapico is self-consciously a "learning-oriented" organization. The managing director (MD) recognizes the need to search actively for better trained workers, new technologies, and improved managerial approaches. But a desire for new resources does not alone guarantee an ability to obtain them. Aapico developed and benefited from a range of network-like relations with outside individuals, groups, and firms, which have been important for the firm's ability to accommodate ever more stringent pressures for enhanced flexibility in areas of quality and process improvements, design capabilities, customization of high-volume production, and process engineering. These network benefits have in turn centered first on increased access to capital, skills, technical and managerial know-how, and markets, and second on enhanced opportunities for collaboration and mutual assistance.

ACCESS TO CAPITAL

Aapico's origins are linked to the capacities and interests of overseas Chinese networks, in this case involving a minor role for the Singapore government. The MD noted, for example, that "it was family ties, not business sense, that got him involved in the project." The MD joined with "friends and relatives from Malaysia, Singapore and Thailand" to buy the original firm (Fairclough 1995: 120). At least part of the Singapore funding came from Singapore Technologies, a government-owned firm whose function is to promote promising technology-based ventures. Aapico began as, and has remained, a privately held firm. It is in fact composed of five firms, one a holding company reflecting the original ownership structure: the Malaysian-born MD owns 30 percent, and the rest belongs to the block of largely passive Singaporean and Malaysian shareholders. Aapico is not highly leveraged; its debt equity ratio as of 1997 was roughly 1.5/1.

Human Resource Development

One, if not *the*, principal challenge for Aapico relates to human resources. Until the downturn and employment cutbacks of 1997, Thailand's supply of skilled personnel at all levels was extremely tight. Beginning in 1990, Thai wage rates were increasing at roughly 10 percent a year, and in some industries, such as electronics, workers were getting annual pay raises of 25 percent (*Bangkok Post* 1997).[19] Compensation levels for local engineers were rising quickly, especially since many were moving into finance rather than manufacturing. Especially troubling was extensive job hopping. In Aapico itself, managers estimated annual turnover rates of 10 percent for newly hired operators prior to reaching six months with the company and for technicians between twenty-five and thirty-five years of age.

In seeking to address these difficulties, Aapico is beginning to introduce ISO-mandated training programs in press parts and to deepen learning-based product development in jigs and dies. The need for internalized learning capacity in tooling is especially important given Aapico's need to develop customized tooling and its opportunity to cross-borrow from different clients: that is, to draw on aspects of one automaker's approach to the build process to develop tooling for another assembler. Complementing intensified training efforts are parallel efforts to reduce turnover through a number of job benefits, internal advancement policies, and seniority bonuses.

These efforts to institutionalize learning across the firm's various operations have been supported to varying degrees by external relations with government agencies and other firms, and through associational and personal relations. It was noted that Aapico has become fully engaged in preparing for ISO certification in press parts. In fact, the firm initiated ISO training efforts prior to coming under pressure from its foreign clients to do so. This initiative helped the firm become one of eight local firms selected to participate in the small-scale ISO promotion program supported by the Thai Ministry of Industry. Under this program, the Thai government paid for a foreign consultant to help Aapico prepare for ISO certification. In addition, Aapico hired a former Honda engineer to develop safety and quality-control programs, first in the firm's joint venture with Sanoh and then in Aapico itself. By the summer of 1995 the QC manager had developed forms for monitoring workflows and establishing the paper trail so critical to ongoing assessment.

But with the possible exception of this Ministry of Industry support for ISO training, Aapico's public sector linkages have not provided significant support for human resources development, technology, or other dimensions of competitive upgrading. This may be seen in Aapico's engineer recruitment efforts. Two members of the jig engineering section are university graduates, and the firm's MD has made numerous attempts to expand such recruitment. But because university-industry linkages are relatively weak, such efforts met with little success. For example, the firm's managing director initiated a scholarship/internship program with the Engineering Department of Thailand's Thammasat University. The firm established a fund to be allocated on a competitive basis to one student per year who would work in Aapico for part of the year. Only one student applied for the program.[20]

Aapico has thus had to rely primarily on an in-house strategy of turning its own technicians into engineers. In addition, Aapico has had to reach beyond Thai borders for some of its key employees. The managing director, who speaks English and Chinese as well as Thai, is a trained engineer with extensive experience in the region's auto industry through Ford dealerships. This linguistic, ethnic, regional, and industry-specific expertise has proven quite useful. It enabled the MD to identify and recruit an individual who has been key to the growth of the firm's jig business: an Australian with over thirty years experience developing tooling for Ford, much of that time in the fragmented markets of Southeast Asia. The Ford connection proved useful as well in the more recent recruitment of two other Ford engineers to direct die and jig production. The MD has also recruited several Chinese from Malaysia and China for some key positions in the Engineering Department. Recruitment of engineers in China has been facilitated by a firm in Wuhan with whom Aapico has a sales tie-up, and by local Communist Party members operating as professional recruiters. The firm's recent expansion into its new facilities has forced it to look even further for skilled personnel. As of the summer of 1997, Aapico had recruited tool and die makers from the Ukraine.

Technology and Management Know-How

Aapico's success depends critically on its access to, and ability to absorb, the technologies and organizational best practices required for export-quality OEM production. The firm is constrained in this regard by the striking weaknesses noted above in Thailand's public sector technology and organizational support services. Far more important have been bilateral and multilateral linkages with other firms (including foreign suppliers with whom the firm has joint ventures or cooperative agreements), assembler clients, competitors, and Aapico's own suppliers.

A core component of Aapico's strategy for responding to new challenges involves expanding ties with *foreign parts firms and service-providers*. These tie-ups include Aapico's joint venture with Japan's Sanoh for brake and fuel pipes, a technical agreement with Japan's Kurata for fuel tanks, another joint venture with Sanoh and Nitto Denka for zinc plating, a sales and installation agreement with Kawasaki Robots, a technology agreement with Kurata, a joint venture with the U.S. firm Arvins, a producer of catalytic converters and exhaust systems, and an electronic programming agreement with PICO.

One benefit from these tie-ups, of course, is access to new assemblers/clients already served by the foreign suppliers. Another benefit is in obtaining state-of-the-art technology and organizational knowledge. The joint venture with Sanoh is intended to introduce high-volume production methods and quality control practices to Aapico, as well as to expand into the production of brake, fuel, and clutch pipes. In part through the Kurata tie-up, Aapico has become a major supplier of some fifteen press parts and fuel tanks for the pickup Ford intends to produce in Thailand. In fact, the firm expects Ford's new operation to absorb some 40 percent of total press-part production. Through the technology agreements with PICO and Kawasaki, the firm has deepened its expertise regarding transfer and assembly line technology necessary for higher-volume jig production.

Japanese trading companies, or *sogo shosha*, also merit note as key mediators in these evolving relationships. Nissho Iwai is a part owner of the joint venture with

Sanoh, and Sumitomo has been key in the tie-up with Kawasaki. In these ventures, the trading companies not only provide information about prospective clients, they also work extensively to prepare the ground for a constructive and harmonious venture. This involves, for example, ensuring that both parties have access to the same information and that Aapico is fully informed about the interests and habits of the Japanese partners. For Aapico, the *sogo shosha* have played a crucial role in establishing and maintaining new relationships. And the firm's managing director expects them to be increasingly important for arranging joint ventures with the new wave of smaller Japanese parts firms that have little overseas experience.

Relations with *assemblers* are also critical sources of technology, and of managerial and organizational expertise. Since Japanese brands dominate Thailand and the rest of the region, we focus here on Aapico's links to Japanese assemblers. Assemblers' interest in promoting more capable suppliers, driven by the Japanese preference for buying rather than making, is the basis for beneficial supplier-assembler relations. It is clear that transplanted Japanese parts firms play an important role in Southeast Asia and promise to play an even more important role with the growth of export-oriented auto investments. But Japanese assemblers have signaled their intention to continue relying on those local firms capable of meeting new requirements and to help local firms develop this capability.

Bilaterally, local suppliers such as Aapico must meet a number of criteria before qualifying as OEM suppliers. In the case of Toyota, for example, prospective suppliers must show satisfactory performance in purchasing management, quality assurance, and component engineering (technology and machinery), in addition to basic cost level.[21] Once a supplier has met these criteria, it must provide a price quotation and undergo a cost study. Once a supplier has been accepted, Toyota provides ongoing pressure to and support for cost reduction and quality upgrading. This involves, for example, visits by Japanese engineers to help with plant layout or quality assurance, joint discussions regarding raw material purchases, and sharing of information regarding new model development. Overseas support and inspection have also been important sources of on-the-job training. Participation in overseas model launches employing Aapico jigs have been very valuable learning experiences for employees in the jig and die sections. The firm has also sent some senior engineers to observe die production in Japan. Similarly, Ford has been very supportive of Aapico's upgrading efforts, especially in its QS 9000 activities, sending consultant engineers to assist where useful.[22]

Assembler relations have been important as well in providing incentives for value improvement and cost cutting. Successful supplier initiatives in value analysis/value engineering often yield "VA/VE points," which are translated into expanded orders for new models or product modifications. Toyota's "cost merit share system" involves (1) breaking down the cost structure of a supplier; (2) asking the supplier to reduce its costs by, say, 10 percent; (3) purchasing the part for the original price for the first year, thus allowing the supplier to increase its own profit by 10 percent; and (4) purchasing the part for the reduced price in the second year.

Multilateral assembler relationships are equally important. Indeed, the Japanese are generally concerned with what Aapico managers refer to as a need to maintain a community of local suppliers. This is done in part by spreading the work among various suppliers, usually at least two per part. In so doing, the assemblers not only increase competitive pressure on their suppliers and avoid vulnerability to holdup by a single firm, they also ensure themselves of an adequate supplier base in the case of unexpected increased demand. In some cases, assemblers organize an ad hoc group of their major suppliers to address a particular challenge. For example, in preparing for its Thai-made vehicle for the ASEAN market, Toyota organized a meeting of its ten largest local suppliers to evaluate these firms' excess capacity before deciding how much work to give to transplants. More often, suppliers operate through assembler-organized groups known as cooperation clubs (Buranathanung 1996: 85–91). These are formal associations of suppliers through which assemblers diffuse basic management practices such as quality control, VA/VE, shipment, and inventory control. Promotion of best practices helps the assemblers to enforce the usual 1–2 percent annual cost-reduction targets required of their suppliers. The clubs are also arenas in which assemblers present their own production goals and ask suppliers for corresponding yearly plans. Participation in the Nissan Diesel Club helped Aapico, for example, to improve its capacity for market projection. Finally, the clubs allow the assemblers to encourage cooperation among the suppliers themselves regarding best practices. Such cooperation sometimes extends to relations among producers of the same product. Aapico's managers insist, however, that the clubs are useful mainly for alerting suppliers to new opportunities, challenges, and information. Actual improvement is up to the firm itself, often operating directly with the assembler.

There is no question that the assemblers dominate these relationships. Yet mutual reciprocity is extensive and important. On the one hand, assembler reliance on suppliers capable of supplying just-in-time, high-quality products has grown due to the intensification of interassembler competition, the shortening of product cycles, reduced in-house capacity to produce key parts and machine-tools, and the increase of vehicles designed for ASEAN markets. For example, Toyota's ASEAN car lacked master drawings for key parts. In Aapico's eyes, these were important signs of Toyota's commitment to and reliance on local firms,[23] a commitment that Aapico would presumably translate into increased investment for Toyota, especially in press parts and dies (Toyota produces its own jigs). On the other hand, to get Toyota's business, suppliers such as Aapico have to prove their commitment by investing in new projects on the assembler's word alone that good effort will be rewarded. Thus, Aapico frequently launches projects with no clear guarantee of full compensation. As one manager noted, "Aapico will accept a B5–10 million job without a purchase order. To make a name for yourself, you have to take a risk." Reciprocity reduces these risks in part because of the nature of contracts and negotiations. While assembler-supplier contracts are quite formal, neither party follows them to the letter. Nonperformance is not typically punished if based on conditions beyond the supplier's control. Indeed, late deliveries, cost overruns and high defect rates will tend to provoke a joint effort to streamline the supplier's cost structure and management practices. Japanese assembler requests to see suppliers' books are fairly common in Thailand and usually accepted. But if weak performance is based on a supplier's refusal to pursue best practices or invest in needed equipment, the assembler will likely drop the supplier.

Aapico also cooperates with *other local parts firms* to a limited degree and under certain conditions. As noted earlier, cooperation within automotive business associations is limited to issues of market sharing and to lobbying activities related to local content and tariff levels. Greater exchange of information related to production upgrading occurs more often within the assembler-sponsored cooperation clubs. And finally, there are also cases of temporary capacity subcontracting among parts suppliers. If Aapico finds itself with insufficient capacity to fill an order, the firm may subcontract part of the order to a rival firm. Such job sharing apparently is confined largely to die production and, even here, to only certain aspects of the production process. Work sharing, to the limited extent it occurs, does not merely preserve Aapico's relationship with its client. It also encourages other firms to provide Aapico with work in lean times. Interestingly, cooperation with other suppliers also strengthens Aapico's capacity to obtain funds. Such cooperation signals to bankers that Aapico (1) will probably have work in slack periods, (2) will be able to satisfy its clients even if it lacks the capacity to fill a particular order, and (3) has a reputation for being a team player. All of this means that Aapico itself is not necessarily interested in seeing its rivals, or at least all of them, go out of business.

Finally, Aapico itself relies on *suppliers* for intermediate goods such as steel, equipment such as machine tools and clamps, and specialized processes such as annealing, wire cutting, heat treatment, and cylinder grinding. Aapico's intent is to support its vendors in the style of its Japanese clients. When the firm wins a bid, say, on a jig program, managers sit down and decide how to divide up the work among existing vendors. The intention is to spread the work evenly so as to maintain existing capacity. The firm also sends its own technicians to supplier factories.

But the firm has not yet worked out a consistent mode of supplier support and its experience in promoting these relationships has not been encouraging. Several years ago, Aapico encouraged one of its foremen to set up a separate shop to subcontract some machining (e.g., of bracket supports) for Aapico. The effort failed, argue Aapico's managers, because of weak entrepreneurialism and a shortage of financing. More generally, continuing quality problems with local suppliers have to this point tended to counteract Aapico's efforts to increase outsourcing, encouraging it instead to continue to emphasize and extend joint-venture in-house production within a network of cross-invested firms. The new zinc-plating joint venture, for example, was established specifically to avoid supplier quality and delivery problems facing its other Sanoh joint venture. In the long run, however, the firm's managers recognize that this solution may prove unworkable. As the firm moves into higher volumes, it will be forced to abandon certain low-tech operations in a process analogous to assembler practices, while relying on other firms for specialized processes. As such, specialty subcontracting will have to expand, forcing Aapico to move toward more systematic relations with vendors.

In summary, Aapico has enjoyed success in different types of flexible production. The firm began its growth by developing a capacity to produce low-technology, custom-designed jigs for Southeast Asia's low-volume markets. As these markets expanded, the firm moved to more rapid production of higher-volume tooling using more advanced technology. It has also prepared itself for a shift from low volumes of moderate quality press parts to a capacity for both high- and low-volume production of export-quality press parts.

Of central importance have been a range of network relations, including overseas Chinese networks, international automotive personnel networks (e.g., Ford connections), and close interfirm linkages, through which the firm has been able to obtain the capital, personnel, and technology necessary for its success. With the exception of Chinese linkages, an absence in Thailand of effective institutional support for collective goods or interfirm cooperation has ensured that Aapico's relational network has largely been strategic in origin, i.e., rooted less in external affiliations and preexisting loyalties than in the efforts of managers of foreign and local firms to forge economically useful relations of trust and cooperation. Choice of partners in these cases relies heavily on industry reputation. But important though strategic considerations are, it must be noted that the *deepening* of strategic relations to the point necessary for significant mutual risk taking depends on a lengthy experience of successful interaction. A recent jig program with Mercedes Benz, for example, began initially with an outsourcing recommendation from a Benz employee and proceeded through several small contracts before Benz was willing to commit to a total turnkey jig program with Aapico. As noted by the tooling director, years of confidence building are necessary for such major programs. This is especially true of relations with Japanese assemblers, who typically enter supplier relations very cautiously, beginning with small orders and withholding information until a supplier has proven itself. Similarly, the Aapico-PICO relationship began with a simple subcontracting arrangement under which PICO managed the electronic programming of a jig assembly project in India, following which the two companies collaborated on several other projects. They now routinely cooperate in formulating project proposals, providing mutual recommendations to prospective customers, and passing work on to one another. And indeed, as noted below in connection with the Arvins tie-up, narrowly calculative joint-venture relations not rooted in continuing trust building may easily rupture under stress.

CONFRONTING ECONOMIC CRISIS

Just as Aapico was completing its major expansion, the firm was forced to confront a drastically changed economic environment. Thailand's overall economic crisis resulted in a drop of almost 40 percent in the country's automobile market from 530,986 in 1996 to around 360,000 in 1997 (*Nation* 1998).[24] Subsequent sales during the first ten months of 1998 were down by over 70 percent from the corresponding 1997 period (*Bangkok Post* 1998).[25] With the country's total automotive production capacity reaching 900,000 units due to recent investments by Japanese and U.S. automakers (including the 135,000-unit capacity at the new Autoalliance plant), Thailand faced a severe overcapacity problem. By consequence, fully half of the fifteen assemblers shut down by October 1997, and only resumed reduced production in late January. In July 1998, Mazda closed its joint-venture auto assembly plant and Thailand-Chrysler entered bankruptcy negotiations with ten major international banks (*Bangkok Post* 1998; 1999).[26] General Motors decided not to start production from its new assembly plant until the year 2000, and when production does begin, it will be at only 40 percent of originally anticipated volume. And during the first half of 1998, Toyota was producing at only 10 percent of capacity. Such huge reductions in auto production have had a devastating effect on local suppliers. Indeed, a mid-1998 industrial survey conducted by Dollar et al. found auto parts makers had been hit harder than firms in other major industries and were most pessimistic about their prospects (Dollar et al. 1998: 9).

Auto industry decline was reflected as well in drastic employment reductions among assemblers (*Bangkok Post* 1998; Dollar et al. 1998: 9–11)[27], with follow-on retrenchments among suppliers, and especially among nonexporting firms. By June 1998, total sectoral layoffs had reached approximately 30 percent,[28] with further layoffs as employers sought to accelerate staff reduction programs in anticipation of new labor legislation increasing required severance payments to displaced workers beginning in August 1998.

Compounding this severe market slump were capital shortages and problematic government policies. The bankruptcy of most of Thailand's finance companies not only undermined credit-based consumer demand but also created liquidity problems for local parts firms. And the government's ability to support local firms was limited by other economic priorities. Even as consumers had less money to spend, the cost of a locally assembled vehicle rose by 40 percent and for a completely built-up unit by 100 percent, reflecting the depreciation of the baht, which increased the cost of imported goods, as well as four tax increases, including higher value-added-tax and tariff rates.

Although assemblers did not pass these costs directly to consumers, they were reflected in assembly cost pressures on parts firms. There were important constraints on the ability of parts firms to reduce costs, however. One constraint was reduced scale economies due to the severe market contraction in Thailand and elsewhere in Asia. A second was the fact that tariffs on raw materials necessary to produce auto parts were up to 40 percent rather than the 0–5 percent requested and anticipated by local parts firms.

Facing these sectoral threats, Aapico had to cope with a drastic reduction in orders from local assemblers. Toyota, for example, substantially reduced its purchases of press parts from Aapico, a problem further exacerbated by GM's delayed production launch. Similarly, the Ford/Mazda Autoalliance joint venture substantially reduced its 1998 fuel tank orders for its new pickup truck. In large part because of Ford's cutback, Aapico press parts sales declined from 70 percent of total sales before the crisis to only 22 percent at mid-1998. Further, Aapico had assumed more than 300 million baht in U.S.-dollar denominated debt to build its new facilities in anticipation of continued rapid growth in the industry, in large measure to meet the requirements of the new GM and Autoalliance assembly lines. It thus faced the daunting task of repaying that loan with greatly diminished revenue.

But despite these new pressures, Aapico was one of very few local auto suppliers to continue to grow during the crisis. While bonuses and wage increments were eliminated, there were no layoffs, and the company is continuing to attract new customers, especially for dies and jigs. That Aapico has done relatively well during so difficult a time can be explained in part by its product and marketing strategies, and in part by access to new financial resources. First, Aapico's preexisting emphasis on innovative jig design and development was critical. As the domestic market declined, increased jig (and to a lesser degree die) exports kept the company afloat, especially through a redirection of exports away from the economically troubled Asian region to more dynamic markets including Morocco, Saudi Arabia, Colombia, and (initially) Brazil. Second, Aapico's continued commitment to QS 9000 certification in parts production, and corresponding progress in training, technology development, and Japanese quality programs across all departments, partly sheltered it from the intense cost competition a number of other Thai parts makers have faced.

Third, and of special interest here, Aapico's close relations with other firms provided a critical resource for dealing with the crisis. In order to manage its huge debt burden, the company has relied on its original shareholders for new infusions of capital. In addition, it has renegotiated its joint-venture capital structures, selling off a portion of its equity in the Able Auto Parts holding company while reducing its capital share in the Sanoh joint venture from 55 percent to 35 percent, as well as selling off its entire 35 percent stake in the Arvins joint venture.[29] And while it had not done so at the time of our interviews, Aapico's management was confident they could, if necessary, request from Honda and Toyota a partial refinancing of their expensive new stamping machines and prepayment of some die orders from Honda. This confidence stemmed from their understanding that their importance to the assemblers, some of whom had relinquished competence in jig and die production, ensured that the "principle would have to come in" to keep them afloat. This assumption was in fact lent credence by Toyota's offer (declined) of supplier credits for parts supplied by Aapico.[30]

External relations have also played a critical role through continued support for the high-value competitive strategy through which Aapico has managed to cope with the crisis. As noted earlier, professional and personal relations, joint-venture and assembler networks, and close relationships with other firms with which Aapico has equipment-purchase and technology-support agreements have been essential for Aapico's success in product, organizational, and skill development. And as lower tier suppliers collapsed during 1998, Aapico's joint-venture "integrated corporate group" brought more and more production in-house to cope with the collapse of the supplier base, and despite heightened recognition of the dangers of overcapacity during market instability.

While the crisis is easing at the time of this writing (*Bangkok Post* 1999),[31] Aapico's success in facing the crisis to this point supports several more general observations regarding longer-term crisis-induced changes in the Thai auto industry. First, it is clear that the crisis has sharply restructured the industry by flushing out lower-value-added producers and labor-intensive, domestic-market-oriented operations which have hitherto been sustained by domestic content, tariff, and equity protection and by rapid market growth. In this sense, earlier strategies driven by precrisis conditions have cast a long shadow on current chances for survival. Instructive in this regard was the observation by the tooling director of the jig design department that reduced customer demand during the crisis permitted the company to further develop and refine its own ongoing QS 9000 and plant-design programs.

Second, those auto supplier firms which have survived, and whose growing competitive edge over other firms creates a cumulative advantage,[32] have generally shared a commitment to constant quality improvement and to technology and product development, and a corresponding ability to shift quickly to new export markets (*Bangkok Post* 1998;[33] Dollar et al. 1998). Third, and closely related to this last point, the Aapico case underscores the great importance of enduring relations with client and partner firms in obtaining financial and technological resources, in enhancing competitive flexibility for success in export markets,[34] and in buffering firms against macrofinancial instability.

Fourth, the demise of many local Thai parts firms, alongside Aapico's experience of increased foreign equity on the part of joint-venture partners, is consistent with a larger perceived pattern of industry denationalization, officially sanctioned by deregulation and liberalization of foreign investment. Anxious to channel foreign funds into the country, the Thai government has relaxed earlier restrictions of the equity holding of foreign partners in local companies (*Bangkok*

Post 1998).[35] Taking advantage of these new rules, and the strong probability that local content will be ended, a number of firms, including Honda, GM, BMW, and Mitsubishi, have expanded their equity in manufacturing and distributorship operations (*Bangkok Post* 1998[36]; Changsorn 1997).

Finally, the question of the larger institutional environment within which firms like Aapico operate reasserts itself powerfully in the context of the crisis. The Chuan government, elected in November 1997 with a strong mandate to contain and manage the crisis, had initially to tread a fine line between contractionary IMF stabilization pressures and industry demands for recapitalization of the finance sector, reduced interest rates, debt restructuring, and expansionary fiscal policy. Partly in response to local pressures, and with financial assistance from the World Bank and the Asian Development Bank, the Thai government has now established an Industrial Restructuring Committee responsible for developing action plans for some thirteen industries, including automobiles and auto parts (*Bangkok Post* 1998).[37] As well, it has instituted an array of new funding and upgrading activities directed at Thai industrial SMEs and especially to automotive and other supplier companies (Deyo 1999). Striking in this regard is a general shift of government assistance from protection toward upgrading and quality improvements to foster export competitiveness, as seen in a new Board of Investment ruling that approved projects be required to institute ISO 9000 programs as a condition for receiving promotional tax incentives (*Bangkok Post* 1998).[38] In support of this approach, the Ministry of Labor and Social Welfare has greatly expanded its industry training programs across the country, and there is renewed effort to activate and redirect a support industry program (BUILD) promoted by the Board of Investment. Of particular interest here is a "vendors meet customers" BUILD program to encourage closer relationships between assemblers and suppliers, and among suppliers themselves.[39]

Paralleling these public goods and collaboration initiatives is a deepening and extension of business-government policy networks, including better linkages to the FTI and chambers of commerce, reactivation of the Joint Public-Private Consultation Committee, creation of an SME board on the stock exchange,[40] and devolution of some Ministry of Industry training and industrial upgrading activities to a new Automotive Institute, in which ministry and industry leaders collaborate in formulating industry support policy.[41] In part, these efforts to further institutionalize government-industry relations stem from intensified lobbying activities by both domestic and foreign companies. A recent government decision to introduce higher import duties on completely knocked-down auto components, for example, may in part be seen as a compromise in meeting demands by GM and other companies to implement the WTO-mandated elimination of domestic content in year 2000, while at the same time responding to strong supplier lobbying through the Thai Auto-Parts Manufacturers Association and the FTI (*Nation* 1998; *Bangkok Post* 1999; *Nation* 1999).[42]

Whether these crisis-induced initiatives will be sustained over the long term is uncertain, although they do signal efforts to create a more supportive institutional environment for business. In this regard, both positive and negative scenarios suggest themselves. A positive scenario is that current tentative changes in sectoral institutions could engender sufficient synergies with existing enclave networks to foster cumulative development of a more supportive governance environment for companies like Aapico. Alternatively, however, without substantial provision by government, industry associations, and educational institutions of substantial collective goods and business assistance, the enclaves of industrial dynamism illustrated by Aapico and its assembly/joint-venture partners could remain confined to the industry enclaves surrounding a few resourceful, foreign-dominated firms, rather than being generalized to the larger population of Thai firms.

NOTES

1. The introduction to this volume distinguishes in this regard between static and more dynamic forms of flexibility, the latter providing a basis for industrial upgrading.

2. A die is a mold used to cut, stamp, or otherwise form metal into specific shapes. A jig is the device that holds the parts of a product, in this case an auto vehicle body, in place as they are welded together.

3. This schema builds on discussions by J. Rogers Hollingsworth (1997) and David Soskice (1999).

4. One study estimates that in 1988 the overall debt-to-equity ratio in autos, electronics, and textiles was around 1.0 if the rollover of short-term debt is considered. See Christensen, Dollar, Siamwalla, and Vichyanond (1993: 3).

5. *Bangkok Post*, "Keeping Violence under Control," 15 February 1998.

6. The 1997 crisis forced a government retreat to offering only infrastructural support for this institute (interview by Manusavee Monsokol with Kantanit Sukonthasap, vice president, Corporate Affairs, General Motors Thailand).

7. *Nation*, "Agreement on Industrial Revamp Near," 4 March 1998.

8. Based on author interviews and participation in an automotive industry upgrading project sponsored by the Ministry of Industry.

9. On agricultural exports, see Christensen (1993); on textiles, Doner and Ramsay (1997); on banking, Hewison (1989); on jewelry, Laothamatas (1991); and on petrochemicals, Vejajiva (1998).

10. GM subsequently postponed production launch to the year 2000 in response to the economic crisis.

11. *Bangkok Post*, "When the Engine Fell Out," 11 March 1998. The Thai domestic market reached 589,126 sales in 1996. Thailand's pickup truck market is the second largest in the world after the U.S.

12. *Bangkok Post*, "Thais Urged to Meet Automotive Standard: Wait and See Attitude Would Be a Mistake," 15 September 1997, Section 2/Business.

13. For example, particularistic and clientelist relations linking firms with government agencies have tended to discourage cooperation.

14. Elimination of local content regulation was subsequently postponed to the year 2000 (Manusavee interview with Khun Kantanit Sukontasap, vice president, Corporate Affairs, GM Thailand.

15. This case is based on fieldwork by Doner and Deyo in July 1995, by Doner in July 1996 and July 1997, by Deyo in June 1998, and by Bryan Ritchie in May 1999. We are very grateful to the employees and managers of Aapico, especially the managing director, Mr. Yeap Swee Chuan; the plant manager, Khun Prakarn Chuenchokesun; the purchasing director; the tooling director, Mr. Brian Cowland; the manager of the Jig Engineering Department, Mr. Peng Hong Jian; and the production manager in charge of quality control programs, Mr. Somphol Thephasdin Na'Ayuthya. None of these individuals is responsible for any errors of fact or interpretation in this draft. We are also grateful to Prof. Linda Lim and the University of Michigan's Southeast Asia Business Program for encouragement, guidance, and financial support for this fieldwork. The 1997 interviews were carried out as part of a Thai Ministry of Industry survey on industrial upgrading.

16. As Aapico's tooling director noted, the company is capable of a much more integrated and efficient process of jig and transfer line development than was Ford, with whom he spent many years.

17. Mass production lines account for almost 30 percent of production processes, but 80 percent of sales. Smaller volume projects, while more difficult, remain important to Aapico inasmuch as customers that purchase mass-produced products also require smaller volume parts (based on Ritchie interviews during May 1999).

18. Interviews with another, larger Thai engineering firm with close ties to Toyota suggest that Toyota emphasizes what it calls total quality commitment. The emphasis here is on customer satisfaction and effective data collection.

19. *Bangkok Post*, "Special Report/Electronics: Warning of Decline Unless State's Help Given," 8 September 1997.

20. This weak response probably reflects two factors. First, Thai engineering students frequently avoided factory work in order to move into finance or marketing, often by studying for an M.B.A. Second, there seems to be a lack of support or encouragement for participation in these programs.

21. Although there are some differences among Japanese assemblers, Toyota's qualification process is similar to those of other assemblers. This information draws on interviews of Toyota Motors (Thailand) officials conducted during the summers of 1993, 1994, and 1995, as well as interviews of Aapico officials.

22. Based on company interviews by Bryan Ritchie in May 1999.

23. There are, to be sure, differences among the Japanese firms. Toyota, with the longest history in Thailand, is known for its solid support of local parts firms. Honda, on the other hand, is a relative newcomer with fewer established local suppliers and a reputation for greater reliance on Japanese transplants. To get Honda's press-part business, Aapico will be forced to subcontract from these firms. But because Honda lacks a local tooling capacity, Aapico may get more of the firm's die and jig business. And even knowing Honda's reputation for lukewarm support of local suppliers, Aapico agreed to build a jig needed for Honda to launch its new Civic model in Thailand soon after the model's launch in Japan. Aapico accepted the project despite very tight deadlines and problems with both engineering and costs. The program did in fact involve fierce negotiations with Honda on engineering, as well as financial losses for Aapico. Still, the program constituted an important learning experience for Aapico as well as an initial step in developing a relationship with

Honda. Aapico's managing director subtly demonstrated to Honda's purchasing officials the firm's commitment and losses, providing a simple cost breakdown of the project. The intention was not to ask Honda for more money, but to ensure that the Japanese were aware of Aapico's commitment. Aapico's managing director was confident that the Japanese would reciprocate in other ways down the line.

24. *Nation*, "Car Makers Suffer from Government Policies," 1 January 1998; *Nation*, "Regional Crisis Puts on Brakes," 1 January 1998; *Nation*, "Gloomy Outlook for Auto Industry," 3 January 1998.

25. *Bangkok Post*, "Exports Play an Increasing Role." *1998 Year-End Economic Review*, 20 January 1999.

26. *Bangkok Post*, "Banks File Bankruptcy Action against TCA," 29 July 1998; *Bangkok Post*, "Local Benz Assembler in Deep Debt Trouble," 23 January 1999.

27. *Bangkok Post*, "Mazda Closes Local Plant, Putting 550 Out of Work," 25 July 1998.

28. Based on data provided to Sununta Siengthai by Khun Alongkorn Chutinant, vice chair of the Auto Parts Industry Group of the Thai Federation of Trade and Industry (26 June 1998). An additional 40 percent of auto-related workers were working only part-time, and severance payouts (three months' pay at Mazda) for those laid off stood at nearly 31 million baht. Dollar et al. (1998) find that a larger percent of auto parts firms than of firms in other surveyed industries have cut employment levels.

29. Based on company interviews by Bryan Ritchie in May 1999. Arvins's more ruthless bargaining stance compared with Sanoh in the handling of the crisis may in part be explained by its somewhat more formal, arms-length joint-venture relationship with Aapico compared with that of Sanoh.

30. Based on Ritchie interviews.

31. *Bangkok Post*, "May Sales Soar 42.8% on Year," 15 June 1999.

32. Aapico's tooling director estimates that the company is now six years ahead of most other automobile tooling companies in Southeast Asia.

33. *Bangkok Post*, "Positivism Amid Sales Drop," *1998 Mid-Year Economic Review*, 30 June 1998; Dollar et al. (1998).

34. The Dollar et al. survey found a strong relationship between exports and ties to foreign firms.

35. *Bangkok Post*, "Draft Almost Ready to Go to Cabinet," 8 August 1998; *Bangkok Post*, "Toyota Stands to Benefit from Easing of Ownership Rule," 8 August 1998. This includes amending the highly restrictive Alien Business Law, under review at the time of this writing.

36. *Bangkok Post*, "Gloomy Outlook for Auto Industry," 3 January 1998.

37. *Bangkok Post*, "Positivism Amid Sales Drop," *1998 Mid-Year Economic Review*, 30 June 1998.

38. *Bangkok Post*, "BoI Eases Cap on Foreign Stakes," 24 November 1998.

39. In particular, subcontractors are encouraged to develop close connections among themselves and to cooperate in sharing facilities and resources. Based on an interview with Dr. Wisan, head of the BoI BUILD unit, conducted by Manusavee Monsakul. See *Bangkok Post*, "Vehicle Makers Will Use More Local Parts," 29 September 1999.

40. In response to industry association pressures, the government has announced plans to list SMEs on a special board of the Stock Exchange of Thailand, thus seeking to address the issue of the lack of long-term finance. *Bangkok Post* "New SET Board Planned for Small Firms," 7 August 1998.

41. Based on Ministry of Industry interviews by Rick Doner and Manusavee Monsakul in July 1999. This program is initially funded under the Japanese Miyazawa regional recovery fund.

42. *Nation*, "Auto Club Wants Local Content Rule to Stay," 29 October 1998; *Bangkok Post*, "Industry Calls for Delay in Tariff Cuts," 16 January 1999; *Bangkok Post*, "Auto Parts Could Be Hit by 35% Duty," 28 January 1999; *Nation*, "Ministry Nod for Increase in CKD Duty," 18 February 1999.

BIBLIOGRAPHY

Bangkok Post (Bangkok). Various issues, 1997–1999.

Brimble, Peter. 1993. *Industrial Development and Productivity Change in Thailand*. Ph.D. diss., Department of Economics, Johns Hopkins University.

Brimble, Peter, and Chatri Sripaipan. 1994. "Science and Technology Issues in Thailand's Industrial Sector: The Key to the Future." Paper prepared for the Asian Development Bank, Bangkok (June).

Brooker Group. 1997. *Automotive Industry Export Promotion Project: Thailand Industry Overview—Final Report Prepared for the Thai Ministry of Industry*, Part V. Bangkok.

Buranathanung, Noppadol. 1996. "The Organization of Parts Procurement in the Thai Automobile Industry." *Chulalongkorn Journal of Economics* 8, no.1: 67-99.

Changsorn, Pichaya. 1997. "Survey Finds Little Changes Among SMEs." *The Nation* 18 (August): B1.

Christensen, Scott, David Dollar, Amar Siamwalla, and Pakorn Vichyanond. 1993. *Thailand: The Institutional and Political Underpinnings of Growth*. Washington, D.C: World Bank.

Christensen, Scott R. 1993. "Coalitions and Collective Choice: The Politics of Institutional Change in Thai Agriculture," Ph.D. Diss., University of Wisconsin.

Deyo, Frederic C. 1996. "Competition, Flexibility, and Industrial Ascent: The Thai Auto Industry." In *Social Reconstructions of the World Automobile Industry*, edited by Frederic C. Deyo, 136–156. Houndsmills, England: Macmillan Press.

———. 1999. *The Politics of Crisis Management: Thailand's SME Sector*. Auckland Working Papers in Development Studies, no. 3. Centre for Development Studies, University of Auckand (September).

Dollar, David, Mary Hallward-Driemeier, Giuseppe Iarossi, and Mita Chakraborty. 1998. "Short-Term and Long-Term Competitiveness Issues in Thai Industry." Paper presented at the UNDC Conference on Thailand's Dynamic Economic Recovery and Competitiveness on May 20-21, 1998.

Doner, Richard. 1991. *Driving a Bargain: Automobile Industrialization and Japanese Firms in Southeast Asia*. Berkeley: University of California Press.

Doner, Richard, and Ansil Ramsay. 1997. "Competitive Clientelism and Economic Governance: The Case of Thailand." In *Business and State in Developing Countries*, edited by Sylvia Maxfield and Ben Ross Schneider, 237–276. Ithaca, N.Y.: Cornell University Press.

Economist (London). 1996. "Bumper to Bumper," 17 August: 50.

Fairclough, Gordon. 1995. "Race to the Finish." *Far Eastern Economic Review* (October 12): 120-122.

Far Eastern Economic Review (Hong Kong). Various issues, 1996–1998.

Felker, Greg. 1997. "The Politics of Technology Development: State, Business and Multinationals in Malaysia and Thailand." Ph.D. Diss., Princeton University.

Hewison, Kevin. 1989. *Bankers and Bureaucrats: Capital and the Role of the State in Thailand.* Southeast Asian Studies series. New Haven: Yale University Press.

Hollingsworth, J. Rogers. 1997. "Continuities and Changes in Social Systems of Production: The Cases of Japan, Germany and the United States." In *Contemporary Capitalism, the Embeddedness of Institutions,* edited by J. Rogers Hollingsworth and Robert Boyer. Cambridge: Cambridge University Press.

Hollingsworth, J. Rogers, and Robert Boyer. 1997. "The Coordination of Economic Actors and Social Systems of Production." In *Contemporary Capitalism: The Embeddedness of Institutions,* edited by J. Rogers Hollingsworth and Robert Boyer. Cambridge: Cambridge University Press.

Laothamatas, Anek. 1991. *Business Associations and the New Political Economy of Thailand: From Bureaucratic Polity to Liberal Corporatism.* Boulder, Colo.: Westview.

Lundvall, B., ed. 1992. *National Systems of Innovation: Towards a Theory of Innovation and Interactive Learning.* London: Pinter Publishers.

The Nation (Bangkok). Various issues, 1997-1999.

Nelson, Richard, ed. 1993. *National Innovation Systems: A Comparative Analysis.* New York: Oxford University Press.

Siengthai, Sununta. 1994. "Tripartism and Industrialization Process of Thailand." In *National Tripartite Consultative Mechanisms in Selected Asian Pacific Countries.* Vol. 2. Geneva: International Labor Organization.

Soskice, David. 1991. "The Institutional Infrastructure for International Competitiveness: A Comparative Analysis of the UK and Germany." In *Economies for the New Europe,* edited by Anthony Atkinson and Renato Brunetta. London: Macmillan/International Economics Association.

———. 1999. "Divergent Production Regimes: Coordinated and Uncoordinated Market Economies in the 1980s and 1990s." In *Continuity and Change in Contemporary Capitalism,* edited by Herbert Kitscheldt, Peter Lange, Gary Marks and Johns Stephens. New York: Cambridge University Press.

Vejajiva, Wichu. 1998. *Beyond Free Markets and Strong States: The Institutional Bases of Petrochemical Development in Thailand.* Ph.D. Diss., University of Chicago.

5

Catching Up and Postcrisis Industrial Upgrading: Searching for New Sources of Growth in Korea's Electronics Industry

Dieter Ernst

Until the Asian crisis began to unfold during the fall of 1997, there was widespread consensus that Korea had consolidated a mix of institutions and policies that were conducive to rapid development and to catching up with the most advanced economies. Korea's achievements had been impressive: within three decades a resource-poor and relatively small country at the periphery of the world economy became a leading exporter of manufactured products. No developing country exceeded Korea in the speed with which it expanded and transformed its manufacturing sector. Yet the Asian crisis illuminated a series of structural weaknesses that were already exerting profound pressures on the Korean model of development. Questions confronting observers today are related to whether the Korean model of late industrialization has failed: Are industrial policies no longer viable? Is there no alternative to convergence with the Anglo-American model of capitalism (Korea Economic Institute of America 1999)? How can growth be sustained in the future? Answers to these questions depend on how one explains the crisis, and indeed on how one defines the Korean model. Whereas most observers of the crisis stress its financial aspects (Stiglitz 1997; Veneroso and Wade 1998; and Krugman 1998), there has been a tendency to neglect the contribution of underlying structural weaknesses in the real economy. Those weaknesses are the focus of this chapter.

A central proposition of the chapter is that the economic structures and institutions that were conducive to catching up in a particular context could not foster the capabilities necessary to guarantee sustained growth. The crisis has further exacerbated the situation: it has dramatically increased the need for industrial upgrading, while at the same time constraining financial resources needed to bring this about. Attempts to return to the *status quo ante* will not provide a solution; nor will success be achieved through the IMF's approach, with its focus on financial reform and a shift to Anglo-Saxon corporate governance structures. Industrial upgrading, defined as substantial changes in a country's specialization and knowledge base that increase its capacity for rent generation (Ernst 2000a), constitutes the medium-term challenge that Korea must master to establish new sources of growth. Industrial upgrading needs to complement the current emphasis on financial and corporate restructuring. We present this argument through an account of the electronics industry, Korea's most prominent example of rapid catching up.[1]

A novel contribution of the chapter is its analysis of how limitations inherent to the Korean model of late industrialization[2] account for a lack of flexibility and truncated upgrading. The focus is on the role of economic institutions, and the coevolution of policies, industry structure, and firm behavior.[3] The analysis centers on three basic limitations of the Korean model that result from a symbiotic relationship between governments and large business groups that are known as the *chaebol*: (1) an extremely unbalanced industry structure gave rise to (2) a narrow knowledge base and (3) a "sticky specialization." Catching up has focused on expanding capacity and international market share for homogeneous, mass-produced commodities such as TV sets, monitors, DRAM, and displays; very little upgrading has occurred into higher-end and rapidly growing market segments for differentiated products and services that require flexible production (e.g., design-intensive ICs and computer products, software, and Internet services). We label this pattern *truncated upgrading* and find it to be one of the principal reasons for Korea's vulnerability to the financial and currency crisis.

The first part of the chapter describes key features of the Korean model that were responsible for rapid catching up in the electronics industry. The next part addresses important structural weaknesses that existed well before the crisis. We review evidence on Korea's sticky specialization on mass-produced commodities and its narrow domestic knowledge base, key causes of weak flexibility and truncated upgrading. We then discuss possible explanations, focusing on the role played by Korea's unbalanced industry structure. In both sections, comparisons with Japan and Taiwan highlight some peculiar features of the Korean model, and consideration is given to the impact of the crisis on economic governance and on prospects for growth. The chapter concludes with a brief discussion of changes necessary to overcome barriers to industrial upgrading. We sketch one possible option for strategic response to the current crisis: an upgrading from product to technology diversification that broadens Korea's knowledge base and at the same time utilizes its traditional strengths in "quick follower mass production."

CATCHING UP IN ELECTRONICS: KEY FEATURES
OF THE KOREAN MODEL

Korea is arguably the most successful example of rapid catching up in the global electronics industry, as well as the most controversial: although it leads Asian producers in its share of the global electronics market, Korea's unprecedented speed of entry into high-risk and very demanding precision component manufacturing, such as DRAM and displays, may signal the limits of what is possible. Indeed, peculiar features of the Korean model, such as a heavy reliance on guided credit and industrial policies and an industry structure dominated by a handful of *chaebol*, have invited heated debate about the model's strengths and weaknesses.

Korea's success has been based on a development model that combines international linkages with a dense, almost symbiotic relationship between the government and the *chaebol*. This approach reflects the nature of the challenge facing Korea when it entered the international electronics markets in the late 1960s. Its main concern mirrored that of the Japanese electronics industry in the early 1950s: to master as quickly as possible those types of production technology that would enable it to capitalize on low labor costs while also reaping economies of scale. Logically, this implied a focus on rapid expansion of capacity and market share for commodity-type products, primarily through exports. Given the limited knowledge and capability base available during this period, the growth of the Korean electronics industry had to occur primarily on the basis of foreign technology. The effective absorption of the latter, however, required proactive investment, industrial, and technology policies.

The Catalytic Role of Foreign Direct Investment (FDI)

Despite the widespread perception, promoted by statist theories (e.g., Haggard 1990; Hikino and Amsden 1992) that FDI played only a minor role in the Korean model of development, electronics exports started to take off only when Korea became a final export platform for a handful of U.S. semiconductor firms (Ernst 1994b: chapter 3). This was made possible by the early willingness of the Korean government to shift to export promotion. Combined with tough labor legislation and the ruthless suppression of labor conflicts, the Electronics Industry Promotion Law of 1969 and the opening of the Masan Free Export Zone in 1970 contributed to a positive foreign investment climate in the industry. The main attractions for foreign electronics companies were Korea's cheap female labor and the incredibly long annual work hours, together with policies favorable to the promotion of export manufacturing.

By opening export channels for assembled chips and for simple consumer devices, FDI played a catalytic role during the critical early phase of the development of the Korean electronics industry. In 1972, foreign firms, of which there were eight, accounted for about a third of Korea's electronics production and 55 percent of its exports; their share in exports fell below 40 percent only in 1980 (Bloom 1992). FDI also exposed Korean workers and managers to new organizational techniques, which, while not necessarily "best practice," contributed to a gradual erosion of highly authoritarian traditional Korean management practices, with their inherent rigidities and inefficiencies. Cost cutting and the need to comply to some minimum international quality standards undoubtedly gave rise to some limited indirect learning effects related to the formation of basic operational capabilities for final assembly, logistics, and facility management (Ernst 1983: 156–166).

A key feature of Korea's catching up in electronics is that, after the mid-1970s, a shift occurred in the center of gravity, away from foreign to local actors. This was due to a number of factors that reflect the changing international investment environment as well as policy design.[4] In semiconductor assembly, for instance, American firms became increasingly attracted by new, low-cost locations in the Philippines and Malaysia, and gradually shifted most of their assembly activities to these two countries. As their capital costs kept rising, these companies were keen to reduce their equity involvement and began to shift to much looser forms of contract assembly, subcontracting, and original equipment manufacturing (OEM) arrangements (Ernst 1997b). In contrast to the U.S. firms' reliance on footloose offshore assembly, most Japanese firms concentrated on factory automation at home and gradually withdrew from offshore assembly activities both in Korea and Taiwan (Ernst 1997a).

The Korean government imposed increasingly demanding requirements on foreign firms to contribute to local value-added and to increase the transfer of technology. By creating fears of a possible "boomerang effect" through involuntary technology leakages, the new requirements probably accelerated the withdrawal of foreign firms, which simultaneously faced rising competition from the increasingly powerful *chaebol*. Confronted with the alternative to either upgrade their existing investments beyond the stage of assembly—and to do so in cooperation with the *chaebol*—or to shift production elsewhere within East Asia, most foreign firms chose the second option.[5]

Symbiotic Ties between Government and *Chaebol*

Korean government policies played an important role in shaping the competitive strengths and strategies of Korean electronics firms. The defining element was the unusually close and symbiotic relationship between the "developmental state" that determined national industrial strategy and huge family-owned conglomerates, the *chaebol*. The latter's strategies were shaped by two closely related state policies: "infant industry" protection and "directed credit."

Korea made frequent use of selective infant industry protection as part of its industrialization strategy, especially in the electronics industry. Import protection enabled producers in a new industrial sector like electronics to exploit learning economies, while export incentives provided the opportunity to reap scale economies not available in the domestic market. Meanwhile, a rich arsenal of directed credit instruments was a hallmark of Korea's industrial policy: access to subsidized credit and tax privileges was coupled with strict performance requirements. The development of Korea's electronics industry fits the pattern of large-scale, capital-intensive latecomer industrialization described by Gerschenkron (1962): easy access to large amounts of patient debt capital was a critical source of competitive strength for the Korean *chaebol*. Korea's heavy reliance on guided credit led to a disproportionately high debt,[6] which sets it apart from Taiwan, where companies have relied much more on equity markets and corporate retained earnings.[7] Table 5.1 documents the consistently and substantially higher debt-equity ratios in Korea versus Taiwan[8].

This development model worked extremely well as long as the goal was to catch up, and as long there was no dependence on highly volatile, short-term capital flows. It succeeded in channeling Korea's large household savings into investments that produced an incredibly fast expansion of industrial manufacturing capacity and international market share.

International Technology Sourcing

The Korean way of building technological capabilities in the electronics industry resembled the Japanese model most closely in its utilization of foreign technology. Rather than allowing foreign firms to establish local subsidiaries and determine the speed and scope of technology diffusion, the government encouraged some of the leading *chaebol* to focus on learning and knowledge accumulation through a variety of links with foreign equipment and component suppliers, technology licensing partners, OEM clients, and minority joint venture partners. The goal was to become quick, lower-cost followers for standard, mass-produced products.

By licensing well-proven foreign product designs and importing most of the production equipment and crucial components, Korean electronics producers were able to focus most of their attention on three areas:[9] (1) the mastery of production capabilities, initially for assembly, but increasingly for related support services and mass production; (2) some related minor change capabilities, ranging from "reverse engineering" techniques to "analytical design" and some "system engineering" capabilities required for process reengineering and limited product customization;[10] and (3) a capacity to ramp up new production lines quickly and at low cost.

The heavy reliance on international technology sourcing enabled Korean electronics firms to reverse the standard sequence of technological capability formation (Dahlman, Ross-Larson, and Westphal 1987). Rather than proceeding from

Table 5.1   **Debt–Equity Ratios in Korea and Taiwan, 1985–1998 (in percentages)**

	1985	1998
Taiwan	120	30
Korea	350	180

Source: SBC Warburg Dillon Reed.

innovation to investment to production, they focused on the ability to operate production facilities according to competitive cost and quality standards. Through reverse engineering and other forms of copying foreign technology, and by becoming integrated into increasingly complex global production networks of American, Japanese, and some European electronics companies, Korean electronics firms were able to avoid the huge cost burdens and risks involved in R&D and in developing international distribution and marketing channels.[11]

Rapid expansion of capacity and international market share would have been impossible had Korean firms tried to start off with a more integrated production system. OEM arrangements have proven to be one of the most cost-effective methods for acquiring core capabilities in production and investment (Ernst and O'Connor 1989). OEM arrangements provide the supplier with a high volume of business, which permits the realization of scale economies. The often tedious and grueling qualification process that any potential supplier has to complete successfully to compete for contracts opens up a variety of learning possibilities with regard to business organization and the use of technology. In addition, customers often provide technical assistance in engineering and manufacturing processes to ensure quality and cost efficiency.

OEM arrangements, however, can also have substantial drawbacks (Ernst and O'Connor 1992). A firm may become locked into an OEM relationship to the extent that it is hindered from developing its own independent brand name recognition and marketing channels. Profit margins are substantially lower in OEM sales than in own brand name sales, which in turn makes it difficult for Korean companies to muster the capital needed to invest in R&D that eventually might lead to the introduction of new products. This constraint is of limited importance, as long as sales volumes through OEM contracts are large and fairly predictable so that, despite low profit margins, total earnings may be substantial. But despite the optimism of many observers during the late 1980s, accumulated technological and organizational capabilities were not sufficient to enable Korean producers to move easily beyond OEM. Rather, the transition to original brand name (OBN) strategies has been exceedingly rough. After years of heavy advertising and public relations efforts, Korean electronics firms must still contend with an image that their products are of inferior quality and reliability. Product development is still conceived mostly in terms of incremental improvement of a given foreign product design. Heavily reliant on OEM manufacturing, Korean companies are very much followers of the latest product designs developed elsewhere, mostly in Japan. Korean firms have a weak capacity to develop new designs and to gather early on the most relevant information about new market trends and customer preferences.[12]

Strategic marketing continues to play a marginal role in the Korean innovation process. The goals of innovation are set by the established foreign benchmark firms. Almost no attempt has been made until very recently to identify undiscovered customer needs and to use this knowledge to develop new markets. It should be mentioned, however, that over the last few years all three *chaebol* active in consumer electronics have identified this passive acceptance of foreign product designs as a major barrier to sustained competitiveness. Since the crisis, there has been widespread experimentation with organizational reforms that are expected to strengthen the link between strategic marketing and innovation management. Many of these attempts are frustrated, however, by the trend toward corporate restructuring arrangements that follow a purely financial logic (author's interviews, September 1999).

The Case of Semiconductors

The essence of the Korean model becomes clear when we look at semiconductors (SC), the crown jewel of Korea's electronics industry. The pace and scale of the capacity and market-share expansion of Korea's semiconductor industry is without precedent. Never before has a country been able to move so rapidly from the position of an insignificant outsider to that of market leader in a highly capital-intensive industry saddled with incredibly high risks and entry barriers. How was it possible that Samsung, together with LG and Hyundai, were able to enter the DRAM market at record speed and to erode the once seemingly watertight grip that a Japanese oligopoly had imposed over this industry since the mid-1980s? Of critical importance was Korea's approach to technological learning[13]. A first characteristic of this approach was a willingness and capacity to spend huge amounts of money on investment and technology acquisition. Between 1983 and 1989, the three *chaebol* are reported to have invested more than $4 billion on production equipment. And while catching up is already quite costly, keeping up and getting ahead leads to an even higher fixed capital cost burden. Thus, annual capital spending increased from $800 million in 1987 to an estimated $1.8 billion in 1993, constituting more than 20 percent of the world's total semiconductor facility investment in that year.

A second important prerequisite of Korea's successful entry into semiconductors was a three-pronged approach to international technology sourcing. This included: (1) early establishment of subsidiaries in Silicon Valley as listening posts for intelligence gathering on technology and market trends, as well as for R&D activities that complemented similar efforts at home; (2) a pervasive reliance on "second-sourcing" agreements, in which the *chaebol* were licensed by leading U.S. and Japanese semiconductor producers to manufacture some of their DRAM designs; and (3) silicon foundry services provided for leading American ASIC (application-specific integrated circuit) companies, such as LSI Logic and VLSI Technology. Based on the gate array or standard cell designs received from these foreign companies, the *chaebol* used their strength in process technology and their capacity to rapidly improve yields to produce ASIC devices at short notice. Forced to comply with the stringent design rules typical for such devices, the *chaebol* thus were able to deepen their knowledge about necessary process improvements.

More recently, there has been a tendency to incorporate this three-pronged approach into somewhat broader package deals aimed at cross-technology-sharing. As the *chaebol* expanded their share in international DRAM markets, they were able to strengthen their bargaining position with regard to licensing agreements. The result is that today cross-licensing and mutual patent swaps link all of the *chaebol* with the leading Japanese and American semiconductor producers. More and more, the *chaebol* are involved in international technology sourcing networks, which include links with other firms (*interfirm* networks) and attempts to tap into key elements of the national innovation systems of other countries (*interorganizational* networks) (Ernst 1997b). These networks now typically cover a great variety of arrangements, ranging from second-sourcing and fabrication agreements to technology licensing and cross-licensing, patent swapping, joint product or technology development, the exchange of researchers and guest engineers, and standard coalitions. Technology acquisition approaches pursued by Korean semiconductor producers have experienced major changes, moving from the reverse engineering of licensed chip designs to much broader and increasingly systemic forms of international technology sourcing.

Advantages and Limitations of the Catching Up Model

It is important to emphasize that Korea's successful catching up in the electronics industry was based on limited and achievable technological learning requirements. One must distinguish between the increasing sophistication of the institutional arrangements for technological learning, especially for international technology sourcing, and the relatively mundane contents of the knowledge thus generated. As discussed below, the main constraining factor remains a narrow specialization concentrated in mass-produced, commodity-type products. Knowledge creation has been confined largely to operational production capabilities of a fairly conventional, mass-production type. While this approach originally constituted the country's chief advantage, making possible a quick late entry into global markets, it also engendered fundamental structural weaknesses that act today as barriers to industrial upgrading in Korea.

PRECRISIS WEAKNESSES: BARRIERS TO INDUSTRIAL UPGRADING

Exogenous and Endogenous Factors

In 1996, before the crisis, Korea experienced a dramatic export crash, leading to a substantial current-account deficit and a dramatic slowdown in growth.[14] This decline was especially prominent in the electronics industry, and affected all major Asian producers (table 5.2). Korea displayed the most dramatic fall: after extremely rapid growth in 1994 (23.7 percent) and 1995 (35.5 percent), its 1996 exports fell by more than 3 percent in U.S. dollar terms. First and foremost, this reflects Korea's heavy reliance on semiconductors, and in particular DRAM, both of which have been subject to intense deflationary pressures since 1996.

Two types of causes for the export crash can be distinguished: *external* causes driven by changes in the international economy, and *internal* ones that reflect structural features peculiar to the Korean model. External causes are relevant, and in comparison with previous years, Korea confronted a substantially more hostile international environment: in 1996, the fall in world export growth from its cyclical peak in 1995 was the largest in fifteen years—from about 20 percent to about 4 percent in U.S. dollars in just one year (World Bank 1998). Much of this was due to accumulated excess capacity in the electronics industry (Ernst 2000c). The sharp depreciation of the yen in 1995 compounded this problem, especially for Korea, whose export structure is similar to Japan's. In 1996, Japan's imports from Korea fell by 8.5 percent.[15]

Of greater importance for our purposes were the *endogenous* barriers to industrial upgrading. These impediments reflected peculiar features of Korea's successful catching up strategy which limited opportunities to increase flexibility: an extremely unbalanced industry structure led to a narrow knowledge base and a sticky pattern of specialization. Easy access to large amounts of patient debt capital has shaped key features of the *chaebol*'s strategy in terms of product specialization, type of production, size of commitment and entry strategy, vertical integration, competition focus, and technology management. Korea's successful entry into the electronics industry was a forced march to develop a mass production capacity that could serve high-growth export markets for *homogeneous* products. In the process, there occurred very little upgrading into higher-end and rapidly growing market segments for *differentiated* products and services.

Upon deciding to enter a sector, the *chaebol* normally move in on a massive scale and in a highly integrated manner. By channeling funds at concessionary terms to a handful of *chaebol*, the state has created powerful domestic oligopolies. Korea's extremely unbalanced industry structure has spawned a peculiar form of competition strategy: firm growth has occurred through "octopus-like"

Table 5.2 A Decline in the Growth of East Asian Electronics Exports, 1992–1998 (% of $million)

	1992	1993	1994	1995	1996	1997	1998
Korea	5.8	6.7	23.7	35.5	−3.3	6.5	−6.7
Taiwan	10.3	10.9	15.4	32.4	8.5	10.5	1.4
Singapore	16.9	25.1	45.0	26.2	5.6	0.0	−10.9
Malaysia	24.4	30.4	37.8	31.2	5.7	2.6	−4.1
Thailand	25.7	16.1	40.3	29.3	12.6	8.9	na
Philippines	na	na	na	na	na	29.2	31.7
China	na	21.5	49.6	36.0	9.1	23.6	13.6

diversification into many different and unrelated industries rather than through an accumulation of knowledge through industrial upgrading. The narrow domestic knowledge base that results has made it difficult to move up the ladder of specialization.

Narrow specialization and limited learning requirements were ideally suited to the original task of overcoming latecomer disadvantages. A focus on commodities was the only realistic entry possibility, guaranteeing access to rapidly growing and relatively open markets. Homogeneous products are based on widely accessible and mature technology and are thus easy to replicate. This allows for limited and achievable technological learning requirements. At the same time, changes in demand patterns are fairly predictable, and interactions with customers play a role only at the margin. Market entry thus essentially depends on the availability of patient capital. In the case of DRAM, for instance, very high investment thresholds have been the main entry barrier.

This development model worked well as long as major export markets kept growing rapidly. This is no longer the case, however, and the result is overcapacity and price wars, as well as a dramatic increase in the country's exposure to debt. A narrow specialization on commodities reduces the scope for rent generation (the "commodity price trap"): commodities such as DRAM are prone to deflationary pricing pressures, which result from periodic over-capacity and price wars (Ernst 2000c). Commodities also display a limited upgrading potential, in terms of technological learning requirements, as long as key inputs are imported. A heavy reliance on imported inputs fosters an "inverted industry pyramid": a rapidly growing mass-production sector based on a very weak base of domestic support industries. Concentration in industrial commodities thus fails to provide sufficient pressure for improving the domestic knowledge base, a weakness that has now becomes a major barrier to a continuous industrial upgrading. A narrow domestic knowledge base constrains necessary improvements in specialization, and indeed may constitute a recipe for "immiserating" growth—an increase in economic activity which results in lower per capita incomes.[16]

Sticky Specialization

Specialization is an important indicator of the degree of industrial upgrading that a country has achieved. Industrial economists (e.g., Baumol, Panzer, and Willig 1982; Nilsson 1996) distinguish specialization patterns that reflect differences in the product composition (homogeneous versus differentiated products) from those that reflect differences in the type of production process (mass production versus flexible production). This taxonomy is based on two criteria: the complexity of technology and the characteristics of demand. It is argued that different market structures will result from these different product compositions and production processes. For differentiated products, for instance, firms can charge premium prices, while for homogeneous products, price competition is the overriding concern. A similar distinction is made for production processes: flexible production is linked to premium pricing, and mass production to price competition.

Modern growth theories have brought technological learning back into the analysis as a key explanatory variable (e.g., Lipsey and Bekar 1995). It is now widely accepted that peculiar features of economic structures and institutions offer quite distinct possibilities for learning and innovation, and hence shape the economic performance of a country (Lundvall 1992). The economic structure determines specialization (i.e., the product mix) and learning requirements (the breadth and depth of the knowledge base). Institutions, on the other hand, shape learning efficiency: they define how things are done and how learning takes place. An important concern is the "congruence" (Freeman 1997:13) of different subsystems, which is necessary to create a "virtuous" rather than a "vicious" circle.

A fundamental problem of Korea's electronics industry is a narrow and sticky product specialization: almost without exception, the *chaebol* have targeted those segments of the electronics industry that require huge investment outlays and sophisticated mass-production techniques for fairly homogeneous products (commodities) like microwave ovens, TV sets, VCRs, computer monitors, picture tubes, and computer memories, especially DRAMs. Overwhelmingly, the focus has been on consumer electronics and components, with companies making only limited inroads into industrial electronics. Burdened with unimpressive products, the *chaebol* have all failed to establish themselves as credible competitors in the more design-intensive sectors of the computer industry.

Revealed comparative advantage (RCA) analysis confirms a highly concentrated product specialization (table 5.3). Trade data for 1996, the year before the crisis, show electronics accounting for almost 29 percent of Korea's merchandise exports. Moreover, product specialization is heavily concentrated within electronics. Three products dominate with a very high RCA: semiconductors (SC) with 3.6, components (Comp) with 2.7, and consumer electronics (CE), with 2.0. And almost 61 percent of Korea's electronics exports consist of components, with semiconductors alone accounting for 40 percent.

A particularly disturbing feature of Korea's specialization pattern is that it combines high investment thresholds and highly volatile income streams: in their choice of sectors, the *chaebol* have exposed themselves to considerable risk resulting from highly volatile markets. Typical examples are DRAM and advanced displays (FPD) that are prone to periodic boom-and-bust cycles and hence do not generate a steady flow of profits. For companies with a high debt-equity ratio, this is obviously not an optimal choice.

Sticky Specialization in Semiconductors

Korea's semiconductor industry displays some important weaknesses. Its wafer fabrication capabilities are excellent or good for a limited number of products: DRAMs (dynamic random-access memories), SRAMs (static random-access memories), and

Table 5.3 Trade Specialization Profiles: RCA and Leading Export Products, 1993–1998

	Korean Share of Electronics in Merchandise Exports (%)											
	1993	*1994*	*1995*	*1996*	*1997*	*1998*						
	28.0	29.7	30.9	28.8	29.2	28.3						
	RCA						*Share in Electronics Exports (%)*					
	1993	*1994*	*1995*	*1996*	*1997*	*1998*	*1993*	*1994*	*1995*	*1996*	*1997*	*1998*
EDP	0.9	0.8	0.8	0.9	0.9	0.7	14.4	11.9	12.2	14.5	15.5	13.9
Storage	0.2	0.3	0.4	0.7	1.3	1.1	0.5	0.8	1.0	1.8	4.1	4.1
Comp	2.4	2.7	2.8	2.7	2.8	2.7	50.1	56.2	62.4	60.8	62.3	63.4
SC	3.3	3.8	4.1	3.6	4.0	3.8	30.4	37.2	45.7	40.3	42.9	45.3
CE	2.3	2.4	2.0	2.0	1.7	1.5	22.5	20.5	16.1	15.6	12.8	12.7
Telecom	0.9	0.9	0.8	0.8	0.6	0.5	3.0	2.7	2.4	2.4	2.1	1.9

Note: EDP = electronic data processing; Comp = components; SC = semiconductors; CE = consumer electronics.

ROMs (read-only memories). Other than that, very little has been achieved, and glaring deficits continue to exist, especially in circuit design. In addition, the industry is based on an extremely weak foundation in terms of the materials and production equipment required. Korea's current annual consumption of semiconductor materials is approximately $600 million, with 70 percent of total consumption being imported (40 percent from Japan and 20 percent from the United States). As for production equipment, 90 percent has to be imported, with 50 percent originating from Japan. It will be extremely difficult to reduce this dependence. Only joint production with leading overseas manufacturers is likely to help.

Probably the most important weakness of Korea's semiconductor industry is a very narrow product range. The three leading Korean semiconductor producers are heavily dependent on computer memories: 80 percent of Samsung's semiconductor revenues come from memories (most of them DRAMs), and in the case of Goldstar (87 percent) and Hyundai (90 percent), this share is even higher.[17] Korea's competitive position in semiconductors thus remains highly fragile. This type of specialization clearly handicaps rent creation: DRAMs are the "bleeding-edge" of the semiconductor industry, prone to periodic surplus capacity and price wars. Current excess capacity for DRAMs is estimated to be around 40 percent. During 1998, this resulted in a 60 percent price fall, after already sharp price declines over the previous two years. Current price levels are below the manufacturing costs of even the most efficient DRAM manufacturer (NEC).

The narrow focus on memory products has very negative implications for the overall structure of the electronics industry. Korea keeps exporting more than 90 percent of its total semiconductor output, while at the same time importing more than 87 percent of its domestic demand. Such an extreme imbalance between supply and demand makes it very difficult to broaden and deepen forward and backward linkages within the electronics industry and to place the industry onto a more viable basis.

It is probably fair to say that Korea's semiconductor industry represents a modern version of the classic monoproduct export enclave, characterized by a minimum of linkages with the domestic economy. There is, however, one important difference: the cost of entering the semiconductor industry is horrendously high, and certainly exceeds that of entering the plantation industry, which is typically associated with the monoproduct export enclave. And even higher is the cost of continuously upgrading the semiconductor industry and maintaining the competitiveness of its exports. Moreover, while Korea's entry into semiconductors has been a major achievement, it should not be interpreted as a move beyond mass production. The very high entry barriers typical for DRAM are due less to their R&D intensity than to their capital intensity, very high economies of scale, and the extremely volatile nature of demand for these devices.[18] Competitiveness in DRAMs centers on the capacity to invest in megaplants churning out a limited variety of standard products, and on the capacity to improve yields and productivity as quickly as possible.

Guaranteed access to patient capital and ample opportunities for internal cross-subsidization place the *chaebol* among the few firms worldwide that could cope with the demanding financial requirements for entering the DRAM business. The *chaebol* also were able to accumulate increasingly sophisticated production and investment capabilities, both in typical mass production industries like cars and consumer durables and in resource-intensive process industries like steel. Yet Korea's entry strategy into semiconductors did not fundamentally differ from its earlier entry into shipbuilding, steel, or the production of picture tubes for TV sets and monitors. Success in DRAMs was based not on strength in research and technology development but on the capacity to raise incredibly large funds for high-risk investments into huge mass-production lines for standard products. High risks in this case do not result from technological uncertainty but from the extremely volatile nature of demand and the periodic emergence of huge surplus capacities.[19] In other words, competition in DRAMs is of a fairly conventional nature, with size, economies of scale, and first-mover advantages being of primary importance.

A Narrow Domestic Knowledge Base

A second important weakness of Korea's electronics industry is a narrow domestic knowledge base. This reflects the coevolution of technological learning and specialization that is central to our model. Coevolution implies that causality works both ways: a narrow specialization on commodities, which is typical for catching up, fails to provide sufficient pressure for an improvement of the domestic knowledge base; in turn, a narrow domestic knowledge base constrains necessary improvements in specialization.

Catching up required a limited set of capabilities: a capacity to absorb and upgrade imported foreign technology and to develop operational capabilities in production, investment, and minor adaptations. The challenges today are different and, in any event, after the crisis, the country simply does not have the foreign exchange required to buy in foreign technology.[20] Korea thus needs to broaden its knowledge base to compete in product design, market development, the design of key components, and the provision of high-end knowledge-intensive support services. Korea's knowledge base remains constrained, however, by three main weaknesses: an insufficient critical mass of R&D and patenting, gross inefficiencies in corporate technology management, and equally important inefficiencies in the country's public innovation system.

An Insufficient Critical Mass of R&D and Patenting

Korea has consistently ranked first among East Asian economies in terms of resources devoted to R&D. In 1996, for instance, Korean R&D expenditures represented 2.79 percent of GDP, far ahead of the 1.86 percent achieved by second-place Taiwan (figures are courtesy of the Korean Development Institute). Korea also led the region in the number of R&D personnel per thousand inhabitants. Nevertheless, there is evidence of an insufficient critical mass of R&D and patenting. Such a constraint matters especially in a highly knowledge-intensive and volatile industry like electronics.

Until around the mid-1980s, Korean electronics firms had little motivation to invest in R&D.[21] Since that time, however, Korea has seen its comparative labor cost advantages erode, while product life cycles have shortened and competition has intensified in the electronics industry (Ernst 1998c; 2000c). This has forced Korean electronics firms to develop their own R&D capacity. Take Samsung Electronics, the industry pace setter: its R&D expenditures, as a share of total sales, increased from 2.1 percent in 1980 to 6.2 percent in 1994 (Kim Linsu 1997a: 141). Overall, Korea's private R&D spending, as a ratio of total sales, increased from 0.36 percent in 1976 to 2.5 percent in 1995. While this is an impressive achievement, it is still less than half of the current R&D/sales ratios of U.S. and Japanese manufacturing companies. And Korea's per capita R&D expenditures of $176.2 (in 1993) lag well behind those of Japan ($762.9 in 1992) and the United States ($540.9 in 1992) (Lall 1997: table 8). In order to reach a "critical mass" for industrial upgrading, R&D investments in Korea still have to grow much further.[22] The extremely tight budgetary constraints imposed by the crisis, however, imply that Korean firms have to withdraw, at least temporarily, from this R&D investment race.

As for patents, Samsung registered a total of 2,310 patents in the U.S. between 1980 and 1996, with most of these registered over the last few years (Mahmood 1998: table 7). In terms of patent intensity,[23] Korea still badly trails major OECD countries; its patent intensity of 10 is only a fraction of that reported for Germany (around 180), Japan (170), the U.S. (140), and the UK and France (slightly below 100).[24] This gap is likely to increase, as the crisis has dried up funds available for this "patent portfolio race."

Inefficiencies of Corporate Technology Management

Patent figures indicate that while Korea spends more than twice as much on R&D than Taiwan, the number of U.S. patents granted to Koreans in 1992 was only 538 compared to 1,252 patents to Taiwanese (Kim Linsu 1997b: 15).[25] Serious problems have been detected with regard to the effectiveness of the *chaebol*'s innovation management (see e.g., Bloom 1992; Kim Sun G. 1995; Kim Youngsoo 1997). While external technology sourcing strategies are highly sophisticated, the organization of innovation *within* these firms follows an outdated centralized R&D model, in contrast to the progressive decentralization of R&D typical today for Japanese, U.S., and European firms.[26] The persistence of hierarchical patterns of firm organization in Korea has important negative implications for the organization of R&D: Korean engineers and technicians are more inclined to work on their own and are much less willing to contribute to a team than are their Japanese counterparts (Oki 1993). Organizing R&D in a centralized manner produces rigid procedures concerning information management and decision making, delaying product design cycles and speed-to-market. In addition, centralized R&D organizations are ill equipped to coordinate the complex requirements of innovation. Feedback loops across the value chain thus remain weak and unreliable, and design, marketing, and manufacturing often proceed in an asynchronous way.

A bias for centralized R&D organizations also has quite negative implications beyond the boundaries of the firm. It is probably one of the main reasons for the still very weak domestic linkages among the different actors in the process of technology generation and diffusion. This applies in particular to linkages between the large electronics manufacturing companies and their suppliers of parts and components.[27] Most of these links are either with foreign companies or are internalized by the leading *chaebol* (Wong 1991; Bloom 1992).

Inefficiencies in the Public Innovation System[28]

Important inefficiencies also exist in Korea's public innovation system. While the government's share of R&D has declined to less than 20 percent, it remains significant, and a serious lack of coordination among R&D programs of different ministries has wasted scarce resources. The current mechanism for setting priorities awards each ministry autonomy over its own program without regard to those of other ministries. Meanwhile, private sector R&D retains a very narrow focus: geared largely to development, especially process reengineering and product customization, rather than research, it actually tends to block opportunities for the kinds of research needed for industrial upgrading. Those *chaebol* that have funds for

research thus neglect it in favor of development activities. This reflects a fundamental mismatch in the allocation of R&D funds and recruitment. Nearly 80 percent of the government's civilian R&D funds go to government research institutes
(GRIs).[29] Yet, due to the recent deterioration of salaries and social status in GRIs,
there is now a heavy brain drain from GRIs to universities. However, Korean universities, which employ 76 percent of the Ph.D. holders, lack the research facilities
and funds to conduct serious research. Receiving less than 11 percent of the government civilian R&D funds, Korean universities are in a much weaker position
than even in Japan, where universities are also quite feeble in terms of R&D.

A further important weakness of the Korean innovation system relates to the
established educational system. Its heavy focus on the training of midlevel managers, engineers, and technicians was an important prerequisite of success during
the catching-up phase. Yet today, as the focus shifts to research, product design,
and market development, the educational system is poorly equipped to cope with
these new requirements.[30]

In short, its earlier success has led Korea's innovation system to a series of new
challenges which it is ill prepared to meet. Structural weaknesses of the system
have been well known and extensively debated within the government and in
management circles for some time, yet the inertia resulting from past success and
established power structures have crippled Korea's ability to adapt its institutions
to the requirements of industrial upgrading. The search for new policy approaches
and new corporate strategies remains constrained by a highly unequal distribution
of economic and political power. We now turn to some of the structural causes for
Korea's truncated industrial upgrading.

An Unbalanced Industry Structure

A distinguishing feature of the Korean model is a dominance of large business
groups that is unrivaled elsewhere:[31] the combined sales of the five largest *chaebol*
grew from 12.8 percent of GNP in 1975 to 35 percent in 1980 and 52.4 percent
in 1984 (Kim Linsu 1993: 2). The *chaebol* dominate sales and exports; they can
recruit the best workers, technicians, engineers, and managers; they have privileged access to investment capital; and their strategies determine the product mix
and the capabilities of Korea's industry.

The extreme degree of concentration is a key variable that distinguishes Korea's
electronics industry from that of Japan (Kohama and Urata 1993: 152). Until recently, Korea's electronics industry was controlled by four *chaebol*—Samsung, LG,
Hyundai, and Daewoo. In 1988, 56 percent of electronics production came from
these four groups, with the first two alone accounting for 46 percent (Bloom 1992:
12). In 1992, the total semiconductor and electronics sale of one company alone,
Samsung Electronics, accounted for 20 percent of the Korean electronics industry's exports (Dataquest 1993). None of the big electronics groups in Japan comes
close to such overwhelming dominance.

Ironically, postcrisis attempts to reform the *chaebol* may reinforce their dominance. Concentration has increased following the break-up of the Daewoo group and acquisition of LG's semiconductor operations by the Hyundai group (Yoo 1999). The Korean electronics industry retains a structure which, according to textbook wisdom, should no longer exist: a tight national oligopoly controlling both domestic production and the domestic market.

Implications for Corporate Strategy: "Octopus-Like Diversification"

Korea's unbalanced industry structure has given rise to a peculiar form of competition strategy that focuses on incessant product diversification, often into technologically unrelated areas.[32] Each time a *chaebol* has reached the limits of "easy" capacity and market share expansion for a particular product, it moves on to a new product group that promises rapid market expansion. Such "octopus-like diversification" has been pushed to the extreme, with the top five *chaebol* in an average of 140 different sectors each. No other country, not even Japan or Sweden, comes close to such an extreme reliance on unrelated diversification.

Here lies one of the most important differences between *chaebol*-type business strategies and those pursued by Japanese electronics firms, which typically have been reluctant to engage in product diversification. A survey of the two hundred largest Japanese industrial firms (Fruin 1992: 318) found that only 40 percent engaged in a limited amount of diversification, with 41 percent of new goods being in the same two-digit standard industrial classification category as the firm's established products.[33] Gerlach (1993) also has shown that Japanese diversification has resulted predominantly in the "spinning-off" of new subsidiaries that retain a certain degree of autonomy from the parent company.

Octopus-like diversification has had important negative implications for capability formation. The *chaebol* have typically used diversification as a shortcut to rapid market-share expansion, without much concern for the depth of the production system that can be generated by such shallow forms of diversification. This has made it very difficult for most Korean companies to accumulate systematically a broad range of technological capabilities for a given set of products. It has also left very little scope for upgrading into higher-end market niches, where premium prices could be reaped. Finally, this opportunistic form of unrelated diversification has precluded a shift to technology diversification.

A Dearth of Innovative Small and Medium-Sized Enterprises

The pervasive role that the *chaebol* have played as engines of growth and industrial transformation sets Korea apart from Taiwan, where small and medium-sized enterprises (SMEs) have been the main carriers of industrial development. Among Asian countries, Taiwan probably has made the most progress toward a balanced industry structure that allows for close and flexible interaction between large business groups and SMEs. This has enabled small firms to grow and to respond quickly to changes in international markets and technology (Ernst 1998b); it may also explain why Taiwan has been able to shield itself better than Korea from the financial meltdown that occurred in much of Asia in 1997–1998. By contrast, in Korea, directed credit has focused consistently on the development of large domestic conglomerates. This has prevented the development of a vibrant domestic SME sector; until very recently, small, innovative start-up companies had little chance to gain access to such credit.[34]

The lack of a vibrant domestic network of SMEs has important negative consequences for learning and specialization. A key issue is whether a firm succeeds in moving beyond imitation based on reverse engineering and on to apprentice-type learning, where a link with a foreign company provides access to both tacit and explicit knowledge (Kim Linsu 1997a: 208–209). This distinction allows us to highlight an important difference in technological learning between South Korea and Taiwan. In Korea, most SMEs are stuck with a focus on imitation based on reverse engineering (Kim Linsu 1997a: chapters 8–9), which has led to a very low learning efficiency for SMEs. The situation is radically different in Taiwan (Ernst 1998b). Especially in the computer industry, Taiwanese SMEs have been exposed early on to apprentice-type learning arrangements with large firms, both foreign and domestic. These relationships have significantly strengthened the flexibility of SMEs, enabling them to shift rapidly from relatively simple to increasingly complex forms of international subcontracting.

The *chaebol*'s dominance in the electronics industry also has had a negative effect on the role of SMEs engaged in the supply of parts and components and other complementary support activities. Although formally independent, most of these firms are tightly integrated into the *chaebol*'s vertical production networks. Until the early 1980s, this had resulted in an industry structure where the leading *chaebol* tended to produce almost everything in-house, from electronics components and electrical accessories to transistors, semiconductors, and precision engineering parts (Wong 1991: 53). One peculiar feature of the Korean electronics industry is that subcontractors work only for one manufacturer, and are thus locked into a fairly closed production network controlled by a particular *chaebol*. Small and medium-sized suppliers have very limited decision-making autonomy, which significantly limits attempts to improve their international competitiveness.

An equally important concern is the extreme concentration of private R&D. Before the crisis, the five leading *chaebol* accounted for nearly 37 percent of Korea's total private sector R&D investment, and the twenty leading *chaebol* for more than 53 percent.[35] Since the crisis, such concentration is likely to have increased. The *chaebol* control the key assets and capabilities of Korea's innovation system, and science and technology decisions thus are overwhelmingly shaped by their strategies. This perpetuates Korea's extremely unbalanced industry structure, despite recent government attempts to give greater attention to the promotion of SMEs capable of developing their own component designs and to improve the competitive conditions for innovative start-up companies.[36]

In sum, a dearth of innovative and aggressive SMEs has severely constrained Korea's attempts to develop higher-end niche markets, one important element of industrial upgrading. This differs markedly from the situation in Taiwan and in the Japanese electronics industry, where SMEs have played an active role in developing such strategies. The *chaebol*-dominated structure that created economies of scale and scope and opportunities for substantial cross-subsidization, appropriate to an era of rapid catching up, has proven ill equipped to foster a dynamic SME sector that could provide key components and critical complementary support services to those very *chaebol*.

CONCLUSION: A PARADIGM SHIFT IN THE KOREAN MODEL?

The vicious circle of weak flexibility and truncated industrial upgrading has increased Korea's vulnerability to the turmoil in international finance and currency markets. In fact, Korea's economy was already weakened when the financial crisis hit.[37] The exhaustion of the Korean model for catching up has important policy implications for other developing economies. While making drastic changes in the financial system is important, these changes need to be supplemented with changes in the real economy: a long overdue process of industrial upgrading requires institutional and policy innovations that can help to remove the barriers to greater flexibility.

Unfortunately, the crisis may have reduced the opportunity for making this move. Recent data on production, trade, and market share show that very little upgrading has occurred in response to the crisis (Ernst 2000c). Korea's electronics industry is confronted with a major dilemma: it must upgrade its competitive position through improved product differentiation and market development capabilities, without losing its traditional strengths in mass production. In contrast to its Japanese, American, and European counterparts, a medium-sized country like Korea, which only recently joined the international market, is less well equipped to cope with the impact of globalization. As a result, head-on competition with market leaders in "high-end" applications is out of the question.

Rather than recommend jumping directly into "technology leadership" strategies, recent research has shown that industrial latecomers may have an intermediate option: "technology diversification."[38] Defined as "the expansion of a company's or a product's technology base into a broader range of technology areas" (Granstrand 1992: 291), such strategies are an attempt to reap technology-related economies of scope.[39] Technology diversification differs substantially from so-called technology leadership strategies, which are defined by their focus on products with a high R&D content. Instead, technology diversification focuses on products which are "based on several . . . crucial technologies which do not have to be new to the world or difficult to acquire" (Granstrand 1992: 300).[40]

For Korean electronics firms, technology diversification could have a number of important advantages. It builds on existing strengths of Korea's approach to technological learning. As technology diversification normally goes hand in hand with an extensive reliance on external technology sourcing, Korean firms could make use of their accumulated capabilities in external technology sourcing, imitation, and adaptive engineering. Technology diversification can also reduce the financial burden and high debt that result from overambitious technology leadership strategies. To the extent that expenditures on R&D will be reduced by the financial crisis, technology diversification can help Korean firms to reduce these costs, and to spread them not only over many markets (countries and segments), but also over many products. Finally, technology diversification may also help to open up new windows of opportunity for international market penetration and for the development of new market niches.

Leading *chaebol* claim that they have already vigorously moved in this direction. They point to a series of technology agreements with leading American and Japanese electronics producers and to a massive increase in R&D expenditures and productive investment. Since 1993, the four leading Korean electronics producers have indeed drastically increased their R&D and capital outlays; they were also planning to increase them even further before the crisis hit (Ernst 1994b). What is important, however, is not the amount of investment expenditures per se, but their allocation among different types of products and production activities.

The real question is to what degree such investments are used to correct some of the basic weaknesses of the Korean electronics industry with regard to product specialization, the organization of production, and accumulated technological deficits. Recent research (Ernst 2000c) has shown that capital spending has been overwhelmingly concentrated on the rapid expansion of mass-production lines for two products (DRAM and LCD). The huge capital spending binge of Korean electronics firms thus clearly has had the primary effect of consolidating the existing product specialization and production organization. In other words, we appear in for more of the same rather than a shift to new products and production activities.

Yet a radical paradigm shift is overdue, as Korea has reached the limits of the old export-led industrialization model, with its emphasis on standardized mass production, OEM exporting, and catching up. Moving beyond these limits will require fundamental changes in the Korean model of economic governance. This is true for government policies and industry structure, as well as for firm organization and strategies. There is an urgent need to redefine the role of government interventions. This does not imply a weakening of the coordinating function of the state (Chang 1998). Rather, overcoming the barriers to industrial upgrading necessitates a strengthening of policies and institutions that can provide the incentives and externalities for technological learning.[41] National policy interventions are required to compensate for these market failures. In addition to the subsidies and tax incentives suggested by Arrow (1962), this also implies a variety of organizational and institutional innovations in policy implementation. A growing body of research on economic policy making in advanced industrial countries has demonstrated that choice is possible, both in the domain of macroeconomic policy making and with regard to industrial and technology policies (see e.g., Berger and Dore 1996). This volume suggests that the same holds true for developing countries. The real question, then, is no longer whether national policies and institutions can make a difference; instead, it is what kind of policies and institutions will prove most conducive for upgrading domestic capabilities and product specialization.

NOTES

My understanding of Korea has been shaped by numerous interviews that I have conducted there over the last two decades. I have also learned a great deal from the writings of Kim Linsu, one of the most thoughtful observers of Korean development, and a number of (mostly Korean) authors I have mentioned in the bibliography. Financial support has been provided by the Alfred P. Sloan Foundation, the Centre for Global Partnership, UNCTAD-SAREC, and the Danish Social Science Foundation. I greatly benefited from theoretical debates on evolutionary economics with George B. Richardson, Chris Freeman, Carlotta Perez, Keith Pavitt, François Chesnais, Bengt-Åke Lundvall, Bo Carlsson, Paolo Guerrieri, Peter Maskell, and Esben Sloth Andersen. Helpful comments are gratefully acknowledged from Rick Doner, Eric Hershberg, John Ravenhill, Stephan Haggard, Martin Bloom, Chang Ha Joon, Chang Sei-Myung, Choi Yongrak, Peter Evans, Gary Gereffi, Kim Hwan Suk, Kim Youngsoo, Lee Won-Young, Lynn Mytelka, and John Zysman. I am of course responsible for the conclusions drawn and for any mistakes.

1. Data on the Korean electronics industry are courtesy of the Electronics Industry Association of Korea (EIAK), the Korea Semiconductor Industry Association (KSIA),the Korea International Trade Association (KITA), and the Ministry of Commerce, Industry and Energy (MOCIE). Additional data sources include the United Nations-COMTRADE trade data base, updated to include 1998; the *Yearbook of World Electronics Data 1998/99* and the 1998 Yearbook of the Information Technology Industry Council, Washington, D.C. (both for market and production figures for the electronics industries); and author interviews conducted over the last two decades.

2. Important sources on the Korean model include Amsden (1989), Wade (1990), Haggard (1990), Kim (1992 and 1997a), Evans (1995), and Chang (1994). Much of this literature is dominated by the developmental state theory. The complementary, catalytic role played by foreign direct investment and global production networks is emphasized in Bloom (1992), Ernst and O'Connor (1992), and Ernst (1994a; 1994b).

3. I use a conceptual framework based on evolutionary theories of innovation and the firm, e.g., Penrose (1959), Richardson (1960), Freeman (1982), Nelson and Winter (1982), Dosi et al (1988), and Kogut and Zander (1993), and their application to economic development, e.g., Bell and Pavitt (1993), Nelson and Pack (1995), Lall (1997), Ernst and Lundvall (1998), and Ernst (2000a).

4. A weakness of "statist" theories has been their neglect of the international investment environment.

5. As a result, Korea today has one of the lowest rates of inward investment in East Asia, even after the crisis-induced attempts by the Korean government to bring foreign investment back into the country as a vehicle for accelerated technology diffusion (Beck 1999).

6. Korea's debt burden is estimated to consist of $450 billion in domestic debt and more than $150 billion in foreign debt. The *chaebol* have an average debt-equity ratio of four to one, and ten of the top 30 *chaebol* have debt-to-equity ratios exceeding five to one. Before the crisis, the following debt-equity ratios were reported by SBC Warburg Dillon Reed: Samsung (473 percent), Hyundai (453 percent), LG (378 percent), and Daewoo (316 percent). Note, however, that the absence of transparent consolidated accounting rules in Korea causes great confusion about accurate debt-equity ratios. Estimates of Hyundai's debt-equity ratio, for instance, range from 1,378 percent (excluding asset revaluations) to 341 percent (the latest official estimate by Korea's Financial Supervisory Commission).

7. In contrast to the Korean government, which used its control of the financial sector to direct credit to a handful of *chaebol*, the Taiwanese government did not try to promote large national champions. Taiwan's industrial policy focused on flexibility and competition: relatively low entry barriers and nondiscriminatory policies enable small firms to enter targeted sectors and to grow. At the same time, the legal system puts relatively few obstacles in the way of bankruptcy. Thus, Taiwan's smaller companies had to rely more on equity markets and corporate retained earnings than did the *chaebol* (Ernst 2000b).

8. It has been argued that such high debt is a prerequisite for catching up (Veneroso and Wade 1998). However, Ernst (1998a) demonstrates two important weaknesses in this argument: it fails to explain why debt-equity ratios are much lower among Taiwanese companies and it fails to address some negative consequences of high debt for firm strategies and industrial upgrading.

9. For the underlying conceptual framework of capability formation, see Ernst, Mytelka, and Ganiatsos (1998).

10. The last two features are typically thought of as strengthening flexibility. Yet as we shall see below, Korean firms remain mired in homogenous products and mass production. Flexibility improvements thus occurred *within* the mass production paradigm.

11. On knowledge outsourcing through global production networks, see Ernst (1997b; 2000b).

12. This contrasts sharply with Taiwan's PC industry, in which early access to market intelligence enables firms to accelerate speed-to-market and to continuously upgrade their products (see San Gee and Wen-jeng Kuo 1998; Ernst 2000b).

13. Two external factors provide the context for discussion of how the Korean way of building technological capabilities may have contributed to this success. The first is a probably unintended, yet very consequential, side effect of the September 1986 U.S.-Japanese agreement on trade in semiconductors: due to the unrealistically high price floors set for DRAM imports into the United States, Korean producers were able to outprice their Japanese rivals at levels that, in 1989, began to generate substantial profits (Ernst 1987). A second external factor was the strategic decision by U.S. semiconductor producers and computer companies to create an alternative, low-cost source for DRAMs in Korea to tame oligopolistic pricing and supply behavior of major Japanese producers (Ernst and O'Connor 1992).

14. The magnitude of East Asia's export slowdown was unprecedented in recent history. The region's export growth reached a peak in the first quarter of 1995. By the first quarter

of 1996, it fell to zero in the East Asia-5 countries and turned negative for other East Asian countries, including China and the newly industrialized countries (World Bank 1998: chapter 2). Korea's average annual growth of exports, for instance, fell from 14 percent in 1990–1995, to 3.7 percent in 1995–1996, to -2.4 percent between January and April 1997.

15. Throughout the period 1990 to 1997, Korea's real export growth mirrored changes in the yen-dollar exchange rate, rising with an appreciation of the yen and falling with its depreciation (World Bank 1998: figure 2.2., p. 21).

16. Differentiated products, on the other hand, are based on new technology whose design features are still fluid and are thus difficult to replicate. This is due to the high entry barriers that result from the substantial R&D outlays required. Close interaction with customers is a critical prerequisite for success. Differentiated products thus require considerable up-front preparatory efforts to enable entry. Their great advantage, however, is that once those initial hurdles have been overcome, these products provide significant rent creation and industrial upgrading potential.

17. In the case of the largest Japanese semiconductor producer, NEC, for example, only 35 percent of semiconductor revenues were generated by MOS (metal oxide on silicon) memories.

18. The minimum efficient scale for producing these devices is now roughly $2 billion of annual sales. This implies that only firms that have reached the critical threshold of 5 percent of world production can compete successfully. For a detailed analysis of entry barriers in different sectors of the electronics industry, see Ernst and O'Connor (1992).

19. For an early model of the volatility of demand and recurrent periodic surplus capacities in semiconductors, see Ernst (1983: chapter 1).

20. According to the Ministry of Trade, Industry and Energy (MOTIE), Korean firms' annual royalty payments more than doubled between 1990 and 1996, from $1.1 billion to $2.3 billion.

21. Explanation for limited R&D expenditures up to that point is provided in Ernst, (1994a: chapter 4).

22. The most vivid illustration is that Korea's total R&D expenditures are only 54 percent compared to GM's R&D budget (Kim 1997b).

23. Patent intensity is measured as the share of a country's patent applications at the European Patent Office per one million inhabitants (EPAT [European Patent Office] data base, as quoted in BMBF [German Federal Ministry of Education and Science] 1998: figures 4.3 and 5.2).

24. The measure of patent intensity for OECD countries, Triad patents, refers to high-quality patents, i.e., world market-oriented patents registered in at least two overseas markets within the Triad region. This means the gap between G7 countries and Korea is even higher than shown by a mere quantitative comparison.

25. Note, however, that by 1996 Korean companies registered 1,567 patents in the U.S., the seventh largest number of U.S. patents registered by foreign companies (figures are courtesy of the Korean Development Institute).

26. Successful innovation requires continual and numerous interactions and feedback among a great variety of economic actors and across all stages of the value chain (OECD 1992: chapters 1-3).

27. A rich body of theoretical and empirical literature shows that both end product manufacturers and component suppliers can reap substantial benefits from vertical production networks. Such networks make possible a shift to a new division of labor in R&D, enabling manufacturing firms to concentrate on system design and final assembly and thus to restrict their R&D primarily to product design and process innovations for

final assembly. Suppliers, in turn, can focus their limited resources on product and process innovations for parts and components and thus can aspire to accumulate specialized technological capabilities. For case studies, see Ernst (1994b; 1997a; 1997b).

28. The following is based on discussions with Dr. Lee Won-Young from the Science & Technology Policy Institute, Seoul.

29. This is much higher than even in France and Japan, two countries where the government traditionally has played a strong role in the national innovation system.

30. Higher education remains a bottleneck for Korea's technological learning. The focus is on classical rather than contemporary material. Too much focus is placed on conformity and memorization, too little on creativity (Kim Linsu 1997a).

31. The only exception is Sweden, where the Wallenberg group, through its holding company Investor, controls companies accounting for more than 40 percent of the Swedish market, while holding only 4 percent of the capital.

32. Literally translated as "financial clique," *chaebol* is defined as " a business group consisting of large companies, which are owned and managed by family members or relatives in many diversified business areas" (Yoo and Lee 1987: 97).

33. The latter figure would be higher—46 percent—if the U.S. SIC code did not classify computers in a different category (35) from other electrical devices (36 and 38).

34. In his important book on the dynamics of Korea's technological learning, Kim Linsu (1997a: 6, 10) argues that "The most serious consequence of the asymmetric promotion of chaebol was the impediment to the healthy growth of SMEs."

35. Oki (1993: 46). The same study found that in the U.S. and Japan the share of the twenty leading firms in total R&D investment was, respectively, less than 31 percent and less than 37 percent.

36. Most observers agree that such policies have had only limited success. A recent survey by the School of Small Business at Soongsil University indicates that 70 percent of government-allocated credit goes to a few relatively large SMEs with strong ties to the leading *chaebol* through subcontracting arrangements. One particularly ironic finding is that many of these small businesses are becoming "mini-chaebol" by branching into various businesses but keeping each of the companies small to maintain access to cheap credit. (*Far Eastern Economic Review,* 19 November 1992: 70). It remains to be seen whether new policy initiatives after the crisis will succeed in breaking this deeply entrenched pattern.

37. A survey of the Korean economy, published well before the financial crisis, states unequivocally, "The South Korean economy is heading for a crisis as the growth that sustained the country's outward-oriented expansion over the past three decades is beginning to run out of steam" (Far Eastern Economic Review, "Focus. South Korea: Trade and Investment," October 23, 1997: 70).

38. For a detailed analysis, see Ernst (1999a).

39. Japanese firms have played a pioneering role in the development of technology diversification strategies. The underlying rationale has been threefold: an attempt to compensate for the increasing constraints on existing manufacturing exports; a deliberate strategy to develop generic technologies that could form the base for penetrating future growth markets; and a reaction to the increasing technological complexity and rising R&D cost of new products (Odagiri and Goto 1993).

40. Empirical research on Japanese, U.S., and Swedish companies has demonstrated the relevance of this strategy. This research has shown that "technological coexistence is more predominant than technological substitution, as seen from the larger number of old tech-

nologies in a current product generation, compared to the number of obsolete technologies" (Granstrand 1992: 305).

41. Markets are notoriously weak in generating technological learning. Markets are subject to externalities: investments in capabilities are typically characterized by a gap between private and social rates of return (Arrow 1962).

BIBLIOGRAPHY

Amsden, Alice. 1989. *Asia's Next Giant: South Korea and Late Industrialization*. New York: Oxford University Press.

Arrow, Kenneth J. 1962. "The Economic Implications of Learning by Doing." *Review of Economic Studies* (June).

Baumol, W. J., J. C. Panzer, and R. D. Willig. 1982. *Contestable Markets and the Theory of Industrial Structure*. New York: Harcourt Brace Jovanovich.

Beck, P. M. 1999. "Foreign Direct Investment in Korea: From Exclusion to Inducement." In *Korea and the Asian Economic Crisis: One Year Later*, by the Korea Economic Institute of America. Joint US-Korea Academic Studies, vol. 9.

Bell, Martin, and Keith Pavitt. 1993. "Technological Accumulation and Industrial Growth: Contrasts Between Developed and Developing Countries. *Industrial and Corporate Change* 2, no. 2.

Berger, Suzanne, and R. Dore, eds. 1996. *National Diversity and Global Capitalism*. Ithaca, N.Y.: Cornell University Press.

Bloom, M. 1992. *Technological Change in the Korean Electronics Industry*. Development Centre Studies. Paris: OECD.

Chang, Ha Joon. 1994. *The Political Economy of Industrial Policy*. London: MacMillan.

———. 1998. "Korea: The Misunderstood Crisis?" Paper presented at the Nordic Research Seminar on the Economic Crisis in East and Southeast Asia on 23–24 January at the Centre for Development and the Environment (SUM), University of Oslo.

Dahlman, C., B. Ross-Larson, and L. Westphal, 1987. "Managing Technological Development: Lessons from the Newly Industrialising Countries." *World Development* 15, no. 6.

Dataquest. 1993. *Vendor Profile Samsung Electronics*. San Jose, Calif. September.

Dosi, G., et al., eds. 1988. *Technical Change and Economic Theory*. London: Pinter Publishers.

Ernst, Dieter. 1983. *The Global Race in Microelectronics*. Frankfurt and New York: MIT Campus.

———. 1987. "U.S.-Japanese Competition and the Worldwide Restructuring of the Electronics Industry: A European View." In *Global Restructuring and Territorial Development*, edited by J. Henderson and M. Castells. London: Sage.

———. 1994a. "Network Transactions, Market Structure and Technological Diffusion-Implications for South-South Cooperation." In *South-South Cooperation in a Global Perspective*, edited by L. Mytelka. Development Centre Documents. Paris: OECD.

———. 1994b. *What Are the Limits to the Korean Model? The Korean Electronics Industry under Pressure*. BRIE Research Monograph. Berkeley: Berkeley Roundtable on the International Economy, University of California at Berkeley.

———. 1997a. "Partners in the China Circle? The Asian Production Networks of Japanese Electronics Firms." In *The China Circle*, edited by Barry Naughton. Washington, D.C.: Brookings Institution Press.

———. 1997b. *From Partial to Systemic Globalization: International Production Networks in the Electronics Industry*, report prepared for the Sloan Foundation, jointly published as *The Data Storage Industry Globalization Project Report 97-02*, Graduate School of International Relations and Pacific Studies, University of California at San Diego, and *BRIE Working Paper # 98*, the Berkeley Roundtable on the International Economy (BRIE), University of California at Berkeley.

———. 1998a. "Catching-Up, Crisis and Industrial Upgrading: Evolutionary Aspects of Technological Learning in Korea's Electronics Industry." *Asia Pacific Journal of Management* 15, no. 2: 247–283.

———. 1998b. *Destroying or Upgrading the Engine of Growth ? The Reshaping of the Electronics Industry in East Asia after the Crisis*. Report prepared for the World Bank. Copenhagen: Department of Industrial Economics and Strategy, Copenhagen Business School.

———. 1998c. "High-Tech Competition Puzzles. How Globalization Affects Firm Behavior and Market Structure in the Electronics Industry." *Revue d'Economie Industrielle* 85: 9–31.

———. 1999. "Industry Structure, Firm Behavior and Technological Learning. How the Crisis Reshapes Upgrading Options for East Asia's Electronics Industry." In *The Economics of Industrial Structure and Innovation Dynamics*. London: Elgar.

———. 2000a. "Globalization and the Changing Geography of Innovation Systems: A Policy Perspective on Global Production Networks." *Journal of the Economics of Innovation and New Technologies*.

———. 2000b. "Inter-Organizational Knowledge Outsourcing: What Permits Small Taiwanese Firms to Compete in the Computer Industry?" *Asia-Pacific Journal of Management*.

———. 2000c. "Moving Beyond the Commodity Price Trap: How the Crisis Reshapes Upgrading Options for East Asia's Information Industries." In *East Asia: Out of the Crisis, Into the New Millennium*. Washington D.C.: The World Bank.

Ernst, D., L. Mytelka, and T. Ganiatsos. 1998. "Export Performance and Technological Capabilities: A Conceptual Framework." In *Technological Capabilities and Export Success: Lessons from East Asia,* edited by D. Ernst, T. Ganiatsos, and L. Mytelka. London: Routledge.

Ernst, Dieter, and Bengt-Åke Lundvall. 1998. "Information Technology in the Learning Economy: Challenges for Developing Countries." In *Evolutionary Economics and Spatial Income Inequality,* edited by Erich Reinert. London: Edward Elgar Press.

Ernst, Dieter, and David O'Connor. 1989. *Technology and Global Competition: The Challenge for Newly Industrialising Economies.* Paris: OECD Development Centre Studies.

———. 1992. *Competing in the Electronics Industry: The Experience of Newly Industrialising Economies*. Paris: OECD Development Centre Studies.

Evans, Peter. 1995. *Embedded Autonomy: States and Industrial Transformation*. Princeton: Princeton University Press.

Freeman, Chris. 1997. "Innovation Systems: City-State, National, Continental and Sub-National." Sussex, England: University of Sussex (December).

Freeman, C. 1982. *Economics of Industrial Innovation*. London: Frances, Pinter.

Fruin, M. 1992. *The Japanese Enterprise System: Competitive Strategies and Cooperative Structures*. Oxford: Clarendon Press.

Gerlach, M. L. 1993. *Alliance Capitalism: The Social Organization of Japanese Business*. Berkeley: University of California Press.

Gerschenkron, A. 1962. *Economic Backwardness in Historical Perspective: A Book of Essays*. Cambridge, Mass.: Harvard University Press, Belknap Press.

Granstrand, O., ed. 1992. *Technology Management and International Business: Internationalization of R&D and Technology.* New York: Wiley.

Haggard, Stephan. 1990. *Pathways from the Periphery: The Politics of Growth in the Newly Industrializing Countries.* Ithaca, N.Y.: Cornell University Press.

Hikino, T., and A. Amsden. 1994. "Staying Behind, Stumbling Back, Sneaking Up, Soaring Ahead: Late Industrialization in Historical Perspective." In *Convergence of Productivity: Cross-National Studies and Historical Evidence,* edited by W. J. Baumol, R. Nelson, and E. N. Wolf. New York: Oxford University Press.

Kim, Linsu. 1992. "National System of Industrial Innovation: Dynamics of Capability Building in Korea." In *National Innovation Systems: A Comparative Analysis,* edited by Richard Nelson. New York: Oxford University Press.

———. 1993. "The Structure and Workings of the National Innovation System in Korea." Paper presented at the conference on Redefining Korean Competitiveness in an Age of Globalization, at the Center for Korean Studies, University of California at Berkeley.

———. 1997a. *Imitation to Innovation. The Dynamics of Korea's Technological Learning.* Boston: Harvard Business School Press.

———. 1997b. "Korea's National Innovation System in Transition." Paper presented at the symposium on Innovation and Competitiveness in Newly Industrializing Economies on 26–27 May in Seoul at the Science & Technology Policy Institute.

Kim, Sun G. 1995. "S&T Promotion Policy and the Incentive Scheme for Technological Capability Building in Korea: Facts and Characteristics." In *Review of Science and Technology Policy for Industrial Competitiveness in Korea.* Seoul: Science & Technology Policy Institute.

Kim, Youngsoo. 1997. "Technological Capabilities and Samsung Electronics' International Production Networks in Asia." In *Rivalry or Riches: International Production Networks in Asia,* edited by M. Borrus, D. Ernst, and S. Haggard. London: Routledge.

Kogut, B., and E. Zander. 1993. "Knowledge of the Firm and the Evolutionary Theory of the Multinational Corporation." *Journal of International Business Studies* 24, no. 4.

Kohama, H., and S. Urata. 1993. "Protection and Promotion of Japan's Electronics Industry." In *Industrial Policy in East Asia,* edited by Ryuichiro Inoue. Tokyo: JETRO.

Korea Economic Institute of America. 1999. *Korea and the Asian Economic Crisis: One Year Later.* Joint US-Korea Academic Studies, vol. 9. Washington, D.C.: Korean Economic Institute of America.

Krugman, Paul. 1998. "What happened to Asia?" Available on-line at http://web.mit.edu/krugman/www/DISINTER.html.

Lall, S. 1997. "Technological Change and Industrialization in the Asian NIEs: Achievements and Challenges." Paper presented at the symposium on Innovation and Competitiveness in Newly Industrializing Economies on 26–27 May, in Seoul at the Science & Technology Policy Institute.

Lipsey, R. G., and C. Bekar. 1995. "A Structuralist View of Technical Change and Economic Growth." In *Technology, Information and Public Policy,* edited by T. J. Courchane. Kingston, Ontario: John Deutsch Institute.

Lundvall, B. A., ed. 1992. *National Systems of Innovation: Towards a Theory of Innovation and Interactive Learning.* London: Pinter.

Nelson, Richard, and H. Pack. 1995. "The Asian Growth Miracle and Modern Growth Theory." Manuscript, School of International and Public Affairs, Columbia University.

Nelson, Richard, and S. G. Winter. 1982. *An Evolutionary Theory of Economic Change.* Cambridge, Mass.: Harvard University Press, Belknap Press.

Nilsson, J. E., 1996. "Introduction: The Internationalization Process." In *The Internationalization Process: European Firms in Global Competition*. London: Paul Chapman.

Odagiri, Hiroyuki, and Akira Goto. 1993. "The Japanese System of Innovation." In *National Innovation Systems: A Comparative Analysis*. New York: Oxford University Press.

OECD. 1992. *Technology and the Economy: The Key Relationships*. Paris: OECD.

———. 1995a. *Reviews of National Science and Technology Policy: Korea. Part I: Background Report*. DSTI/STP(95) 16. Paris: OECD.

———. 1995b. *Reviews of National Science and Technology Policy: Korea. Part II: Examiners' Report*. DSTI/STP (95)15. Paris: OECD.

Oki, Toshie. 1993. "Technology Development in South Korea." *RIM. Pacific Business and Industries*, Vol. III. Tokyo: Center for Pacific Business Studies, Sakura Institute of Research.

Penrose, Edith T. 1959. *The Theory of the Growth of the Firm*. Oxford: Oxford University Press.

Richardson, G. B. 1960. *Information and Investment*. Oxford: Oxford University Press.

San Gee and Wen-jeng Kuo. 1998. "Export Success and Technological Capability: Textiles and Electronics in Taiwan." In *Technological Capabilities and Export Success: Lessons from East Asia*, edited by D. Ernst, T. Ganiatsos, and L. Mytelka. London: Routledge.

Stiglitz, Joseph. 1997. "How to Fix the Asian Economies." *New York Times* (31 October).

Veneroso, F., and R. Wade. 1998. "The Asian Financial Crisis: The Unrecognized Risk of the IMF's Asia Package." Paper presented at the Nordic Research Seminar on the Economic Crisis in East and Southeast Asia on 23–24 January at the Centre for Development and the Environment (SUM), University of Oslo.

Wade, Robert. 1990. *Governing the Market: Economic Theory and the Role of Government in East Asian Industrialization*. Princeton: Princeton University Press.

Wong, Poh-kam. 1991. *Technological Development through Subcontracting Linkages*. Tokyo: Asia Productivity Organization.

World Bank. 1998. *East Asia: The Road to Recovery*. Washington, D.C.: World Bank.

Yoo, Sangjin, and Sang M. Lee. 1987. "Management Style and Practices of Korean Chaebols." *California Management Review* 29, no. 4.

Yoo, Seong Min. 1999. "Corporate Restructuring in Korea." In *Korea and the Asian Economic Crisis: One Year Later*. Joint US-Korea Academic Studies, vol. 9. Washington, D.C.: Korean Economic Institute of America.

6

Politics, Institutions, and Flexibility: Microelectronics Transnationals and Machine Tool Linkages in Malaysia

Rajah Rasiah

This volume's introduction emphasizes the need to go beyond simple descriptions of flexible production. Its challenge is to explain flexible performance by addressing both the roles of various institutions in facilitating flexibility and the origins of these institutions. The present chapter addresses these concerns by exploring a puzzle: How do we explain contrasting levels of transnational subcontracting and local machine tool development in one industry—microelectronics—across two regions of the same country—Malaysia?

We emphasize subcontracting behavior because of its link to success in an industry—microelectronics and, especially, semiconductors—where the need for flexibility is quite clear. This industry has undergone extensive changes in product and process developments in the last decade. Intense competition and volatile price fluctuations have driven firms to shorten product cycles and cut production costs. The rising importance of quick interfacing between product innovation, manufacturing, and marketing on the one hand and extensive production reorganization on the other has forced firms to raise operative flexibility at all levels of production and distribution (Rasiah 1994). While in-house flexibility has been central, its success has required a concomitant response in extrafirm provision of resources such as training, capital (including machinery), materials, and services (including marketing). Due to the rising sophistication of microelectronics production, the need for such resources applies even to the lower-end manufacturing activities such as assembly and test.

Given inherent information asymmetries, scale economies, and dynamic gains accruing to innovations, serious doubts exist as to the capacity of purely arms-length, market-type arrangements for providing such resources (Richardson 1960; Richardson 1972; North and Thomas 1970; Kaldor 1979; Alt and Chrystal 1983;

Rasiah 1997). Even when complementary support services are involved, scale economies, externality issues, and uncertainty associated with dissimilar activities present significant collective action problems. This of course is where institutions can play a constructive role in coordinating firms and individuals (Wilkinson and You 1992; Rasiah 1995).

But what kind of institutions playing what kinds of roles and at what costs? New growth economists generally accept the reality of market deficiencies, but they contend that nonmarket interventions by governments are likely to generate far more costs than gains (see Helpman and Krugman 1989; Lucas 1988). This chapter goes beyond the state-market dichotomy to examine relationships between firms as well as between the state and firms. At the interfirm level, we examine the benefits of transnational corporation (TNC) subcontracting to and support for local machine tool firms (LMFs) in Malaysia.[1]

But this begs the key question of why such subcontracting actually occurs. A functionalist explanation would suggest that certain kinds of interfirm relations emerge to reduce the transaction costs resulting from some combination of asset specificity, transaction frequency, and uncertainty (Williamson 1985; Coase 1937). But because this research shows significant intranational variation in interfirm arrangements in the same industry, and involving most of the same firms, this chapter explores what might be called second- and third-level explanations of flexibility. The second level involves institutions in the provision of collective goods that promote the strengthening of both local machine tool firms and their linkages to microelectronics TNCs. At the third level, we argue that variations in subcontracting linkages and supporting institutions are a function of political factors that vary within Malaysia. More specifically, we focus on the position of ethnic networks within the broader political dynamic of state-federal relations in Malaysia.

This chapter is, then, a sort of natural experiment: by holding constant a range of firm, industry, and national incentive factors, it is possible to evaluate the weight of other independent variables that differ across the two regions under study. Pursuing this strategy, the next section of this chapter begins by reviewing the cross-regional differences in the dependent variables: there are more developed local machine tool firms and interfirm linkages within the semiconductor industry in Penang than in the Kelang Valley. It then presents the puzzle more clearly by reviewing the factors common to the two areas. The third section begins to explain the cross-regional variation by focusing on differences in the support institutions: due to what we might call different "regional systems of innovation" (Best 1990; Saxenian 1994) something akin to an agglomeration economy has emerged, albeit still underdeveloped, in Penang, whereas the Kelang Valley is characterized by vertical integration within the TNCs and a general lack of support institutions. The fourth section pursues a political explanation of these differences through an investigation of the interaction among social networks, ethno-class alignments, ethnic networks, ethno-class relations, and party alignments. The final section summarizes the findings in light of several broader concerns: the question of whether trust is simply a second-best mechanism for dealing with underdeveloped markets; the value of institutional density for flexibility; and the question of convergence.

VARIATION IN MACHINE TOOL LINKAGES AND FLEXIBLE PRODUCTION SYSTEMS

TNC Shifts to Flexible Production

We are interested in the degree of subcontracting by microelectronics TNCs with local machine tool firms and the strengths of these local firms. To this end, eight microelectronics TNCs, of whom seven were U.S. firms, were surveyed (table 6.1). Local suppliers were traced from the eight microelectronics transnationals (table 6.2). The interview response rate was 72.0 and 44.4 percent from the two regions respectively.[2] All TNCs in the sample have introduced flexible production techniques. This has been a gradual process. Initial investments in the early 1970s by semiconductor firms, including Intel, Advanced Micro Devices, and National Semiconductor, involved simple assembly of imported inputs for export. All exports went back to parent firms before being sold to wholesalers and retailers. Work organization typified neo-Taylorism—referred to as flexible casualization by Sabel (1986) or as the low road to industrial restructuring by Sengenberger and Pyke (1991) and Hirst and Zeitlin (1991). Under such circumstances, microelectronics transnationals were not only little interested in deepening skills and establishing training facilities in Malaysia, but also saw limited need to broaden proximate machine tool supply capacities. Being essentially

Table 6.1   Microelectronics Transnationals, 1993

Firms	Year of Inception	Equity (%)	Location	Flexibilization Efforts	Substantial Flexibilization
AA	1972	USA (100)	Kelang Valley	1983	1988
AB	1973	USA (100)	Kelang Valley	1982	1989
AC	1980	USA (100)	Kelang Valley	1984	1990
AD	1972	USA (100)	Penang	1982	1989
AE	1973	USA (100)	Penang	1980	1984
AF	1973	USA (100)	Penang	1983	1989
AG	1973	USA (100)	Penang	1984	1989
AH	1973	Japan (90); Malaysia (10)	Penang	1975	1978

Source: Author's interviews, 1993.
Note: Fictitious firm names were used to protect confidentiality.

Table 6.2   Local Machine Tool Suppliers, Penang and the Kelang Valley, 1993

Firm	Ownership (equity %)	Location	Inception Year	Process Techniques	Employees	Sales (RM million)	Products
BA	L$_C$(100)	Penang	1979	TMS, JIT, QCC	45	2.5	Precision components
BB	L$_C$(100)	Penang	1983	TMS, JIT, TQM, QCC, SPC	22	1.4	Precision parts, automated machinery
BC	L$_B$(60) L$_C$(40)	Penang	1988	TMS, Codified instructions	15	0.3	Precision fabrication
BD	L$_C$(100)	Penang	1987	QCC and SPC	34	1.5	Precision parts, automated machinery
BE	L$_C$(100)	Penang	1991	TMS, Codified instructions	17	0.3	Precision parts
BF	L$_C$(100)	Penang	1976	JIT, TQM, TMS, TPM, QCC, SPC	200	20.0	Precision components, automated machinery
BG	L$_T$(100)	Penang	1978	Codified instructions	22	2.6	Precision parts, molds, and dies
BH	L$_C$(100)	Penang	1984	JIT, SPC, QCC	85	10.0	Precision components
BI	L$_C$(100)	Penang	1980	JIT, TPM, QCC, TMS	68	15.0	Precision parts, automated machinery
BJ	L$_C$(100)	Penang	1984	JIT, TPM, QCC, TMS	40	2.5	Precision parts

Table 6.2 Local Machine Tool Suppliers, Penang and the Kelang Valley, 1993 (Continued)

Firm	Ownership (equity %)	Location	Inception Year	Process Techniques	Employees	Sales (RM million)	Products
BK	L$_C$(100)	Penang	1950	JIT, TQM, TPM, QCC, TMS	120	10.0	Precision parts, automated machinery
BL	L$_C$(100)	Penang	1980	JIT, TQM, TPM, QCC, SPC	40	1.7	Automated machinery
BM	L$_C$(100)	Penang	1982	JIT, TQM, TPM, QCC, SPC	128	12.0	Simple parts fabrication, jigs, fixtures, molds, and dies
BN	L$_C$(100)	Kelang Valley	1988	Codified instructions	18	0.15	Molds, dies, jigs, and fixtures
BO	L$_C$(100)	Kelang Valley	1988	Codified instructions	14	0.36	Jigs, fixtures, molds, and dies
BP	L$_C$(100)	Kelang Valley	1984	Codified instructions, QCCs	32	0.56	Simple parts fabrication, molds, dies, jigs, and fixtures
BQ	L$_C$(100)	Kelang Valley	1975	TQM, QCC	69	2.5	Parts fabrication, jigs, fixtures, molds, and dies

Source: Author's interviews, 1993.

Note: Abbreviations used under "Ownership" are as follows: L$_C$ = Local Chinese; L$_I$ = Local Indian. Abbreviations for process techniques are as follows: JIT = just in time; QCC = quality control circle; SPC = statistical process control; TMS = time motion study; TPM = total preventative maintenance; TQM = total quality maintenance. Fictitious firm names were used to protect confidentiality.

a primary economy, Malaysia also offered few internally generated productive capacities. The country lacked a dynamic industrial policy to facilitate the creation and management of institutions to support industrial deepening and widening (see Rasiah 1997). Manpower development institutions were relatively weak. The labor force was composed primarily of school leavers—though relatively high literacy rates and fluency in English made these workers easily trainable.

The pattern of work organization showed some signs of changing in 1975, when the single Japanese microelectronics firm in the sample began introducing just in time,(JIT) principles and achieving substantial application of these methods by 1978. Employing minimum stock turnaround (MST) techniques and small group activities, this firm was using both flexible and Taylorist work organizations in the 1970s and early 1980s. But it was in the 1980s that changes from the old systems to flexible production systems occurred throughout the industry as a consequence of competition, volatility of demand, shortened product cycles, and falling prices. During 1980–84, the majority of semiconductor firms, owned by American capital, began to introduce flexible production systems, superimposing cellular manufacturing using quick changeovers and multiproduct lines, total preventative maintenance (TPM), and statistical process control (SPC) onto state-of-the-art human resource techniques such as total quality management (TQM), quality control circles (QCCs), small group activities, and JIT (Rasiah 1987; 1994). In 1984, Intel was the first non-Japanese semiconductor firm to introduce a JIT system. Pressed by the U.S. headquarters to cut costs as the mid-1980s cyclical crisis struck the industry and prices crashed, Intel's Penang facilities used JIT to double productive capability after cutting its workforce from four thousand to two thousand. By the mid- to late 1980s, all firms irrespective of ownership had begun introducing flexible production techniques and integrating innovative capacity with execution throughout the division of labor, thereby reducing hierarchies and making them interlock in the process (table 6.2). The sharp fall in labor reserves from the late 1980s left even industrial and consumer electronics firms introducing flexible production strategies (Rasiah 1995; 1996a). Downsizing occurred again in 1995, when a glut in the electronics market depressed demand.

The (Uneven) Growth of Subcontracting

The absorption of flexible production techniques from the 1980s and the shortening of product cycles intensified process/layout reorganizations and machinery modifications in the microelectronics TNCs. These modifications were aided by increasing automation, which displaced some of the more mundane tasks and those requiring dexterity. The result was to allow workers to manage numerous machines and to handle tasks such as simple machinery repair, quality inspection, and problem solving. This not only made workers more flexible, it also encouraged a horizontal integration of the technical division of work in some of the electronics firms (Rasiah 1994). However, these changes were so rapid that importing new machinery whenever production concepts or design layouts changed became too costly. *It made more sense to improve and modify equipment than to replace it.* This in turn raised demand for proximate machine tooling and prompted all the microelectronics TNCs to establish machinery support divisions to coordinate such service activities.

However, this need for equipment modification resulted in the growth not of in-house machine tooling capacity but of subcontracting to local machine tool firms. The microelectronics transnationals were reluctant to expand in-house machinery repair capacities due to the dissimilar product lines involved. But local machining firms were not capable of providing high precision tooling when the TNCs first needed it in 1980 (Rajah 1994).

How then do we explain this expansion of outsourcing? Three factors were key: the difficulties of controlling labor in different product lines within each TNC; the minimum scale efficiency required to amortize investments in expensive computer numerical controlled (CNC) machines; and the volatility of demand (Rasiah 1994; 1998). Moreover, foreign independent machine tool firms were hesitant to relocate production facilities to Malaysia, despite some encouragement by the microelectronics TNCs. The result was a significant growth in the potential for outsourcing of precision tooling to local firms. But while latent demand grew strongly in all locations of microelectronics firms, the local share of machinery outsourcing and related services has tended to show a distinct variance between Penang and the Kelang Valley. Local microelectronics suppliers in the two regions also demonstrate substantial differences in productive capability.

Two distinct patterns of supplier networks have emerged in Penang and the Kelang Valley. In total, the eight TNCs reported machine tool sourcing from twenty-five firms in Penang and nine firms from the Kelang Valley. And as shown in table 6.2, Penang's machine tool firms are not only greater in numbers, they also show a wider and more sophisticated range of products. The technological depth of Penang's supplier firms, as measured by precision and human capital indices, is clearly superior to the Kelang Valley's supplier firms (table 6.2). Also, all Penang supplier firms interviewed regarded microelectronics transnationals as key to their development. Substantial inflows of technology involving American microelectronics firms, and gradual two-way interfacing with software and hardware, has helped local firms upgrade technological capabilities. Only BO among the four Kelang Valley supplier firms considered microelectronics transnationals to be an important agent for its growth.

The technology trajectory of local machine tool firms in Malaysia has involved several stages of development, ranging from the production of simple crude parts that are subsequently fabricated into final components by other firms, to original design (ODM) and original brand manufacturing (OBM).[3] None of the local machine tool firms studied here have participated in ODM and OBM, though six firms—all in Penang—reported possessing designing capabilities. The prime cutting-edge machinery used in production is still imported by the microelectronics firms in the sample, as none of the local supplier firms have managed to move up to ODM and OBM activities. Nevertheless, within the limited range of machinery and component markets entered by local firms, suppliers in Penang tend to enjoy production capabilities superior to supplier firms in the Kelang Valley. Penang firms (using the proxies: share of precision production and testing machinery indices, engineer and technician/machinist indices, and level of precision tolerance) tend to show higher productive capabilities.

Penang and Kelang Valley machine tool firms also demonstrate considerable differences in their technological relationships with microelectronics transnationals. Machine tool firms in both Penang and the Kelang Valley remained backward in the 1970s. From simple fabrication, several of Penang's local machine tool firms have gradually moved up the technology trajectory, while those of the Kelang Valley have generally remained entrenched in stage one and two activities. Technological deepening in the former has involved substantial technology transfer from microelectronics transnationals. In addition to providing upfront capital and guaranteed markets, microelectronics firms have also developed prototypes and subcontracted them out to local machine tool firms. Process and product know-how was transferred and the development of local firms was monitored by the principal buyers. As the local firms participated actively in fulfilling the quantitative and qualitative needs of the microelectronics transnationals, the latter's self-expansion efforts led to swift technological deepening in the former (Rasiah 1994). As the local firms passed through the learning cycle, the relationships changed to involve increasing in-house participation in technology development. BF, BI, BK, and BM subsequently managed to gain sufficient synergies to participate actively in the development of their own capabilities. Increased in-house development capabilities enabled BF and BK to attain relative freedom from their patron transnationals in the 1990s. Local machine tool firms hardly enjoyed similar technology transfer from microelectronics transnationals in the Kelang Valley, despite the dominance of American ownership. Relying strongly on in-house technology development from the 1970s through the 1990s, machine tool firms in the Kelang Valley failed to achieve similar levels of technological deepening.

The lack of consequent development in supplier networks has resulted in increased in-house workshop machine tool production in Kelang Valley microelectronics transnationals. However, some microelectronics transnationals have also begun purchasing machinery from Penang's machine tool firms.[4] The growing reputation of Penang firms has led microelectronics firms in the Kelang Valley to woo for establishing subsidiary operations in the Kelang Valley. As a result, BK, BF, and BI reported considering starting subsidiary machine tool operations in the Kelang Valley.[5]

Overall, backward sourcing by microelectronics transnationals in Malaysia has been very limited, due largely to the fact that wafers are overwhelmingly imported. The share of local production inputs in microelectronics transnationals in

1993 ranged from 0.5 percent in AC to 7.5 percent in AE.[6] Although the pecuniary share of machine tool inputs sourced by most microelectronics firms has been relatively small—ranging from 2.5 percent by AC to 33.7 percent by AE in 1993—it has risen steadily in Penang firms. The average share over the period 1988 to 1993 ranged from 1.2 percent in AC to 18.5 percent in AE.[7] When AE is excluded, the next best figures come from AG, which sourced 8.3 percent of its machine tools from local firms on average over the same period. As noted earlier, local machine tool firms have yet to break into ODM and OBM activities. Overall sales of local machine tool firms linked to microelectronics transnationals have, however, expanded considerably. From virtually scratch operations at inception, local machine tool firms' sales rose to almost eighty million ringgits in 1993. BF recorded gross sales of RM20 million in 1993 (table 6.2). Here again, Penang firms show a superior performance record compared to Kelang Valley firms. All five firms that achieved gross sales figures of at least RM10 million in 1993 are located in Penang.

More effective institutional coordination has also helped Penang LMFs to enjoy greater resilience than Kelang Valley firms during times of crisis. The downswing in the global electronics market in 1995–1998 put pressure on the suppliers. The appreciation of the ringgit from 1994 caused many more problems for the machine tool firms in Penang than for those in the Kelang Valley. Imports became cheaper and exports more expensive as Penang firms competed with foreign suppliers. The minor fabrications undertaken by Kelang Valley firms made them less exposed to external competition. The better government-business coordination mechanisms in Penang led to efforts by the state to assist mature Penang firms in upgrading into higher value-added activities and relocating subsidiaries in China, the Philippines, and Indonesia. BF started production operations in China and the Philippines and also considered locating in Thailand. BM started production operations in Indonesia. Rising production costs (including skilled labor), tariffs, and the need for proximity to purchasers were suggested as causes of these firms' internationalization of production. Both firms reported having enjoyed tremendous support from the local Penang government in negotiating their investments abroad.

Also, the financial crisis that struck in 1997 caused serious liquidity problems for the LMFs, as borrowing became extremely difficult until 1999. Machine tool firms in the Kelang Valley faced considerable problems. The contraction of demand resulting from a slowdown in the electronics industry and a highly conservative credit strategy in which equities dominate asset ownership helped Kelang Valley firms avoid a serious crash. Several Penang LMFs had even lower equity/asset ratios due to their easier access to loans. The falling demand in 1995–1998 and the liquidity crisis of 1997–1998 affected their operations considerably, forcing some smaller LMFs to fold. The bigger LMFs enjoying greater access to government-business coordination networks managed to sustain their access to loans despite the high interest rates faced in 1997–1998.

Similarities in Penang and Kelang Valley

Whatever the classifications used, it can be seen that Penang's local machine tool suppliers have generally experienced higher growth and technological deepening than their counterparts in the Kelang Valley. Yet the regions exhibit a number of similarities that would seem to preclude such differences. First, the microelectronics TNCs in both regions are almost completely American owned. And although the initiator of flexible production in Malaysia was a Japanese firm (in 1975) operating in Penang, the exclusion of local personnel from key decision making discouraged the firm from subcontracting to local machine tool firms or developing such firms on its own. Thus, if anything, the initiation of flexible production by a Japanese firm emphasizing in-house capacity might be seen as an obstacle to the growth of local subcontracting in Penang.

Second, the technical level of local machine tool firms in both regions was similarly low when the TNCs began to exhibit interest in subcontracting. Local firms were mainly backyard workshops engaged in simple fabrication and foundry work, with little experience in precision engineering and no automated machinery development capacity (Rasiah 1998). Third, exchange-rate fluctuations, which would seem to have favored local machine tool sourcing after 1985, applied to both regions. And, as shown elsewhere, currency fluctuations accompanied such developments rather than stimulating them (Rajah 1994). Fourth, since ethnic Chinese (as opposed to ethnic Malays—*Bumiputera)* dominated the positions of TNC purchasing agents and the ownership of the LMFs in both regions, the potential for ethnic-based networking was largely the same in Penang and the Kelang Valley.

Fourth, the microelectronics industry in both regions operated under similar sets of national development incentives. In response to slow manufacturing growth, rising unemployment, and ethnic riots in the late 1960s, the federal government adopted a number of measures to attract employment- and export-generating investment. These included the relaxation of the ethnic objectives of the New Economic Policy in regard to equity and employment, the establishment of industrial estates (some eighty-six between 1962 and 1984), and the creation of free-trade or export-processing zones. These measures triggered an influx of transnational electronics firms into Malaysia. And although Penang became an especially attractive site for electronics investment, table 6.1 shows that microelectronics TNCs also moved into the Kelang Valley.

Finally, federal government incentives were not initially conducive to the growth of local subcontracting in either region. Located in FTZs, semiconductor firms could obtain tariff exempt imports as long as the items came from outside the principal customs area. And until 1986, local firms themselves faced tariffs on imports, including specialty steel, and had no incentives to export (Rasiah 1998).

The federal government eventually launched a number of programs to encourage local sourcing. These include the Subcontract Exchange Program (SEP) and the Vendor Development Program (VDP), launched in 1992 and specially designed to promote subcontracting linkages for *Bumiputera* firms in the electric/electronics industry. The SEP has had only modest success in stimulating subcontract relations between local firms and microelectronics transnationals, even after the enactment of the 30 percent local sourcing condition in 1991 for firms applying to enjoy financial incentives (Malaysia 1994: 260). The VDP involved TNCs as "anchor" companies supporting small and medium firms with *Bumiputera* participation in equity of 70 percent and employment of 55 percent. Government support included subsidized loans and technical assistance offered through the Industrial Technical Assistance Fund (ITAF) and subsidized loans through a *Bumiputera* venture trust, Permodalan Usahawan Nasional (PUNB). Participation in this program within the electronics industry has so far largely involved consumer and industrial electronics firms. Few of them, however, have established links with microelectronics firms. Sapura and Sharp were the initial anchor firms. This program has helped create *Bumiputera* controlled suppliers from scratch within a short time in the electronics industry. The government planned to create eighty new vendors over the sixth and seventh Malaysia plans (Vijaya Letchumy 1993).

EXPLAINING VARIATION IN SUBCONTRACTING AND SUPPLIER BASES: SUPPORT INSTITUTIONS

Penang's ability to make use of TNC shifts to develop proximate machine tool sourcing owes much to the provision of collective goods and services by the Penang state government and related institutions, especially the Penang Development Corporation (PDC) and the Penang Skills Development Center (PSDC). It should be emphasized, however, that these institutions did not themselves strengthen local machine tool firms. Rather they acted as catalysts, creating an environment conducive to the upgrading of local firms by TNCs, both individually and collectively. Beginning in the 1970s, the PDC, led by Penang's chief minister, Dr. Lim Chong Eu, spearheaded a successful effort to attract microelectronics TNCs. The PDC went beyond Malaysia's generous investment incentives for export-oriented firms. It promoted the largest number of free-trade zones among the Malaysian states. It expanded the state's infrastructural attractions by offering subsidized land, water, and electricity. It promised to ensure coordination of customs regulations and power supplies. And it did so through an aggressive, personal campaign in which PDC officials, led by the chief minister, visited the heads of firms such as Intel, NS, and Advanced Micro Devices. Four managing directors of American semiconductor firms reported that:

> Penang's chief minister was among the earliest and most active political leader from Southeast Asia to knock on our doors. . . . He gave us a certain assurance that got our commitment to relocate here.[8]

Overall, the PDC worked closely with TNCs to stimulate export-oriented processing, assembly, and testing activities. The export-oriented thrust was so successful that Penang was removed from the list of underdeveloped states in 1974.

The establishment of TNCs in turn provided some impetus to the growth of local machine tool firms. For example, National Semiconductor opened a machine tool facility in the 1970s which acted as a prime training ground for cutting-edge hardware machine tool activities. Trainees from this facility eventually became founders of several local firms (BI, BG, and BJ). As we shall see, however, significant spin-offs did not occur without some outside help (Micro Machining was the exception). During the 1970s, most semiconductor firms sourced their machine tool supplies from abroad. Only minor fabrication and repair work was done in-house. Intel initially opened a separate machining firm, Intel Automation, but subsequently closed this facility as local suppliers grew.

Rapid growth resulted from the supportive intermediary role of the Penang state government. Working closely with the Chinese Chamber of Commerce, the PDC actively promoted spin-off relationships between local businessmen and transnationals. This partly involved simple exhortations: the chief minister himself increasingly advised the PDC to promote local sourcing of components by transnationals.[9] These exhortations were supplemented by early and active efforts at matchmaking: in the mid-1970s, the state government began inviting local managing directors to meet with their counterparts from TNCs located in Penang's FTZs. This resulted in the first links between Advanced Micro Devices (AMD) and Eng Hardware, a small workshop, founded by a Chinese traditional physician, that was to become one of Penang's most successful machine tool firms (Rasiah 1998).

These early efforts were backed up by coordination of services and provision of information critical to more extensive matchmaking. All eight semiconductor firms in Penang in 1986—irrespective of ownership—considered the state government as having been proactive in stimulating machine tool spin-offs (Rasiah 1987). Transnationals' reliance on the PDC's effectiveness in coordinating security, providing infrastructural support, and quelling labor unrest enabled the latter to promote local sourcing actively. The PDC also compiled a list of local suppliers in the metal, plastics, and packaging industries from 1985; the list, which has been updated annually since, shows detailed information on productive capacities of local firms. In addition, the PDC actively organized meetings, vendor/buyer fairs, visits, and promotions to match and strengthen links between foreign transnationals and local firms. In at least a few cases between 1989 and 1993, the PDC, with support from Penang's chief minister, helped three of Penang's local machine tool firms obtain important tax benefits. Finally, the PDC encouraged the growth of industry-wide bodies—business councils—with which it could negotiate and exchange information. Given serious information asymmetry problems associated with backward small and medium firms, PDC's role here has been critical in effecting linkage coordination.

The state government also played a key role in addressing labor market imperfections. Not surprisingly, poaching and skills shortages became serious problems with the expansion of subcontracting in the 1980s. PDC's strategy was twofold. First, it helped organize successful efforts to reduce poaching of skilled employees within the semiconductor and supporting industries. The importance of these industry-specific efforts is reflected in the fact that, while poaching has been reduced in these sectors, it has continued to be a problem in other Penang industries, such as garments. Second, the PDC encouraged the growth of industry-wide training by coordinating the formation of the PSDC in 1989. This coordination involved providing financial incentives: the PDC negotiated with the federal government to obtain double tax deduction for corporate contributions to PSDC training programs. It also involved encouraging the organization of both foreign and local firms. The PSDC has thus been driven by public-private sector collaboration in which foreign and local firms play central roles in curriculum design; the PSDC is now a major training ground for local machine tool firms in the development of capacities in areas such as time measurement, precision engineering, and JIT (Rasiah 1994; 1998). In its first year of operation, almost nine thousand people went through its courses, and by the mid 1990s, the PSDC had fifty-one participating companies (Churchill 1995).

Penang state support also helped to encourage the interfirm linkages necessary to reduce the risks incurred by local machine tool firms venturing into new precision tooling and machinery operations. The pioneering case of Intel and Eng Hardware merits note here. When Intel decided to expand its sourcing to local firms, no local firms had the confidence or resources to diversify from simple jigs, fixtures, molds, and dies into precision tooling. With the backing of the PDC, however, Intel was able to convince Eng Hardware to upgrade its operations. Intel provided critical up-front capital, prototypes, and engineering support (Rasiah 1998). In essence, PDC support provided both parties with the assurance necessary to enter into the relationship.

This did not lead to a monopolistic position for Eng. Its efforts with Eng having been successful, Intel supported other local firms as well. In fact, the individual most responsible for initial supplier development, Intel managing director Lai Pin Yong, used Intel staff cooperative funds to establish local firms, e.g., Shinca, Unico, Shintel, and Samatech. Initially, at least, all of these firms were led by former Intel employees. The result was to cut supply bottlenecks and foster competition among prospective suppliers.

Finally, the government supported collective efforts to facilitate the supply of at least one important input. As noted above, high tariffs impeded the capacity of local firms such as Eng to obtain specialty steel. To address this problem, several firms organized a steel trading company through which to obtain large quantities of specialty steel from abroad at significantly lower cost than if each firm purchased separately. The trading company subsequently established a joint venture in 1988 to perform some upstream activities, before selling the imported steel to machine tool firms.[10]

To sum up, something akin to an agglomeration economy or cluster emerged in Penang's semiconductor production during the 1980s. Such economies, if successful, generate what Schmitz has termed "collective efficiency," i.e., "the competitive advantage derived from both external economies and joint action" (Schmitz 1997: 14; see also Scott 1995; Oakley 1985; Baum and Haveman 1997).[11]

We can identify several benefits of external economies in the context of Penang. First, vertical (subcontracting) and horizontal linkages among firms have reduced the costs of knowledge diffusion, especially tacit, noncodified knowledge critical for technological growth of local firms. Second, clustering has resulted in several kinds of "depot effects": the sharing of physical infrastructure and support for the emergence of a specialized local supplier of at least one intermediate input—steel—and stimulation of a pool of specialized skills. Finally, initial achievements of both TNCs and local machine tool firms have shown the potential for success, implicitly reduced risks of investment, and therefore stimulated follow-the-leader behavior, especially on the part of the local firms. Put somewhat differently, initial investments led to informational externalities regarding the feasibility of production in the area (Baum and Haveman 1997: 311). All of these factors have reduced entry barriers to new firms and thus encouraged competition.

More deliberate cooperation—joint action—has also enhanced the competitive potential of the industry's firms in several ways. Through public support for private-sector collective action, the PSDC has been an important source of training and skilled personnel. Government matchmaking support was also an important, albeit indirect, factor in reducing Intel's risks in supporting local machine firms and in reducing the latters' risks in investing in the assets required for more precision tooling. The result was to increase the level of trust and to reduce the need for vertical integration. Indeed, contrary to Williamson's (1985) argument that trust only emerges as a second-best alternative to undeveloped market institutions, the Penang experience suggests that trust can be a mechanism of governance capable of ensuring more effective coordination of production than ordinary arms-length markets. Lastly, publicly supported industry discussions constituted fora for collective action to reduce the kinds of short-term, predatory labor market practices, i.e., poaching, that would undermine the industry's long-term viability.

This does not, however, occur in the Kelang Valley. Although that area's small- and medium-scale firms have had the same long entrepreneurial experience and potential linkage development effects as their Penang counterparts, they have enjoyed little state support. This has left them facing severe market failure problems. Not only are microelectronics transnationals badly positioned to identify small- and medium-scale firms' potential capabilities, as this would require detailed scrutiny and monitoring, but the TNCs themselves have received little encouragement to do so. Hence, both microelectronics transnationals and local machine tool firms have been reluctant to engage actively in upgrading the technological capabilities of the latter. Local machine tool firms not only face financial problems—including accessing subsidized loans and technical assistance from the credit guarantee schemes and the ITAF—but they are also insufficiently prominent to attract the attention of potential transnational clients. Indeed, interviews show that the list of small- and medium-scale firms promoted by the government includes relatively few machine tool firms operating in the Kelang Valley. Active state promotion has taken place in institutes such as the *Bumiputera* venture trust PUNB, but this has involved stringent ethnic-based conditions that exclude ethnic-Chinese-owned machine tool firms.

This lack of political support has restricted the establishment and strengthening of sourcing relationships between microelectronics transnationals and local machine tool firms. The intermediary coordination role played by the PDC in Penang has been missing in the Kelang Valley and its state (Selangor). Hence the Selangor Skills Development Center (subsequently renamed Selangor Human Resource Development Center), which was modeled after PSDC, has yet to attract participation of local firms in training. Absent state efforts through socialization of risks and other support services, microelectronics transnationals in the Kelang Valley reported a lack of motivation to develop local machine tool capabilities. Unlike in Penang, where a proactive state leadership has played a critical role in stimulating links between local firms and microelectronics transnationals, state leadership in the Kelang Valley has generally avoided such a role. As the managing director of AA reported in 1995,

> We are for greater local sourcing as that would raise our productive flexibility and lower costs. Suppliers here are not in the same class as those in Penang. They do not perform high precision engineering. In fact, we have been acquiring some precision tools from Penang's local machine tool firms. . . . Penang's success in creating a fairly mature local supplier base has been possible because of its local state's visionary and proactive role. The state leadership has worked closely, both formally and informally, with multinationals in Penang on many areas for mutual benefit. We do not enjoy such an experience here in Selangor and Kuala Lumpur. Our official contacts with government bodies have always been with MIDA [Malaysian Industrial Development Authority] and MITI [Ministry of International Trade and Industry]. These two bodies only encourage local sourcing through formal investment guidelines but do not actively participate in building relationships.

EXPLAINING VARIATION IN SUBCONTRACTING AND SUPPLIER BASES: SOCIAL AND POLITICAL FACTORS

To explain this intranational contrast in institutional support for supplier linkage and development, we must acknowledge the potential benefits of ethnic networks. But networks are not productively activated outside of enabling factors in the broader political environment. A fuller explanation must also acknowledge the roles of ethno-class alignments, developmental preferences or objectives on the part of state/political elites, and party alignments providing state elites with some degree of leverage vis-à-vis national elites.

Ethnic Networks

The growth of Penang's microelectronics industry owes much to relations among local ethnic Chinese based on school ties, friendships, and community organizations. Within the private sector, Lai Pin Yong, Intel's pioneering local managing director, was part of a (Chung Ling) high-school-based "old boys' network." Lai's support was important in the establishment and expansion of firms by several members of this group, including the founder of Eng Hardware. Ethnic Chinese purchasing officers in the TNCs also played important roles in fostering the growth of local firms, in some cases run by friends and relatives, to satisfy the need for cheaper suppliers, when even smaller and infrequent orders were involved. Some of these purchasing officers, as well as some engineers, actually started their own supplier firms on the basis of their strong contacts with TNC clients (Metfab, Prodelcon, and Rapid Engineering were established by engineers from Micro-Component Technologies). This network also linked the public and private sectors. The founders of some of the earliest successful local machine tool firms had been friends with the Penang chief minister prior to the industry's growth.[12] Finally, all of these individuals were active within the Chinese Chamber of Commerce, an organization that worked with PDC officials to promote local subcontractors.

But ethnic Chinese networks are not limited to Penang. TNC purchasing agents in the Kelang Valley were ethnic Chinese, as were owners of Kelang Valley machine firms. And during the 1970s, intra- (Chinese) ethnic networking throughout the country was strengthened by Chinese concern over federal efforts to raise *Bumiputera* participation in the economy (Khong 1991). Further, as noted in this volume's introduction, networks, ethnic or otherwise, can often end up as incestuous, closed distributional arrangements characterized more by lock-in than by market-oriented growth. The challenge then is to explain why the networks in Penang constituted a relatively effective spin-off mechanism. Put differently, why did the network in Penang become stronger and efficiency-oriented?

Ethno-Class Politics and State-Federal Relations

As is evident from the preceding discussion, active support by the Penang chief minister and PDC officials played a critical role in promoting ethnic-based linkages between TNC officials and LMFs. This support reflected an ethnic convergence between public and private sectors in Penang, a convergence that has been reinforced by the Penang state's political sensitivity to the needs of small and medium-sized firms. This contrasts with an ethnic divergence and general lack of political support for small and medium-sized firms (SMEs) in the Kelang Valley. Explaining this variation requires addressing, first, ethno-class alignments at the national level and, next, the coalitional bases, leverage, and developmental objectives of elites at the two state levels in Penang and the Kelang Valley (Selangor state).

Class tensions in Malaysia have exhibited strong ethnic undertones. While Malaysia's ruling party, UMNO—the United Malays National Organization—has enjoyed political dominance they had little control of the economy in the 1960s (Cham 1979; Jomo 1986; Hua 1983). The persistence of high poverty levels among *Bumiputeras*, Chinese control of the local economy, and growing interethnic inequalities;[13] the relative failure of state trusts to raise the living standards of the *Bumiputeras;* and frustrations among emerging *Bumiputera* entrepreneurs surrounding their inability to establish a hold on the economy culminated in bloodshed on May 13, 1969. The New Economic Policy (NEP), launched in 1971, was predicated upon targets for ethnic-based poverty alleviation and economic restructuring (Malaysia 1971; 1976). Government policy has subsequently been designed not only to stimulate growth, but also to achieve restructuring—particularly to improve the economic status of *Bumiputeras*.[14]

But since Malays constitute roughly 60 percent of the population (the Chinese constitute some 30 percent and Indians and others the rest), UMNO has not been able to govern the country on its own. It has ruled as a first among equals in coalitions with other, elite, ethnic-based parties: the Malaysian Chinese Association and the Malaysian Indian Congress. Smaller parties in the ruling coalition are also largely ethnic based. Political support drawn along ethnic lines has enabled the UMNO-led Alliance and National Front coalitions to rule the country since independence in 1957. This alliance involves ethnic cooperation among the upper class throughout the country—*Bumiputera* and Chinese political and business elites. SMEs, most of which are owned by ethnic Chinese, did not figure prominently in the coalitional base of any of these groups. This highlights an ethno-class divergence between the local firms with the greatest potential for successful subcontracting and the ruling political coalition.

This national structure of politics is effectively replicated in the Kelang Valley, but not in Penang. This difference has resulted in quite different consequences for local machine tool firms. The Kelang Valley was a major center for colonial economic activities. The area's importance rose following independence: one of its cities, Kuala Lumpur, remained the administrative and commercial capital of Malaysia; its principal port, Port Klang, replaced Penang as Malaysia's chief port; and Subang and, after 1998, Sepang, have each been the site of Malaysia's biggest international airport. In addition, like the federal ministries, Malaysia's prime industrial promotion agency, the Malaysian Industrial Development Authority (MIDA), and other industrial parastatals are also mainly located in the Kelang Valley. Indeed, the federal state has generally been the de facto economic governance agent in the Kelang Valley. The synergies associated with good infrastructure and federal administrative and commercial centers obviously attracted many transnationals.

But this concentration of national institutions in Selangor has also meant that state officials have neither the interest in promoting local ethnic Chinese machine tool firms nor the instruments or leverage to do so. *Bumiputera*-dominated UMNO has ruled Selangor since Malaysia's independence, with the ethnic-Chinese-dominated *Democratic Action Party* relegated to a minority role. Staffed primarily by *Bumiputera* employees, the Selangor Economic Development Corporation (SEDC) has hardly enjoyed ethnic-based networking potential with ethnic Chinese purchasing officers in the TNCs. Given the proximity of the country's capital, transnationals generally coordinated their security, infrastructural support, and labor relations operations with federal institutions. The local state institutions have thus generally been bypassed by the microelectronics transnationals. The SEDC's role has been limited to infrastructure development and the leasing of industrial land. In fact, its function stops once the firms have located in their new premises. It has played no formal role in the promotion of local sourcing. Without pressure to promote LMFs or the institutional leverage to do so, state officials have not attempted to make use of existing ethnic Chinese networks for developmental purposes.

As noted earlier, nationally coordinated programs to stimulate subcontracting have experienced only modest success in Selangor state. With a few exceptions, the Chinese business community involved in metal, tooling, foundry, rubber, and plastic works enjoyed little support in accessing electronics transnationals.[15] Federal financial incentives associated with local sourcing also failed to generate local sourcing levels comparable to those in Penang.

In sum, ethnic divergence in the Kelang Valley—between the small and medium business community and the UMNO-dominated political leadership both at the state and federal levels—blocked political support for the ethnic-Chinese-controlled small- and medium-scale businesses.

Penang, in contrast, is characterized by ethno-class convergence between local machine tool firms and the state's political leadership. At first glance, this would seem to result simply from the fact that Penang is Malaysia's only state with a majority (60 percent) ethnic Chinese population. But simple demographics does not explain the class basis of this coalition, i.e., why SMEs, as opposed to big business, find strong supporters among state officials. Nor does it explain the significant leverage Penang state officials have exhibited in their industrial promotion efforts. After all, although Malaysia is officially a federal system with thirteen states, the latter do not exercise much control over their own finances. In 1991, for example, Penang was allowed to keep just 1 percent of the $397 million in revenues it raised (Churchill 1995: 65). And finally, demographics does not explain how and why state support for local machine tool firms in Penang has generally led to efficiency rather than simple unproductive rent seeking.

The importance of ethnic Chinese SMEs to Penang's political leadership is rooted in the needs and objectives of Gerakan, a largely Chinese political party that has governed the state since 1969. Gerakan's rise is rooted in Penang's postindependence difficulties. After Singapore, Penang's Georgetown had been the second most important trading port in Malaya during British colonialism. With a free port status, the island had enjoyed substantial economic activity for 181 years. Independence and the subsequent shift in trade to the Kelang Valley led to its decline. Munro (1964: 132) described the island as being "besieged by depression, spiraling inflation, labor unrest and political instability." Penang's future looked even bleaker following the revocation of its free port status.

With 60 percent of Penang's population (including mainland Province Wellesley) being Chinese, the launching of the NEP and the ICA was seen as a major brake on Penang's progress. As the NEP clearly represented an effort to eradicate poverty and restructure the economy along ethnic lines, Gerakan won the state elections in 1969 under opposition banners. It joined the ruling coalition in the early 1970s. Faced with a deplorable socioeconomic situation in which the unemployment rate in the state had reached 15.2 percent (PDC 1971)—nearly twice the national rate of 8.0 percent in 1970 (Malaysia 1971)—and the impending national drive to support the development of *Bumiputeras,* the Gerakan-led state government aggressively promoted economic growth by looking to foreign capital as the major platform to generate investment and jobs for its predominantly Chinese electorate. PDC was formed to spearhead this task. And the effort was facilitated by the federal government's removal of local ownership conditions on export-oriented investments. By 1984, Penang had the biggest number of FTZs among the Malaysian states, viz. Bayan Lepas, Prai, Prai Wharf, and Pulau Jerejak (Kamal and Young 1985).

Local state support for transnationals, however, led opposition political parties and nongovernmental organizations to criticize the "sustainability" of such developments. Also, the Gerakan government had to convince its supporters among small- and medium-scale businessmen that transnational expansion would generate spin-offs for local firms. Hence, when the export processing activities remained as offshore enclaves and real wages in the zones declined in the 1970s (see Rasiah 1996a), the local state leadership began to face serious pressures.

To engage local businesses in the new economy, the state leadership began to encourage strongly the formation of consultation committees to assist their development. Hence, when developments in microelectronics transnationals stimulated proximate machine tool sourcing as discussed earlier, the channels for matching local SMEs with them had already emerged. As microelectronics activities expanded, Penang began to experience severe labor shortages. In response, the PDC undertook measures to move the industry from low-wage assembly to more skill-intensive production.[16] The PSDC, initially funded by twenty-six foreign producers, was key to this effort.

In retrospect, the initiatives undertaken by Penang state officials to attract TNCs and link them to locally based, higher value-added production are similar to Singapore's strategy (see Poh-Kam Wong's chapter, this volume). This resemblance is perhaps not surprising given that both Singapore and Penang lack natural resources and are Chinese-dominated areas in a broader Malay region. But Singapore is a sovereign state and thus able to offer a wide range of investment incentives. Penang's leadership, on the other hand, operates within a federal system dominated by UMNO and Kuala Lumpur.

How then do we account for PDC's ability to undertake what was a relatively independent industrial policy? Part of the explanation no doubt lies with the fact that while the federal government is concerned primarily with *Bumiputera* promotion, it is also sensitive to the country's need for continued economic dynamism. Penang's hand was undoubtedly strengthened by its generation of exports and attraction of foreign capital.

But equally if not more important has been Gerakan's role within the broader dynamics of Malaysian party competition. After its initial victory in Penang, Gerakan joined the national, UMNO-led Alliance coalition, despite the fact that UMNO's traditional Chinese partner is the Malaysian Chinese Association. In doing so, Gerakan helped UMNO achieve the two-thirds majority necessary to assure the passage of the NEP in Malaysia's parliament. In addition, Gerakan's strong performance helped to weaken opposition to the Alliance by the Chinese-dominated DAP, which narrowly lost the state elections in 1990. Gerakan's position as both a successful agent of growth and a buffer against stronger political opposition thus allowed the party some relative autonomy (vis-à-vis national authorities) to promote its own policies (Rasiah 1987; 1993).

Finally, it is necessary to explain the fact that the PDC's support for local subcontracting did not result in simple coddling and bailing out of inefficient machine tool firms. The question is especially important given the general tendency of ethnic networks to become closed and the fact that, in a few cases, initial supplier linkages were based less on proven supplier capacity than on personal relationships and even an exchange of "sweeteners" between local firms and TNC purchasing agents. Two factors—market pressures and hard budget constraints—seem to have limited the cost of rent seeking and the amounts of rents obtained by local firms. In the long run, the purchasing agents' own positions within the TNCs depended on the performance of local suppliers. The latter were thus exposed to constant pressure for both higher quality and lower price, in addition to receiving financial and technical support from the transnational client. The purchasing agent's leverage as a principal vis-à-vis the supplier was constrained by his position as an agent for the TNC.

Reinforcing this market pressure was the PDC's lack of capacity for or interest in bailing out inefficient firms. As noted earlier, the Penang state government lacked control over its own tax revenues. Reinforcing these hard budget constraints was the fact that Gerakan's political dominance depended on relatively broad-based support within the Chinese community. Preferential backing for one particular firm would have undermined this coalition.

CONCLUSION

This chapter has argued that variation in the capacity for flexible production, viewed through the growth of local subcontractors, reflects the interaction of external market forces with societal, institutional, and political factors at the local and national levels. In both Penang and the Kelang Valley, pressures on microelectronics TNCs for product and process customization provided a strong impetus for proximate local machine tool sourcing and the intensification of employee training both in-house and externally. Only in Penang, however, did state institutions build on existing ethnic networks to help private actors help themselves. This involved a combination of positive externalities (reduced costs of knowledge diffusion, depot effects, stimulation of specialized skills, and follow-the-leader behavior) and deliberate joint action (provision of training and skilled personnel, matchmaking, and encouraging standards of behavior with regard to poaching).

But institutions are themselves embodiments of collective action problems. Their shape and supportive capacity are thus a function of broader politics. In Malaysia, this broader politics is bound up with ethno-class politics. Ethnic congruence in Penang—particularly the small- and medium-scale business community aligned with the Gerakan party—enabled relatively strong political support and direct matching efforts linking microelectronics transnationals with local machine tool firms. This, along with the state leadership's relative autonomy from the federal government, facilitated efforts to stimulate local machine tool sourcing by microelectronics transnationals. The smooth coordinating role played by the Penang state government and the PDC has created strong cooperative relations between them and the transnationals. Hence, despite Penang's backward starting point, proactive state-level support for local firms helped tap the spin-off potential that emerged from growing flexibilization of production in electronics transnationals.

This chapter thus reinforces several points relevant to development in general and flexible production in particular. It supports the argument that flexible production is facilitated by societies characterized by dense institutional environments, in this case, ethnic networks (Hollingsworth and Boyer 1997). Trust, engendered by such environments, can be more than just a second-best alternative to formal governance mechanisms promoting arms-length transactions.

But the chapter also suggests that such institutional environments are most productive under public-private sector interactions through which information is widely diffused and industry-wide goods and services are transparently available to firms in exchange for market-conforming performance (Biddle and Milor 1997: 300–301). Such public-private linkages are in large part a function of the coalitional bases of political leaders. In the Malaysian case, we have emphasized the benefits of ethno-class congruence. But there are limits to the generalizability of Penang's particular coalitional arrangements. Taiwan, for example, has developed a highly flexible economy based on both horizontal and vertical subcontracting (Fields forthcoming). Yet Taiwan's coalitional arrangements are quite distinct from those in Penang: as noted in this volume's introduction, Taiwan's political economy has traditionally been characterized by a split between mainland-based political leadership and an indigenous, Taiwanese private sector, especially among SMEs. What links Taiwan and Penang is the common existence of dense societal networks with commercial potential, pressures on the political leadership to make efficient use of these networks, and the political leadership's relative autonomy to do so.

NOTES

Institute for Malaysian and International Studies, Universiti Kebangsaan Malaysia. The fieldwork reported in the paper was undertaken in 1993 through United Nations Conference for Trade and Development (UNCTAD) funding. Helpful comment from Rick Doner is gratefully acknowledged.

1. The assumption of this paper is that effective subcontracting with capable local suppliers enhances firm and industry performance in the presence of market volatility and rapid technological change. There is, however, no aggregate data showing that those microelectronic TNCs engaged in subcontracting performed better with regard to market share, time to market, profitability, etc. However, as noted below, the TNCs themselves acknowledge the need to introduce flexible production systems and the advantages of proximate outsourcing of tooling functions. Indeed, the greater flexibility offered by the more integrated Penang region stimulated stronger local sourcing than in the less integrated Kelang Valley region (see below).

2. The firms that did not respond claimed to have information records or to be too busy to meet datelines required. Discussion on the backward sourcing of land, building, energy, and water has been avoided, as these items are generally accessed from local aegis even in less-developed sites, and therefore do not involve the TNCs.

3. The trajectory typically involves five stages. Stage one is the fabrication of simple, crude parts which are then fabricated into final components by more developed suppliers or the microelectronics transnationals themselves. The second stage involves the manufacture of jigs, fixtures, molds, and dies with low-precision levels. Stage three is characterized by high-precision engineering of small-batch components. Stage four involves the production of small batches with high-precision requirements, the manufacture of semiautomated machinery, or both. In stage five, firms undertake large-volume precision engineering of components, small-batch fully automated machinery, or both. Firms in stage five generally possess original equipment manufacturing (OEM) capability, i.e, they enjoy the capacity to supply orders using their own production capabilities. Given the cumulative and complementary nature of these stages, firms in the higher stages in the technology trajectory also often perform the lower operations. It is only when firms pass through stage five that ODM and OBM stages emerge. But even firms enjoying OBM capacity may also perform manufacturing activities of the lower production stages.

4. For example, AC bought four automated wire bonders from BF. AA acquired six wire bonders from BK in Penang in 1990, while its subsidiary in Seremban acquired eight wire bonders from BK in 1992.

5. Interviews in 1993.

6. These figures exclude building and service expenses.

7. Among other things, the average figure takes into account large machinery purchases during major upgrading exercises.

8. Interview conducted in 1986 by the author.

9. Interviews with PDC officials conducted by the author in 1986.

10. The joint venture was between A Assab and Uddeholm (PDC 1993: 70).

11. Schmitz (1995: 536) uses the term *cluster* rather than *industrial district* because the latter presumes the development of extensive interfirm divisions of labor, whereas *cluster* connotes only a geographical and sectoral concentration of firms whose division of labor remains an empirical question.

12. Teh Ah Bah, the founder of Eng, rented Chief Minister Lim's house before expanding his operations.

13. Although foreign capital enjoyed higher control of the domestic economy (Saham 1980; Lim 1975; Rasiah 1995).

14. The Industrial Coordination Act (ICA) of 1975 imposed NEP conditions on equity and employment for manufacturing enterprises with employment size and paid-up capital exceeding twenty-five employees and RM250,000 respectively. Although these conditions were not applied to export-oriented firms, such as the microelectronics TNCs, they did apply to potential local machine tool subcontractors.

15. The local subcontract assembly operations of Carsem and Unisem are located in Ipoh, Perak.

16. PDC's involvement with the Chinese-dominated urban and industrial zones was so strong that the *Bumiputeras* through UMNO pressured the state to set up the Penang Rural Development Authority (PERDA) to protect their interests. PERDA's creation was intended to help develop *Bumiputera*-dominated rural areas and to prevent PDC's acquisition and sale of rural lands for industrial and service use. Despite the intense rivalry between PDC and PERDA, the latter has had a quiet existence. Inequalities between the two became so stark that the latter abandoned its traditional preoccupation with primary activities (mainly agriculture and fishing) to venture into manufacturing in the 1990s.

BIBLIOGRAPHY

Alt, J. E., and K. A. Chrystal. 1983. *Politic Economics.* Berkeley: University of California Press.

Baum, Joel A. C., and Heather A. Haveman. 1997. "Love Thy Neighbor? Differentiation and Agglomeration in the Manhattan Hotel Industry, 1898–1990." *Administrative Science Quarterly* 42: 304–338.

Best, M. 1990. *The New Competition.* Cambridge, Mass.: Harvard University Press.

Biddle, Jesse, and Vedat Milor. 1997. "Economic Governance in Turkey: Bureaucratic Capacity, Policy Networks, and Business Associations." In *Business and the State in Developing Countries,* edited by Sylvia Maxfield and Ben Schneider. Ithaca, N.Y.: Cornell University Press.

Cham, B. N. "Toward a Malaysian Malaysia: A Study of Political Integration." Ph.D. diss., University of Alberta.

Churchill, Paul Reyes. 1995. "Local Government Initiative in Southeast Asia: Toward a New Growth Model." *Journal of Asian Business* 11, no. 1: 40–76.

Coase, R. H. 1937. "The Nature of the Firm." *Economica* 16, no. 4: 386–405.

Doner, R. 1991. "Approaches to the Politics of Economic Growth in Southeast Asia." *Journal of Asian Studies* 50, no. 4: 818–849.

Evans, P. 1992. "The State as Problem and Solution: Predation, Embedded Autonomy, and Structural Change." In *The Politics of Economic Adjustment*, edited by S. Haggard and R. R. Kaufman. Princeton: Princeton University Press.

———. 1995. *Embedded Autonomy: States and Industrial Transformation*. Princeton: Princeton University Press.

Fields, Karl. Forthcoming. "Is Small Beautiful? The Political Economy of Taiwan's Small-Scale Industry." In *The Four Asian Tigers, Economic Development and the Global Political Economy*, edited by Eun Mee Kim. San Diego: Academic.

Haggard, S. 1990. *Pathways from the Periphery: The Politics of Growth in the Newly Industrializing Countries*. Ithaca, N.Y.: Cornell University Press.

Helpman, E., and P. R. Krugman. 1989. *Trade Policy and Market Structure*. Cambridge: MIT Press.

Hirst, P., and J. Zeitlin. 1991. "Flexible Specialization Versus Post-Fordism Theory: Evidence and Policy Implications." *Economy and Society* 20, no. 1.

Hollingsworth, J. Rober, and Robert Boyer. 1997. *Contemporary Capitalism: The Embeddedness of Institutions*. New York: Cambridge University Press.

Hua, W. Y. 1983. *Class and Communal Politics in Malaysia*. London: Zed Press.

Jomo, K. S. 1986. *A Question of Class*. Kuala Lumpur: Oxford University Press.

Kaldor, N. 1979. "Equilibrium Theory and Growth Theory." In *Economics of Human Welfare: Essays in Honour of Tobor Scitovsky*, edited by M. J. Boskin, 271–291. New York: Academic.

Kamal, S., and M. L. Young. 1985. "Penang's Industrialization: Where Do We Go From Here." Paper presented at the "Future of Penang Conference," Penang, Malaysia.

Khan, M. 1989. "Corruption, Clientelism and the Capitalist State." Ph.D. diss., Cambridge University.

Khong, H. L. 1991. "The Service Sector in Malaysia: Structure and Change." Ph.D. diss., Cambridge University.

Lim, L. Y. C. 1978. "Multinational Firms and Manufacturing for Export in Less Developed Countries: The Case of the Electronics Industry in Malaysia and Singapore." Ph.D. diss., University of Michigan, Ann Arbor.

Lucas, R. E. 1988. "On the Mechanics of Economic Development." *Journal of Monetary Economics* 22, no. 3–22.

Malaysia. 1971. *The Second Malaysia Plan 1971–1975*. Kuala Lumpur: Government Printers.

Malaysia. 1976. *The Third Malaysia Plan 1976–1980*. Kuala Lumpur: Government Printers.

Malaysia. 1994. *Ministry of International Trade and Industry Report*. Kuala Lumpur: Government Printers.

Mardon, R. 1990. "The State and Effective Control of Foreign Capital: The Case of South Korea." *World Politics* 43, no. 1: 111–138.

MIDA. 1988. *Investment in the Manufacturing Sector: Policies, Incentives and Procedures*. Kuala Lumpur: Malaysian Industrial Development Authority.

Munro. 1964. "Untitled mimeo," Penang, Malaysia.

North, D. C., and R. P. Thomas. 1970. "An Economic Theory of the Growth of the Western World." *The Economic History Review* 22, no. 1: 1–17.

Oakley, Ray. 1985. "High Technology Industries and Agglomeration Economies." In *Silicon Landscapes*, edited by Peter Hall and Ann Markusen. Allen and Unwin.

PDC. 1971. *Annual Report*. Penang, Malaysia: Penang Development Corporation.

Rasiah, R. 1987. *International Division of Labor*. Translated from Malay. Master's thesis, Universiti Sains Malaysia (Published in 1993 by Malaysian Social Science Association).

———. *Pembahagian Karja Antarabansa: Industri Semikonduktor di Pulau Pinang*. Kuala Lumpur: Malaysian Social Science Association Press.

———. 1994. "Flexible Production Systems and Local Machine Tool Subcontracting: Electronics Component Transnationals in Malaysia." *Cambridge Journal of Economics* 18, no. 3: 279–298.

———. 1995. *Foreign Capital and Industrialization in Malaysia*. New York: St Martin's.

———. 1996a. "Changing Organisation of Work in the Electronics Industry in Malaysia." *Asia Pacific Viewpoint* 37, no. 1: 21–38.

———. 1996b. "Innovations and Institutions: Moving Towards the Technological Frontier in the Electronics Industry in Malaysia." *Journal of Industry Studies* 3, no. 2: 79–102.

———. 1997. "Ethno-class Politics and Economic Development in Malaysia." In *Political Economy of Malaysia*. Sydney: Oxford University Press.

———. 1998. "From a Backyard Workshop to a Modern Machine Tool Factory: Eng Hardware." *Looking Inside the Black Box: Industry Technology Development in Malaysia*, edited by K. S. Jomo, G. Felker, and R. Rasiah. London: Routledge.

Richardson, G. B. 1960. *Information and Investment*. Oxford: Oxford University Press.

———. 1972. "The Organisation of Industry." *Economic Journal* 82, no. 3: 883–896.

Sabel, C. 1986. "Changing Models of Economic Efficiency and their Implications for Industrialization in the Third World." In *Development, Democracy and the Art of Trespassing*, edited by Alejandro C. F. Diaz et al. Notre Dame, Ind.: Notre Dame University Press.

Saham, J. 1980. *British Industrial Investment in Malaysia 1963–1971*. Kuala Lumpur: Oxford University Press.

Saxenian, Analee. 1994. *Regional Advantage: Culture and Competition in Silicon Valley and Route 128*. Cambridge, Mass.: Harvard University Press.

Schmitz, Hubert. 1995. "Collective Efficiency: Growth Path for Small-Scale Industry." *Journal of Development Studies* 31, no. 4: 529–566.

———. 1997. "Collective Efficiency and Increasing Returns." Institute of Development Studies/Working Paper #50. Sussex: IDS.

Scott, Allen J. 1995. "The Geographic Foundations of Industrial Performance." *Competition and Change* 1: 51–66.

Sengenberger, W., and F. Pyke. 1991. "Small Firm Industrial Districts and Local Economic Regeneration: Research and Policy Issues." *Labour and Society* 16, no. 1.

Vijaya Letchumy. 1993. "SMI Development Programmes." Paper presented at MITI/MIDA/FMM seminar, "Domestic Investment in the Manufacturing Sector," Penang, Malaysia.

Wilkinson, F., and J. I. You. 1992. "Competition and Cooperation: Towards an Understanding of the Industrial District." Small Business Research Centre, Working Paper No. 88. Cambridge University.

Williamson, O. E. 1985. *Markets, Hierarchies and Relational Contracting*. New York: Free Press.

7

Flexible Production, High-Tech Commodities, and Public Policies: The Hard Disk Drive Industry in Singapore

Poh-Kam Wong

Over the last three decades, the Asian newly industrialized economies (NIEs) and, more recently, the ASEAN countries and China have become the manufacturing powerhouses of the world, producing an increasing range of industrial and consumer goods that were previously manufactured only in the advanced industrialized countries. In the global electronics industry, for example, the four Asian NIEs accounted for more than one-third of the electronics imported into the United States in 1995.

The search for low-cost and abundant labor was the main impetus for multinational corporations (MNCs) from advanced countries to relocate their manufacturing operations to the Asian NIEs in the late 1960s and 1970s. Yet the redistribution process continued in the 1980s and 1990s, despite rapidly rising labor costs in these countries. Singapore, for example, has experienced a rapid escalation of wage and industrial land costs over the last two decades and today ranks among the most expensive places to manufacture products in East Asia outside Japan. Despite this, Singapore continues to attract a record amount of manufacturing direct foreign investment (DFI) from the United States, Japan, and Europe.

While rising productivity has clearly been a major factor in maintaining Singapore's overall manufacturing competitiveness in recent years, it is argued in this chapter that another significant contributing factor is the changing nature of transnational offshore production in East Asia. While low-cost production is still important, other considerations—like time to ramp up production, reliability of supply-chain networks, and responsiveness to rapid changes in product mix—are becoming increasingly critical as well. We can use the term *flexible production capability* to encompass these additional dimensions of manufacturing performance, which are of growing importance for a wide range of industrial and consumer products.

The need for flexible production capability arises from a number of global competitive trends that have been well identified in the literature, e.g., "time-based competition" in the face of a shortening product life cycle (Stalk and Hout 1990), increasing product variety to secure blanket coverage of a market (as in the case of Toshiba and the laptop computer market), niche differentiation (Hamel and Prahalad 1994), and "mass-customization" to offer a variety of customized yet low-cost products and services (Pine 1994).

Despite the general recognition of such global trends, there have been few empirical studies that examine the extent to which the East Asian NIEs have actually succeeded in providing low-cost yet flexible production capability. Do they arise naturally from their unique resource endowments, or was there a significant government or institutional role in transforming these endowments into a "supply infrastructure" that facilitates flexible production? If the latter is the case, how do these institutional mechanisms work, and can they be replicated in other developing countries? This chapter examines how one Asian NIE, Singapore, was able to establish significant flexible production capability in a global, technologically fast-changing industry, namely, the magnetic hard disk drive (HDD) industry.

From the perspective of studying flexible production capability in East Asia, HDD represents a relevant choice of industry for several reasons. As we shall show below, not only has the industry experienced significant redistribution of production to East Asia, but even more remarkably, this has taken place in the face of very rapid product technological innovation, which in turn imposes requirements for rapid manufacturing process innovations (Abernathy and Utterbeck 1978). Furthermore, the final assembly stage of the industry has exhibited a relatively high degree of geographic concentration, with close to half of the world's production located in Singapore. This high agglomeration poses interesting questions, on which we believe the flexible production perspective is able to shed significant light.

The industry is also one of the few electronics assembly industries where American firms continue to perform well against the Japanese. We will suggest that this is not a coincidence, but the result of American firms' ability to leverage the flexible production capability of East Asia. And finally, we shall argue that the Asian financial crisis, having reduced costs in the region while intensifying the need for rapid time to market combined with high yields, has only strengthened the position of East Asia in general and Singapore in particular in this industry.

In the next section of the chapter, we present a brief overview of the historical evolution of the global HDD industry, highlighting the salient features of the pattern of internationalization of its production network. The third section examines how the geographic concentration of a cluster of HDD final assembly operations in Singapore resulted in the codevelopment of a network of supporting industries there. The fourth section seeks to analyze how the creation of this local supply infrastructure in turn contributes to the flexible production capability of the final assembly process. Finally, we offer some concluding observations and policy implications in light of the Asian financial crisis.

HISTORICAL EVOLUTION OF THE GLOBAL MAGNETIC HARD DISK DRIVE INDUSTRY

The magnetic Hard Disk Drive (HDD) industry has enjoyed phenomenal growth since the emergence of the personal computer industry in the early 1980s. Today, the industry is estimated to have a global output worth US$34 billion, with about 105 million disk drives being shipped in 1996 (Disk/Trend 1997). Although the industry had its beginnings in the production of mass storage devices for mainframe computers, and later produced for minicomputers, the industry as we know it today started when the 5.25-inch "form-factor" drive was introduced for the emerging PC market in the early 1980s. Today, while large capacity drives for mainframes and large network servers are still important, the industry is driven primarily by the growth of demand for PCs, since practically every PC comes equipped with some form of hard disk drive. What constitutes large capacity has also become a moving definition: while gigabyte drives were unthinkable just five years ago, they are now minimum requirements for most PCs being shipped.

The emergence and ascendancy of the small form-factor (5.25-inch or less) HDD market heralded an architectural revolution (Abernathy and Clark 1985) that rapidly destroyed most of the existing vertically integrated large disk drive makers (Christensen 1993). Driven by increasing PC market demand for higher storage capacity in smaller volumetric space on the one hand, and dramatic technological advances on the other, the industry has witnessed very rapid product and process technological change. The storage capacity of HDD has been expanding every year, while the volumetric dimensions of disk drives continue to shrink. The industry has witnessed three generations of read/write head technologies (ferrite head to thin film head to MR head), increasing improvement in media and substrate technologies, and increasing sophistication of servo-control mechanisms and the integrated circuit chipsets that manage data storage and transfer.

These rapid product technological changes have in turn sparked significant process technological improvements. Increasing miniaturization requires increasing precision in the mechanical components and their subassembly processes. There is also an increasing need for automation in the various stages of assembly and testing.

Although the industry has attracted many new entrants over the years, rapid technological changes have resulted in several shakeouts in the industry, resulting in an increasing concentration of players over time (Christensen 1995). By 1994, the top ten firms alone commanded over 92 percent of total world production, with the top five capturing 72 percent (Disk/Trend 1996). With the acquisition of Conner by Seagate in 1996, the share of the top five in 1996 was estimated to have increased to 86 percent (IDC 1996). Despite constant new product innovations, product differentiation advantages tended to be short-lived, as these innovations were quickly imitated or leapfrogged by other competitors (see Disk/Trend, various years). Consequently, price competition has become the norm except during the very brief window at the beginning of each new product lifecycle. Indeed, intense competition has driven the unit cost of storage from over U.S.$20/Mbyte to U.S.$0.1/Mbyte over a period of less than ten years (Frank 1997).

Characterized by fierce rivalry, the HDD industry continues to stand out as one of the few electronics manufacturing industries where American firms have consistently dominated and prevailed over their Japanese competitors. While Japanese success in overtaking pioneering U.S. firms in many industries is attributed to their manufacturing process excellence and ability to achieve continuous cost and quality improvements, this has clearly not happened in HDD. Indeed, American players predominate throughout all segments of the HDD markets, from low end to high end. The overall share of American companies in the global HDD market has been estimated at 85.6 percent in 1994 (Disk/Trend 1996), and rose to 88.4 percent in 1995 (Gourevitch et al. 1997). Of the top ten players in 1994, seven were American, and only three Japanese (ranked seventh, ninth, and tenth). With the exception of Quantum, which relies on a Japanese partner (MKE) to assemble practically all of its drives, all U.S. HDD majors assemble their own drives, if mostly outside the United States. Indeed, the HDD industry has been characterized by a high degree of internationalization of production right from the start of the growth of the small form-factor drives for PCs. In 1995, it was estimated that only 5.1 percent of the final assembly output of HDD was located within the United States; 13 percent was located in Japan, 11.2 percent in Europe, and over two-thirds in Southeast Asia (Gourevitch et al. 1997).

GEOGRAPHIC CONCENTRATION OF HDD
ASSEMBLY OPERATIONS IN SINGAPORE

The first assembly operations of small form-factor HDD outside the United States were established by Tandon and Micro Peripherals in Singapore in 1981, but these were short-lived. The first significant HDD assembly operation was started one year later, in 1982, by Seagate, a year after the company was founded in the United States. Interviews with industry informants suggest that Tom Mitchell, director of operations of Seagate at that time, was primarily responsible for the decision to start component sourcing and, later, drive assembly in Singapore. Seagate chose Singapore for a number of reasons: the immediate availability of facilities and relevantly skilled labor from a floppy disk drive manufacturer that had just closed its operation in Singapore; quick and generous offers of investment incentives by the Economic Development Board (EDB), the government investment promotion agency in Singapore; the general availability of well-trained, English-speaking workers and engineers; and the presence of U.S.-

trained, experienced engineers who were able to manage the start-up of production on short notice and with little supervision.

Seagate's initiative was quickly followed by its leading U.S. competitors, such as Maxtor, Miniscribe, and CDC (known later as Imprimis), in 1983–1984. A second wave of major new HDD investments came to Singapore shortly after the 1985 recession: Micropolis, Conner, Rodime (from Scotland), and Western Digital (see table 7.1). New HDD investments in Singapore continued through the late 1980s and early 1990s in the form of aggressive expansion of facilities by most of the existing large firms, as well as new start-ups by a number of smaller players. More recently, both IBM and MKE (the manufacturing partner of Quantum) have also started HDD assembly operations in Singapore. By 1996, therefore, each of the six largest HDD companies in the world had established a significant manufacturing presence in Singapore. Besides newcomers IBM and MKE, the other four HDD majors have expanded their HDD assembly operations in Singapore over the years, even though they all have redistributed the assembly of lower-end products or lower value-added subassembly operations to other countries in the region, including Thailand (Seagate), Malaysia (Western Digital, Conner, and Maxtor), China (Conner), and the Philippines (Seagate).

The agglomeration of HDD assemblers in Singapore over the years has made Singapore the single most important location in the world for HDD assembly operations, accounting for 40–50 percent of the world's total production in recent years. Table 7.2 shows the rapid growth of HDD production in Singapore over 1987–1995. Output value grew four-fold from S$3.4 billion in 1987 to S$13.9 billion in 1995, while employment increased from 12,500 to over 31,600. In terms of exports, the number of disk drives shipped from Singapore-based HDD makers increased from 3.8 million units in 1986 to 40.3 million units in 1995, or an average compound growth rate in exported units of 30 percent per annum (table 7.3).[1]

The dominance of Singapore as a location for HDD assembly was particularly striking for U.S. companies. By 1996, with the exception of Hewlett-Packard (HP), every one of the eight largest major American HDD producers had located production facilities in Singapore. (HP has since decided to exit the HDD business.) As can be seen from table 7.4, the Singapore assembly operations of the top six U.S. HDD producers accounted for more than one-third of the worldwide employment provided by these companies. Indeed, Seagate was the largest single manufacturing employer in Singapore, with fifteen thousand employees, even before its recent acquisition of Conner. It is also interesting to note that, while some of the companies that started HDD operations have since been taken over by competitors or have exited from the business entirely (e.g., Rodime exited in 1991, Imprimis was acquired by Seagate in 1989, and Myrica from Taiwan exited in 1994), none of the surviving players that started operations in Singapore (with the exception of Syquest) have relocated entire manufacturing operations out of Singapore in favor of other locations.

Table 7.1 Hard Disk Drive Assembly Operations in Singapore

HDD Company in Singapore	Year Founded	Year Established Operations in Singapore	Current Status
Micro-Peripherals	1980	1981	Exited from Singapore in 1982
Tandon	1981	1981	Exited from Singapore in 1987
Seagate Technology	1979	1982	na
Computer Memories	1980	1982	Exited
Miniscribe	1980	1983	Acquired
Maxtor Peripherals	1982	1983	Acquired by Hyundai in 1994
Microscience	1952	1984	Exited
Micropolis	1979	1986	Acquired by Singapore Technologies in 1996
Rodime	1981	1987	Went bankrupt in 1991
Conner Peripherals	1985	1987	Acquired by Seagate in 1995
Unisys	na	1987	Exited from Singapore in 1989
Western Digital	1970	1988	na
Syquest	1982	1989	Exited from Singapore in 1996
Imprimis (CDC)	na	1979	Acquired by Seagate in 1989
PrairieTek Corp	1986	1990	Exited in 1991
Unigmatics	1980	1991	Exited
Myrica	1991	1991	Went bankrupt in 1993
Integral Peripherals	1990	1992	na
Ministor	1991	1992	na
Quantum (MKE)	1980	1994	na
JTS	1994	1994	Procurement only; no production in Singapore
IBM	na	1995	na

Source: Compiled by the author from various press reports.

Table 7.2 Growth of Singapore's Hard Disk Drive Industry (SSIC 38412), 1987–1995

Year	Number of Establishments N	Number Output S$mn	Estimated Employed L*	Value Added S$mn	Wages S$mn	Fixed Asset (K) S$mn	Sales S$mn	Total Export S$mn	Estimated Profit S$mn
1987	7	3,359	12,516	1,231	na	na	3,256	na	na
1988	8	3,920	21,532	1,326	na	na	4,890	na	na
1989	12	5,341	25,425	1,418	372	na	5,420	5,312	681
1990	13	7,355	28,335	1,842	426	na	7,381	7,055	1,013
1991	12	7,064	27,691	1,780	449	444	7,038	6,391	775
1992	15	8,267	28,695	2,238	533	468	8,285	7,693	888
1993	11	8,919	25,923	2,107	464	307	8,985	8,504	777
1994	13	11,282	30,178	2,762	574	439	11,289	10,670	1,013
1995	12	13,899	31,629	2,892	701	709	13,975	12,736	1,053

	Output	Employment	Value Add	Fixed Assets
		Growth % p.a.		
1987–1995	19.4	12.3	11.3	na
1991–1995	18.4	3.4	12.9	12.4

Source: Economic Development Board, Report on the Census for Industrial Production, various years.
*L = number employed

Table 7.3   HDD Exports from Singapore, 1986–1995

Year	#Units (mn)	Exports (S$bn)
1986	3.8	1.9
1987	6.1	3.3
1988	8.6	4.9
1989	10.1	5.5
1990	14.9	7.2
1991	14.7	7.0
1992	20.8	9.0
1993	23.2	9.5
1994	32.3	11.1
1995	40.3	13.5
	Growth % p.a.	
1986–1995	30.0	24.3

Source: Trade Development Board, 1996.

Coevolution of Supporting Industries in Singapore

The rapid growth of HDD assembly activities in Singapore has induced a correspondingly rapid development of various supporting industries. These include electronics components industries such as printed circuit board (PCB) and printed circuit board assembly (PCBA), flex-circuits, and connectors; die casting, metal stamping, precision machining, and plating of various mechanical components such as baseplates, covers and actuator arms; and various subassembly operations associated with this precision engineering work. Except for the disk media, read/write heads, magnets, spindle motors, and integrated circuits, most of the precision parts and components that go into HDDs assembled in Singapore are sourced locally or within Southeast Asia. A significant proportion of production in PCBs, PCBA, and flex-circuits occurs in Singapore as well, although there has been a trend toward outsourcing from Malaysia.

Table 7.4   Profile of the Six Largest Global HDD Assemblers in Singapore, 1995

HDD Assembler	Estimated No. Units Shipped (mn)	Total Worldwide Employment	Employment in Singapore
Conner	11.7	10,000	3,100
Maxtor	7.0	7,500	4,500
Quantum	19.3	9,000	na
Seagate	16.7	60,000	15,000
Western Digital	12.3	7,600	2,100
IBM	10.5	na	1,300
Total	77.5	94,100+	26,000+

Source: Globalization of Data Storage Industry Project, UC—San Diego.

Table 7.5 shows the estimated pattern of input sourcing for three HDD assemblers in Singapore in the early 1990s. Overall, a conservative estimate of the proportion of inputs which consist of precision engineering and PCBA services sourced from Singapore is about 25 percent, which implies total local purchasing of about S$1.4 billion in 1990, or about S$2.1 billion in 1994. These estimates imply that purchase by the HDD industry contributed about one third of the total output of Singapore's precision engineering and contract manufacturing industry in 1990, and an even higher proportion in 1994 (40 percent).

More than a hundred precision-engineering and contract manufacturing firms in Singapore are known to be suppliers to the HDD industry. While many of these were established to serve other electronics industries in Singapore and later moved into supplying the HDD industry, a significant number started with the establishment of the industry itself. Many of these firms today continue to supply not only the HDD industry, but also various electronics manufacturing and assembly industries in Singapore, including consumer electronics, computers, and other peripherals like ink-jet printers, monitors, and telecommunications equipment. Nonetheless, among the largest local precision-engineering and contract manufacturing firms, supplying to the HDD industry has played a very important part in propelling their growth.

Table 7.5   Typical Sourcing Structure of HDD Assemblers in Singapore

A)   Seagate (1990)
    39% of components (surface mount assemblies, precision parts) in Singapore
    22% of disk media, ICs from U.S.
    15% of motors, magnetic heads from Japan
    24% of others from Thailand, Malaysia, and other Asian countries

B)   Western Digital (1990)
    30% of surface mount assemblies and precision parts in Singapore
    34% of disk media, ICs from U.S.
    21% of motors, magnetic heads from Japan
    15% of others from Taiwan, India, and Europe

C)   Maxtor (1994)
    PCBA from Taiwan, Hong Kong, and Singapore
    Heads from U.S., Malaysia, and Thailand
    Disks from U.S., Malaysia, and Singapore
    Motors from Japan and Thailand
    Flexlead from U.S., Malaysia, Singapore, and the Philippines
    VCM from Singapore

Source: (A) and (B), Economic Development Board; (C), Y. J. Lim (1995).
Note: IC = integrated circuit; PCBA = printed circuit board assembly; VCM = voice coil mechanism.

Table 7.6 shows the extent of dependence on HDD business among seven of the largest Singaporean precision-engineering or contract manufacturing firms that were recently listed on the Singapore Stock Exchange. The dependency ratios range from

Table 7.6   Extent of Dependence of Singapore Firms on HDD Firms as Buyers

	Products/Services Provided	% Sales to HDD Customers			Customer Since
Cam Mechantronics	Baseplates, covers, precision machining, die casting, and subassembly	Conner	1991 1993 1994	93.1% 70.9% <60%	1988
Seksun	Precision machining	Seagate	1991 1993	15.9% 13.7%	1986 1988
		West. Digital	1991 1993	7.1% 1.0%	
		Total dependence on HDD in 1993 = 37%			
Uraco Engineering	Precision machining, metal stamping, die casting, and assembly	Seagate	1992 1994	34.2% 39.4%	1984 na
		Maxtor	1992 1994	23.5% 11.3%	na na
		West. Digital	1992 1994	5.5% 9.3%	
		Micropolis	1992 1994	11.6% 4.7%	
		Total dependence on HDD in 1994 = 90%			
Tri-M Technologies	PCBA and contract manufacturing	Conner	1991 1993 1994	89.7% 85.5% <70%	na
First Engineering	Precision-injected molded plastic	Iomega	1992 1994	9.9% 15.2%	na
		Conner	1992 1994	10.4% 9.9%	na
		Total dependence on HDD in 1994 = 35%			
MMI	Baseplates, covers, and VCM subassembly	Conner Seagate	1994 1996	99.0% 86.0%	1989
		(post merger with Conner)			
		MKE Toshiba	1996 1996	5.0% 2.4%	1995 1995
		Total dependence on HDD in 1996 = 93.4%			
Armstrong	Acoustic foams and top cover gaskets	Seagate	1992 1994	25.7% 19.9%	1986
		Maxtor	1992 1994	5.7% 10.3%	na

Source: Compiled from respective companies' initial public offering (IPO) prospectus.

about one-third to 96 percent. Although comprehensive data are not available for smaller precision engineering firms, quite a few are known to be almost 100 percent dependent on HDD assemblers. Thus the HDD assembly industry is a very important customer for the products and services supplied by these Singapore-based firms.

The contribution of the HDD assembly industry to the development of the local supporting industries can be gauged not only in terms of the volume of demand generated, but also in terms of the extent to which it has induced technological upgrading of these industries. An earlier study shows that both direct and indirect transfer of technology from the electronics assemblers to their supporting industries has been substantial (Wong 1992). More importantly, it shows that there was a large technology investment inducement effect, whereby the supporting industries demonstrated a higher propensity to invest in technological upgrading when they perceived that a long-term relationship with their buyers would reduce the market risk involved. All the major HDD assemblers were covered in that study.

Another indication of the importance of HDD majors to technological upgrading of local supporting industries is that, in the early years of the Local Industry Upgrading Program (LIUP), launched by the Singapore government to facilitate technology transfer from MNCs to local suppliers in general, all the HDD assemblers were selected for participation. A recent study (Wong 1997) covering the sources of technology acquisition by 109 manufacturing firms in Singapore included about a dozen precision-engineering and contract manufacturing firms that are known to be suppliers to the HDD industry. These firms indicated that "learning from the product specification and feedback from customers" was the single most important source of technological learning for these firms, ahead of recruiting experienced engineers and their own in-house R&D.

The growing technological capability of local supporting industries in Singapore is reflected in the emergence of a cluster of local precision-engineering firms which have achieved listing on the Singapore Stock Exchange. Most of these firms have benefited from being suppliers to the HDD industry at key stages of their corporate growth. As shown in table 7.6 (above), many of them continue to be key suppliers to the industry, although some have diversified their customer base since. Nearly all of them have since internationalized their operations, expanding to neighboring ASEAN countries and China.

SUPPLY INFRASTRUCTURE AND FLEXIBLE PRODUCTION

Having highlighted how the establishment of HDD operations in Singapore has led to the codevelopment of local supporting industries in Singapore, I shall now examine in more detail how the codevelopment of this local supply infrastructure has in turn contributed to increasing the production flexibility of the major HDD firms operating in Singapore, and the significance this has had for the global competitiveness of the HDD firms.

Location-Specificity of Supply Infrastructure

The local supply infrastructure of manufacturing operations like HDD assembly consists of two components: resources that are internal to the firm and resources external to the firm that are supplied locally. The resource-based theory of the firm (Barney 1991) suggests that, for a local supply infrastructure to provide a unique source of competitive advantage, the resources available through this local infrastructure must be specific to the locality and not easily made accessible or duplicated at other locations. This location-specificity can arise in two ways: (1) immobility of the individual asset or resource (e.g., manufacturing process engineering knowledge accumulated by engineers on the job in a manufacturing plant) or (2) agglomeration economies arising from synergies and scale economies of the different component assets or resources. In the latter case, even if individual factors are mobile or easily imitated elsewhere, the duplication of the entire cluster of factors is difficult.

Our field interviews with HDD firms in Singapore suggest two major sources of location-specific resources that confer significant differentiating advantages to the supply infrastructure in Singapore when compared to other locations. The first is the presence of a significantly large pool of process engineering skills and knowledge which is fairly specific to the HDD industry, but by and large *not* firm-specific. The second condition is important because it helps to increase the effect of agglomeration economies. Supporting the lack of a firm-specific effect is the fact that the major American HDD firms in Singapore appear to have achieved fairly similar levels of process capability (Christensen 1995), and that there has been frequent movement of managerial and technical personnel between the companies.

The second source of location-specific advantages is the presence of a sizable cluster of high-capability precision-engineering supporting firms that provide inputs to the HDD assembly operations. This supporting industry can be divided into two value chains: the "direct materials" chain, which produces components or subassembled parts that are used in the drive itself, and the "indirect materials" chain, which produces the tools and dies, the automation engineering services for the design and maintenance of assembly equipment, and other services like clean room design, factory layout, and materials requirement planning systems. The first value chain itself consists of several related processes, including metal stamping, die casting, machining, and surface treatment (plating, etc.). Because of the job-shop nature of these precision-engineering works, precision-engineering firms tend to be small, and few are completely vertically integrated. Similarly, very few precision-engineering firms are internationally diversified. Because of the close interrelationships of the different precision-engineering value chain operations (e.g., die casting, machining, and plating), having many players performing the different operations in close geographic proximity provides the advantage of facilitating fast and flexible response in the supply of the finished parts to the HDD assemblers. In transaction-cost terms, the risks of opportunism by sellers are reduced when there is a large pool of diverse suppliers in close proximity. In other words, agglomeration economies arise from both economies of scope and scale of the precision-engineering cluster.

While the clustering of buyers (the HDD assemblers) certainly facilitated the development of a larger and more varied cluster of precision-engineering firms, there has been another contributing element: the production capacity of these precision engineering firms was not taken up entirely by the supply of precision parts to the HDD industry. Because the precision and quality requirements of HDD components were among the most stringent of all electronics products, firms that had mastered the capability to supply mechanical components to the HDD industry were typically able to supply precision parts to other electronics manufacturing industries as well. Because Singapore has been able to attract a large number of manufacturing firms in a wide range of electronics industries over the years, the size and diversity of Singapore's precision-engineering supporting industry is thus much more than can be sustained by HDD requirements alone. The agglomeration economies of Singapore's precision-engineering cluster have thus been increased due to the mobility of supply capacity between HDD and other electronics sectors.

The second value chain of supporting services also benefits from close geographic proximity. Firms offering tool and die or process automation services need to interact closely with engineers and technicians at the production shop floor to facilitate fast response and feedback. Moreover, because the skills and assets of these firms are generic to support a wide range of electronics manufacturing industries, the HDD industry can draw upon the larger pool of supply for such expertise. The presence of a much larger electronics industry in Singapore since the early 1980s also helped to create the scale economies needed to support a critical mass of competent local consulting firms specializing in advanced manufacturing facility design and development services, such as clean room design and energy optimization services. Such local firms as Supersymmetry and Perdana Consulting have contributed importantly to the rapid commissioning of new assembly plants not only in Singapore, but also, in later years, elsewhere in the region, as in Malaysia and Thailand.

In addition to precision-engineering and facility development services, the early development of PCBA capability in Singapore constituted an important supporting industry to HDD assembly. PCBA capability hence added to the agglomeration economies of Singapore's supply infrastructure, especially in the earlier years, when this capability was less widely diffused in the region. Like precision engineering, PCBA capability (and, more generally, contract manufacturing capability) is a generic capability that is deployable across a wide range of electronics manufacturing production. However, unlike precision engineering, the value chain activities for PCBA operation can be more easily integrated and, indeed, a number of large, multinational firms that specialize in PCBA have emerged globally (e.g., SCI and Solectron from USA, Pentex from Germany, and Venture and Flextronics from

Singapore). Thus, there are less compelling reasons for geographic clustering of PCBA activities, with the possible exception of transport costs.

The other major HDD inputs are disk media and read/write heads. The subassembly of read/write heads is among the most labor-intensive of operations. Consequently, although this operation was originally started by Seagate in Singapore, it was the first activity to be relocated to a lower labor cost location like Thailand. The growth of Seagate's head-assembly operation in Thailand has in turn induced investment by head makers such as Read-rite in Thailand to be geographically close to Seagate.

Until recently, there was little reason for disk media to be clustered in close proximity to the HDD assemblers. However, some industry analysts have suggested that, with the increasing density of data being squeezed into the disk media, reduced yield arising from disk contamination in the assembly process is becoming an increasing concern. A technological reason for the disk media manufacturers to be located closer to the drive assemblers, therefore, is that yield problems can be more easily diagnosed and isolated. This is indeed beginning to happen, as discussed below.

Supply Infrastructure and Flexible Production Capability

HDD firms are increasingly having to pursue both rapid product innovations and continuous cost cutting to survive the intense global competition. This competitive requirement translates directly into pressure to develop and maintain flexible production capability. How important, then, are the two components of location-specific supply infrastructure identified above to enhancing the flexible production capability of HDD firms in Singapore?

To address this question, we need to examine the requirements of flexible production in some detail. As is widely discussed in the industrial engineering literature, the concept of manufacturing flexibility is quite complex (see for example Sethi and Sethi 1990). Field interviews at several HDD assembly plants in Singapore suggest three key components of production flexibility.

Rapid Production Ramp-Up Capability for Major New Products

Because of increasingly short product life cycles, each new generation of drives that incorporates the latest product technology innovations must reach the market fast to take optimal advantage of the first mover's window of opportunity. Hence, HDD assemblers must be able to ramp up production of new drives quickly. This production volume capability in turn requires rapid tooling, fast response in the supply of components (especially those that represent new designs not shared with older product lines), fast process engineering development and commissioning of new production lines, and a responsive logistics management system to cope with the spike in volume. Rapid ramp up also extends to rapid development and commissioning of new manufacturing facilities.

Product Mix Flexibility

In between major new product innovations, the HDD assemblers face rapid changes in the mix of market demand for specific products. (The "sweet spots," as the most popular storage/form-factor configurations are known, can shift several times a year.) The HDD assemblers must therefore be able to maintain sufficient product mix flexibility, which in turn leads to requirements for fast set-up time and operations management flexibility. HDD assemblers must also be able to ramp down quickly to avoid being stuck with obsolete models.

Continuous Process Improvement Capability

Finally, HDD assemblers need to have the capability to continuously improve the manufacturing process to achieve higher yield/quality and to drive down cost. This calls for "continuation engineering" skills such as progressive automation of assembly process steps, speeding up of drive testing, and design of more flexible work stations that can handle a wider range of product configurations. The challenge is to have the flexibility to implement regular engineering changes and frequent fine-tuning of the operations management procedures, while ensuring that the throughput of the system is not adversely affected in the process.

To achieve a high level in each of the three dimensions of flexible production capabilities mentioned above, HDD assemblers need to be able to draw upon a significant pool of industry-specific process engineering skills, both within the assembly plant and in the related supporting industries.

Manufacturing Process Engineering Skills

Recent studies of the introduction of automated procedures by electronics firms in Singapore suggest that, in addition to lowering operational costs, achieving greater flexibility has been a major motivation (Wong and Ngin 1997). Other studies, such as those devoted to Singapore-based HDD assemblers (Seagate, Conner, Western Digital, Micropolis), confirm the importance of flexibility as a major objective of automation investment (Wong et al. 1997). These case studies also found that the HDD assembly plants automated a substantial part of their operations through their own, locally developed in-house process engineering capability. Indeed, although new product development activities remain located in their parent headquarters in the U.S., all the manufacturing plants have introduced some form of concurrent engineering, with their process engineers closely involved early in the product design phase, e.g., during extended postings to the U.S. headquarters. As several of the senior engineers interviewed suggested, the highest process engineering capability of HDD makers now resides in the engineers in Singapore plants, not in the United States. In one plant, there was a clash between Singapore engineers and engineers from U.S. headquarters over how to design and implement a new automated process in the Singapore plant. The Singapore team eventually prevailed when their approach was demonstrated to be superior.[2]

The high level of process engineering capability among HDD plants in Singapore can also be seen from the fact that, when HDD companies have opened assembly operations elsewhere in the world, they have often resorted to the use of Singaporean engineers to transplant their process design and operations knowledge to these other plants. One early reported case was the Conner assembly plant in Scotland, which was a replica of the Singaporean operation built by Singaporean engineers.[3] Less dramatic, but just as important, the Singaporean HDD operations have regularly transferred older production lines to other parts of the region (e.g., Seagate in Thailand, Conner in China, and Western Digital in Malaysia). Indeed, the Singaporean HDD operations have taken on the role as "transfer stations" for HDD assembly operations in some companies: they are typically given the task of developing the process to make the latest product lines, and after these stabilize and mature, the Singapore operations are subsequently required to transfer the process to alternative, lower-cost locations. Thus, despite significantly higher wage and land costs, Singapore has been able to maintain a competitive position as the hub for "lead" manufacturing plants.

On a more general level, the high level of process engineering capability among Singaporean engineers working in the HDD plants has been acknowledged by senior managers of HDD companies as being a key factor in their decision to invest in, or expand production of, new HDD product lines in Singapore. Thus, when IBM established their HDD assembly operation in Singapore in 1995, nine out of the top ten senior management and engineering positions were filled by experienced managers and engineers who had previously worked for Conner in Singapore, rather than by people from the IBM plant in the United States. The ability of IBM to shift its entire mass production lines from San Jose to Singapore within six months attests to the capabilities of Singaporean production managers.

Related Supporting Industry Infrastructure

The availability of a sizable, technically sophisticated precision engineering support industry has been commonly cited by senior managers in the HDD industry as being a key factor in favor of HDD assembly in Singapore. For example, Singapore is credited with having developed a "diffused" supporting infrastructure that "can quickly transform design into hardware without deep, high volume commitments, and at the same time provide the flexibility to accommodate the required growth when high volume became a reality. . . . [H]ere, you don't have to be one of the "Fortune 500" to get a vendor's attention" (Di Bene 1992). Similar assessments were reported by various senior managers of HDD assemblers when they were interviewed by the local press on the occasions of their announcements of new investment or facility expansion in Singapore. For example, a recent published interview with Seagate management in Singapore cited close relationships with suppliers, flexibility to change lines quickly to respond to customers' requirements, and constant and continuous improvement in the manufacturing process as its "productivity secrets."[4] Also, in a study covering three HDD firms in Singapore, all cited close relationships with suppliers as their key competence (Phun 1997).

Recent interviews by the author with senior management in a number of HDD manufacturers in Singapore confirmed the importance that these companies attached to the contribution of local precision-engineering firms for their ability to ramp up production fast and to adjust production mix quickly. Indeed, when these HDD makers have redistributed some of their more mature product lines to neighboring countries, they have often replicated their buyer-supplier relationship with Singaporean precision-engineering firms by inviting these firms to start up operations in these countries. For example, when Conner started HDD assembly in Penang, Singaporean firms were involved in the clean-room design, in automation equipment development, and in factory commissioning, while a number of Singaporean precision-engineering firms set up operations in Penang to supply to Conner.

Flexible Production Capability and Competitiveness

While quantitative estimates of the competitive advantages of locating production in Singapore versus locating in other locations are hard to come by, it is striking to note that all the surviving independent major HDD makers that have increased their market shares over the last ten years have had significant production activities in Singapore. In contrast, the previously "captive" makers (those that produce HDDs for computers they produce), DEC, HP, and IBM, have all lost significant market shares in the same period, despite being acknowledged by the technology press as having among the most advanced product technology for HDD.[5] The inability of these companies to match the merchant makers (those that produce for sale to computer makers) in terms of manufacturing costs and flexibility is a major factor in their loss of competitive position. Indeed, HP and DEC have since decided to exit the market entirely.

Coincidentally, the Japanese HDD majors, which have chosen to locate production within Japan until very recently, have also seen their collective share of the global HDD market shrink over the last ten years. A number of senior managers of U.S. HDD companies in Singapore who were interviewed by the author suggested that, aside from the inability of the Japanese to match the U.S. HDD firms in product technology, the "hard" automation approach of the Japanese to mass production has been a disadvantage against the "agile," fast ramp up/ramp down capabilities of U.S. HDD firms.

The increasing importance of flexible production capability to competitive advantage in HDD assembly operations can also be seen in terms of the emerging cost structure of HDD assembly. As can be seen from table 7.7, derived from an industry estimate (Lim 1995), direct-assembly labor cost represents only 3 percent of the total cost of production of one HDD assembler in Singapore, with

Table 7.7   Estimated Cost Structure of a HDD Assembler in Singapore, 1994

Cost Composition of Assembling a Drive	%
PCBA	36
Heads	21
Disk	14
Motor	5
Flexlead	3
VCM	2
Others	8
Materials-related subtotal	89
Freight	1
Direct labor	3
Indirect labor	3
Facilities related	1
Depreciation	2
Other overheads	1
Total	100

Source: Y. J. Lim (1995).

input-materials-related costs accounting for almost 90 percent. Consequently, the flexibility and cost competitiveness of the input supply infrastructure has a much bigger impact on the overall competitiveness of the HDD assemblers than do direct labor costs. Indeed, because yield levels for new high-end drives tend to be low, even a slight improvement in yield through process engineering improvements may contribute more to cost reduction than a significant reduction of direct labor cost (Hampton 1996; Gourevitch et al. 1997).

Similarly, the razor-thin margins on component parts like baseplates and actuator arms can be wiped out by excess inventory holding and transport costs; hence the importance of close geographic proximity. To the extent that these two sources of flexible production capability are still not yet widely available in competing countries for HDD assembly, like Malaysia, Thailand, and the Philippines, Singapore can expect to continue to command a competitive edge—despite its unfavorable costs relative to other Southeast Asian and Northeast Asian countries (table 7.8).

The Influence of Government and Other Institutional Factors

While the development of the supply infrastructure for HDD production in Singapore would not have happened if American HDD majors had not been driven by competitive pressures to look for production locations in Asia, the Singapore government played a critical role, not only in channelling the HDD in-

Table 7.8   Regional Cost Data Comparison, 1993 (U.S.$)

Data comparison	Singapore	Malaysia (Penang)	Indonesia (Batam)	China (Shenzhen)	Thailand
Exchange rate	1.527	2.59	2,165	8.68	25.05
Base labor rate per month					
Operator	382	232	138	55	105
Engineer	1048	619	360	182	327
Manager	1637	967	490	302	458
Provident fund/ workmen's compensation	20–22	13–14	2–6	39	0–4.5
Rental psf	1.05	0.46	0.79	0.9	0.13
Foreign exchange control	Liberal	Liberal	Liberal	Chaotic	Liberal
Corporate tax % year end 1994	27	37	15–35	15–33	37
Pioneer status tax incentives (%)	100	70	nil	100	nil

Source: Y. J. Lim (1995).

vestment to Singapore, but also in facilitating the development of the supply infrastructure itself.

The success of Singapore's overall MNC-driven industrial development strategy has by now been well documented (see e.g., World Bank 1993; Wong 1995). Openness to trade and financial flows, the generous tax incentives to encourage DFI, and the proactive DFI promotion efforts of the government through the EDB have been important factors in establishing Singapore as a major offshore production platform in Asia for MNCs from Europe, the United States, and Japan since the early 1970s. Other important factors include the heavy investment in public infrastructure and human resource development supplemented by a liberal immigration policy to attract foreign skills and talents, use of English as a medium of education, policies to foster harmonious industrial relations, and a transparent and efficient government (World Bank 1993). The early emphasis on attracting DFI, when most of the countries in the region were still not that favorably disposed to inward investments, gave Singapore the crucial "first mover advantage" that enabled her to accumulate agglomeration economies as a regional manufacturing, transport/communications, and financial/business services hub (Wong 1995).

Generous tax incentives and an efficient government bureaucracy have facilitated business start ups and have undoubtedly contributed to Singapore's ability to attract new investments as well as to encourage expansion and upgrading of existing facilities. For example, the recent move by IBM to transfer its assembly operation from San Jose to Singapore benefited not only from generous tax incentives, but also from significant practical, facilitative assistance from various government agencies concerned to ensure that IBM could establish and start up its production operations on very short notice. Similarly, the continuous upgrading and expansion of Seagate's operations in Singapore have benefited from significant tax incentives.

From the perspective of logistics and supply-chain management, it is also clear that the presence of world-class transport and communications infrastructure in Singapore has contributed to making it a preferred location for final drive assembly, despite its high wage cost. Given the imperative of reliable global supply sourcing and quick time to market, efficient and low-cost manufacturing operations can be undone by bottlenecks in the transport system, including customs clearing, as the U.S. firm JTS found when it started its HDD assembly operation in India.

Beyond these factors, the Singapore government has also contributed to the development of the precision-engineering industry cluster. One contribution was the early public investment in a large number of training institutions for precision-engineering skills, which provided the critical human resources for the subsequent development of the precision-engineering industry (Soon 1992). As the skill levels demanded by the industry increase over time, the training programs are also upgraded steadily, with increasing emphasis placed on training at the university undergraduate and postgraduate levels. Another facilitating factor was the early establishment of an innovative Local Industry Upgrading Program (LIUP), targeted at upgrading local industries that supply to MNC manufacturers (Soon 1994). Many of the local firms that received assistance through LIUP were in the precision-engineering cluster. A third contributing factor was the establishment of public R&D institutions and programs focusing on precision-engineering capability development. These include the GINTIC Institute of Manufacturing Technology (GIMT) and other precision-engineering-related research centers at the universities and polytechnic institutes. Finally, many of the precision-engineering firms that have grown successfully have benefited from the various financial assistance programs for SMEs, which were biased toward local enterprises deemed "promising" (PLEs).

Proactive government policy has also contributed to the development of a reservoir of HDD manufacturing process engineering skills, primarily by augmenting the supply of well-trained engineers through heavy investment in tertiary engineering education and training. Liberal immigration policy and active government programs to attract foreign talents have also helped. Incentives were also given to HDD manufacturers to invest in automation and to adopt computer-integrated manufacturing technologies. The establishment of GIMT and, more recently, of a Magnetic Technology Centre (MTC; later expanded into a Data Storage Institute, DSI), are also contributing to increasing the HDD manufacturing process capability of Singapore through publicly funded, but industrially driven, R&D programs.

It is important to recognize that many of the government policies targeted at promoting the HDD industry and its local supply infrastructure have been informed by an explicit industry cluster development strategy (MTI 1991; Porter 1990). As is evident from the *Strategic Economic Plan* formulated in 1991, the government explicitly recognizes the need to promote industrial development as an integrated cluster linking downstream end-product industries, upstream supporting industries, and enabling capabilities. In line with this strategy, there was strong emphasis on intergovernment agency coordination in formulating industrial policies and implementing industrial promotion programs. There was also strong emphasis on involving all the various players in particular industry clusters in policy formulation dialogue and implementation consultation. Industry players are also strongly represented in the board of government agencies responsible for industry and technology promotion, industrial training, and the development of tertiary educational institutions.

Application of this cluster industry promotion approach to the HDD industry is going beyond building the precision engineering and PCBA supporting industries. Since the mid-1990s, the EDB has focused on attracting disk-media-related companies to locate their production in Singapore as well. As of 1997, four such companies (Hoya, StorMedia, Seagate, and Mitsubishi) have commenced production in Singapore, suggesting the possible emergence of another important subcluster in the HDD industry value chain. Moving upstream, a number of the HDD assemblers in Singapore have established drive design activities there, facilitated by increasing collaboration with the publicly funded DSI. With more than twenty participating corporate members, DSI has strategically expanded R&D capabilities in areas that complement the HDD majors, such as head-disk integration and tribology, coding and signal processing for magnetic recording, and servo systems for precision motion. Besides serving the magnetic HDD industry, DSI is strategically positioned to help support the complementary development of an optical storage industry, another emerging cluster that EDB has identified for promotion in the future.

CONCLUSION

The importance of agglomeration economies arising from location-specific supply infrastructure clearly depends on the industry concerned, given that different industries have different technology characteristics and consequently may exhibit different supply structure requirements (Porter 1990). Indeed, within the same industry, different component supplies may exhibit differences in their economies of scale and need for close interaction with user firms, with quite different implications for optimal spatial patterns of location for supporting industry activities. This helps explain why, in the HDD industry, disk media and read/write heads have traditionally been geographically dispersed worldwide instead of being concentrated near the location of final assembly. Thus, the generalizability of the importance of localized supply infrastructure must be predicated on the nature of the industry involved. What constitutes "local" supply is also likely to change over time, as transport and communications technologies improve and regulatory barriers decline between regions and countries.

The above caveats notwithstanding, this analysis of the special case of HDD assembly in Singapore suggests that the production of complex assembly products that are subject to rapid technological change, short product life cycles, and intense competition are likely candidates for production agglomeration. Singapore was able to exploit the demand for flexible yet low-cost production capability by U.S. HDD assemblers through a combination of policies that reinforced the forces of agglomeration economies. It may have been partly due to luck that Seagate initially chose Singapore for its first offshore production site, but the subsequent concentration of HDD assembly activities in Singapore was the result of a dynamic interaction between increasing demand for flexible production capability and the growing agglomeration of a local supply infrastructure reinforced by government policies. Government policies promoting DFI by HDD assemblers, coupled with conscious programs to promote the development of local supply infrastructure, have reinforced the agglomeration advantage that Singapore has created in HDD assembly—despite the rising costs and increasing competition for DFI by neighboring countries, as shown in table 7.8. If low-cost competition had been the sole factor, it is unlikely that Singapore could have maintained the high degree of concentration of HDD assembly activities that it has achieved up to now.

To the extent that this observation is generalizable to other industries, there are significant policy implications for developing countries in general, for it suggests that just providing abundant low-wage labor is not sufficient to compete for a share of global industries in which flexible production capability is important. Another implication is that government policy does matter, not only in terms of targeting industries to attract, but also in terms of promoting the development of local supporting industry infrastructure. While the mainstream industrial economics literatures tend to emphasize the inability of government to pick winners in emerging industries or technologies, it may be easier for governments in late-industrializing countries to target industries and firms that have already established themselves in the advanced industrial countries. The Singapore experience suggests in particular the usefulness of an integrated industry cluster development strategy. Our analysis of the development of the HDD industry in Singapore thus lends support to the argument by Borrus (1994) that the development of flexible yet low-cost production capability in East Asia by U.S. MNCs has contributed to the success of these MNCs with respect to their Japanese competitors. This strategic alliance has also served the host countries in East Asia well.

In the HDD industry, the achievement of flexible yet low-cost production has certainly been a major contributing factor in the continuing dominance of U.S. players over their Japanese competitors, which until recently have relied on hard automation of mass production facilities in Japan. It is also interesting to note that practically all the American HDD firms that have *not* leveraged East Asian flexible production capabilities have not done very well. The recent decision by MKE (the Japanese manufacturing partner of Quantum) and IBM to locate their production in Singapore suggests a belated recognition of regional location as a source of competitive advantage in this industry.

A potential policy implication of the above is that American competitiveness in a global industry like HDD may in fact be strengthened through a strategic partnering of advanced U.S. product technologies and East Asian (non-Japanese) manufacturing process capability, rather than weakened as some may suggest. This is a proposition with profound implications for future patterns of national competitiveness.

A third observation is that, as HDD assembly activities continue to be upgraded in Singapore, a pattern of complementary regional specialization appears to be emerging in Southeast Asia, with lower-end drives being assembled in countries like Malaysia, China, and the Philippines, and more labor-intensive stages of operations being located in Thailand, Batam (Indonesia), and the Philippines, while intermediate operations like drive repair and media polishing are being located in Malaysia. While these countries constantly compete against one another to move up the technological ladder of manufacturing, the resulting larger, regional clustering of HDD-related activities helps to provide the whole of Southeast Asia with a *regional agglomeration advantage* with respect to other regions (such as Latin America). In this sense, the spread of HDD-related activities throughout Southeast Asia adds to the advantage of Singapore as a regional hub for high-end HDD manufacturing activities.

A fourth implication of our analysis of the HDD industry in Singapore is that the supply infrastructure for an industry need not be "imprisoned" within that industry, but may in fact represent broad capabilities that can be leveraged to support a wide range of industries, thereby strengthening the host country's overall industrial production capability and flexibility. The concern that developing countries may become vulnerable by being too dependent on "footloose" global MNCs (those not firmly rooted in a host county) has *not* been borne out in the case of the HDD industry. Singapore's strong position as a regional manufacturing hub has benefited significantly from the presence of the HDD assemblers. A major exodus of such industries has not occurred despite rising wage costs. More importantly, even if such an exodus were to occur in the future, or if HDD as an industry were to go into decline due to technological substitution by other storage technologies such as recordable CDs, DVDs, or flash memories, the pool of flexible manufacturing process engineers and the precision-engineering supporting industries that have been built up would likely be able to redirect their capabilities to other industries. Indeed, the advanced precision and flexibility requirements of complex assembly products like HDD may indeed have prepared the foundations for Singapore's entry into other technologically sophisticated industries.

Finally, although most of the analysis for this chapter was completed before the onset of the Asian financial crisis, the conclusions of the chapter remain unchanged in the aftermath of the crisis. Indeed, recent developments support the importance of flexible production capability as a driver for the global hard disk drive industry overall and as a factor in the continuing competitiveness of Singapore as a location for the industry. To begin with, while the financial crisis that broke out in the second half of 1997 has crippled economic growth in much of East Asia, it has not reduced the region's competitiveness as a production platform for the electronics industry in general and magnetic HDD in particular. In fact, with the significant depreciation of local currencies against the U.S. dollar and the reduction of labor-market tightness throughout the region, the cost competitiveness of East Asia versus other regions has actually been enhanced. Consequently, there has been no diversification of production away from East Asia.

Secondly, to the extent that the economic slowdown in Asia has been translated into lower growth in demand for HDDs, it may have contributed to the over-supply situation for the HDD industry in 1999. More importantly, the rapid pace of technological improvement has continued unabated, with drive capacities continuing to increase while unit price per megabyte of storage continues to fall. Both these developments are exerting increasing pressure on the HDD majors to become even more flexible in their production capabilities. While some consolidation of the industry has occurred, and resulted in some retrenchments in the HDD industry in Singapore, large-scale redistribution away from Singapore has not taken place. Although Western Digital has relocated some drive assembly activities to Malaysia, Maxtor has expanded production capacity in Singapore; and while Seagate has retrenched some staff in Singapore, this is part of a worldwide reduction effort. Singapore has been able to maintain its role as a major production hub because the set of conditions that facilitated production flexibility in Singapore have not been eroded by the Asian financial crisis. Interestingly, a new drive company has recently chosen to enter the emerging market for microdrives by completely outsourcing production to JIT, a Singaporean contract manufacturer.

NOTES

This chapter is a revised version of "Creation of a Regional Hub for Flexible Production: The Case of the Hard Disk Drive Industry in Singapore," which appeared in *Industry and Innovation* 4 (December 1997). The research for this project has been partially funded by the Data Storage Industry Globalization Project at the University of California, San Diego, and by a research grant from the National University of Singapore.

1. Export figures in table 7.3 differ slightly from those in table 7.2, due possibly to inclusion of reexport totals in the former.
2. Private communication.
3. *Fortune*, 13 August 1990.

4. *Electronic Business Asia*, February 1997: 37–43.

5. The latter three firms are deemed "captive" in the sense that they produce HDDs solely for in-house consumption, rather than for sale on the open market.

BIBLIOGRAPHY

Abernathy, W. J., and J. M. Utterbeck. 1978. "Patterns of Industrial Innovation." *Technology Review* 50, no. 7.

Abernathy, W. J., and K. Clark. 1985. "Innovation: Mapping the Winds of Creative Destruction." *Research Policy* 14: 3–22.

Barney, J. 1991. "Firm Resources and Sustained Competitive Advantage." *Journal of Management* 17: 99–120.

Borrus, M. 1994. "Left for Dead: Asian Production Networks and the Revival of U.S. Electronics." In *Japanese Investment in Asia,* edited by E. M. Doherty. San Francisco: Asia Foundation.

Christensen, C. M. 1993. "The Rigid Disk Drive Industry: A History of Commercial and Technological Turbulence." *Business History Review* 67, no. 4: 531–588.

———. 1995. "The Drivers of Vertical Disintegration." HBS Working Paper 96-008, Boston.

———. 1997. *The Innovator's Dilemma: When New Technologies Cause Great Firms to Fail.* Boston: Harvard Business School Press.

Di Bene, J. T. 1992. Presentation to the EEE Convention on 25 July 1992, Winchester Island, Singapore.

Disk/Trend. Various years. *Rigid Disk Drives Report.*

Economic Development Board. Various years. *Census of Industrial Production.* Singapore: Government Printers.

Economic Development Board. 1992. *The Disk Drive Industry.* Singapore: EDB.

Frank, B. 1997. "Rigid Disk Drive Price Trends." *IDEMA Insights* (March/April).

Gourevitch, P., R. E. Bohn, and D. McKendrick. 1997. *Who Is Us? The Nationality of Production in the Hard Disk Drive Industry.* Data Storage Industry Globalization Project Report 97-01. University of California, San Diego, March.

Hamel, G., and C. K. Prahalad. 1994. *Competing for the Future.* Boston: HBS Press.

Hampton, S. M. 1996. *Process Cost Analysis for Hard Disk Manufacturing.* Data Storage Industry Globalization Project Report No. 96-02, University of California, San Diego.

International Data Corporation (IDC). 1996. *Storage Bulletin* (December).

Lim, Y. J. 1995. *Is Singapore Losing Its Attractiveness to Be the Key Manufacturing Centre for the Disk Drive Companies?* MBA Advanced Study Project Report, National University of Singapore, Graduate School of Business.

MTI (Ministry of Trade and Industry). 1991. *Towards a Developed Nation: The Strategic Economic Plan.* Singapore: Government Printers.

Ng, J. K. 1989. *Competitive Strategies in Emerging Industries: A Study of the Mini Rigid Disk Drive Industry.* MBA Advanced Study Project Report, National University of Singapore, Graduate School of Business.

Pang, S. F. 1996. *Technological Trends and Their Impact on Management Strategies in the Disk Drive Industry.* MBA Advanced Study Project Report, National University of Singapore, Graduate School of Business.

Phun, K. M. 1997. *Product Centric vs. Competence-Based Competition.* B. Eng. thesis, National University of Singapore, Department of Mechanical & Production Engineering.

Pine, B. J. 1994. *Mass Customization.* Boston: Harvard Business School Press.

Porter, M. 1990. *The Competitive Advantage of Nations.* New York: Free Press.

Sabel, C. F. 1989. "Flexible Specialization and the Re-emergence of Regional Economics." In *Reversing Industrial Decline?* edited by P. Hirst and J. Zeithin. Oxford: Berg.

Sethi, A. K., and S. P. Sethi. 1990. "Flexibility in Manufacturing: A Survey." *International Journal of Flexible Manufacturing Systems* 2: 289–328.

Soon, T. W. 1992. "Human Resource Development and Management in Singapore." In *Human Resource Development and Utilization in the Asia-Pacific: A Social Absorption Capacity Approach*, edited by P. K. Wong and C. Y. Ng, 21–30. Singapore: ISEAS.

——. *Enterprise Linkages: Examples from East Asia*, edited by S. Meyannathan. Washington, D.C.: World Bank/EDI.

Stalk, G., Jr., and T. M. Hout. 1990. *Competing against Time.* New York: Free Press.

Tan, G. H. 1995. *The Precision Engineering Sector and the National Competitive Advantage of Singapore in the Hard Disk Drive Industry.* M.B.A. Advanced Study Project Report, National University of Singapore, Graduate School of Business.

Tan, W. T. 1992. *Hard Disk Drive Manufacturing: An Industry Analysis.* M.B.A. Advanced Study Project Report, NUS-GSB, Singapore.

Teo, K. C. 1990. *A Study of Electronic Subcontractors in Singapore.* M.B.A. Advanced Study Project Report, National University of Singapore, Graduate School of Business.

Trade Development Board. Various years. *External Trades Statistics.* Singapore: TDB.

Wong, P. K. 1992. "Technological Development through Subcontracting Linkages: Evidence from Singapore." *Scandinavian International Business Review* 1, no. 3: 28–40.

——. 1995. "Competing in the Global Electronics Industry: A Comparative Study of the Innovation Networks of Singapore and Taiwan. *Journal of Industry Studies* 2, no. 2: 35–62.

——. 1996. "Technology Transfer and Development Inducement by Foreign MNCs: The Experience of Singapore." In *Industrial Strategy for Global Competitiveness of Korean Industries*, edited by K. Y. Jeong and M. S. Kwack. Seoul: Korea Economic Research Institute, 1996.

——. 1998. "Technology Acquisition Pattern of Manufacturing Firms in Singapore." *Singapore Management Review* 20, no. 1: 43–64.

Wong, P. K., and P. Ngin. 1997. "Automation and Organizational Performance: The Case of Electronics Manufacturing Firms in Singapore." *International Journal of Production Economics* 52, no. 2.

Wong, P. K., et al. 1997. "Critical Success Factors in Implementing Manufacturing Automation: Evidence from Singapore's Electronics Industry." Singapore: NUS-CMT Working Paper.

World Bank. 1993. *Lessons of East Asia: Singapore—Public Policy and Economic Development.* Working paper. Washington, D.C.: World Bank.

Yap, N. J. 1993. *A Manufacturing Start-Up Company in the Electronic Supporting Industry.* M.B.A. Advanced Study Project Report, National University of Singapore, Graduate School of Business.

Conclusion

Network Governance, Flexibility, and Development amid Crisis

Frederic C. Deyo, Richard F. Doner, and Eric Hershberg

The cascade of financial crises that pummeled one East Asian economy after another beginning in the second half of 1997 has called into question the much-vaunted East Asian miracle. The dramatic events that swept the region at that juncture were largely unanticipated, and because most of the research upon which the chapters in this volume are based was completed just as the crisis began to unfold, initial drafts of the chapters did not take into account the impact of the crisis on the region's economies or on the institutional underpinnings of East Asian success. However, a key attribute of the case studies is that they underscore the degree to which the creative destruction inherent to capitalist economies was always as salient in Asia as it was elsewhere. Popular accounts of the Asian model may have conveyed an image of ceaseless industrial advance predicated on highly rational organizational structures and a uniquely consensual culture which were presumed to combine in such a way as to maximize both efficiency and equity. Contributors to this volume, in contrast, emphasize the pervasive uncertainties that, even in the best of times, have tested the capacity of export-based industries in Asia to respond to competitive pressures. Throughout the region, they find that engagement with global markets has generated losses as well as gains for firms, for workers, and for localities. The crisis has exacerbated uncertainty and increased the costs of failure to respond rapidly to changing conditions, but neither uncertainty nor the potential for failure were absent prior to the events of 1997.

It is in part due to the uncertain consequences of insertion in volatile markets that economic actors enter into the multiplicity of institutional arrangements that the authors describe in their empirical studies of industrial performance in East Asia. But there is no direct functional link between economic necessity and institutional emergence. A central point of this volume is that while flexibility has been critical to success in many of the most dynamic sectors of East Asian industry, firms are not always able to meet the challenges that confront them, and that even when they do succeed, both the nature of productive flexibility and the social and institutional contexts in which economic activities are embedded vary widely. The aim of this volume has been to illuminate the conditions that dictate whether flexibility is a precondition for success, to analyze the kinds of flexibility that are imperative in different industries, to reveal the institutional arrangements—the governance structures—that facilitate or impede flexible production, and to identify the social and political factors that account for these structures in distinct sectoral and national settings.

This concluding chapter begins with a brief consideration of some of the principal findings of our empirical studies in light of the provisional hypotheses put forth in the volume's introduction. In the ensuing section, we address the relationship between flexible production and equity. Our emphasis here is on the impact of changing types of flexible production, themselves influenced by global economic changes such as East Asia's economic crisis, and on the conditions encountered by workers and small and medium-sized enterprises (SMEs).

HYPOTHESES

Pressures for Flexibility?

The case studies illustrate that pressures for flexibility are ubiquitous. Whether in low-technology clothing and footwear, medium-technology automobiles and consumer electronics, or high-technology disk drives, developing-country firms face strong and growing pressures to bring products to market quickly, efficiently, and with ever higher quality. The cases also demonstrate diversity with regard to the relative importance of scale, cost, and design. Some sectors, such as fashion clothing and machine tools for multinational semiconductor producers in Penang, involve quick time-to-market with relatively small volumes. But in many of the most successful industries of contemporary East Asia, economies of scale are such that mass customization is often more appropriate than small batch production. This pattern is evident in Wong's account of the disk drive industry. On the one hand, time to market is critical, products need to be tailored to specific niches ("sweet spots"), and quality must be flawless. On the other hand, there are huge periodic pressures for quick ramp-up into high-volume production. A similar phenomenon is evident in the case of the Korean semiconductor industry, analyzed by Ernst, and the Thai auto parts producer Aapico, described by Deyo and Doner, where the need to enhance quality coincides with a shift to higher volumes. Taiwanese footwear manufacturers also engage in mass customization, since success in all industry segments requires the capacity to produce new models quickly and in high volumes. But even within and between high-volume industries there are significant differences. For example, within the footwear industry, cost is a critical variable in some instances, while quality of design is more important in others.

Similarly, design and cost pressures, while important for auto parts firms, are less exacting than for disk drive producers who face product life cycles of under one year, huge capital costs, and price reduction requirements from PC makers whose own products are continually falling in price.

The experience of over three years of financial and economic instability in East Asia highlights an additional point concerning the linkage between pressures associated with environmental volatility and the capacity of firms to adapt flexibly. Most of the analyses in this volume focus on pressures derived from the sorts of market volatility described above—shifting consumer tastes; demands for enhanced quality; lower prices; quicker speed to market; and so on. Yet the macroeconomic volatility triggered by the crisis imposes uncertainties of a quite different nature. Largely unprecedented in the region, these powerful pressures have brought about sharp declines in demand across a number of sectors, while simultaneously adding to existing constraints on prices. The result may have been to further undermine entrenched strategies of market-cum-hierarchy mass production regimes that have in the past been successful in grappling with market volatility.

This point seems especially useful in explaining the difficulties facing South Korea in contrast to Taiwan. As Ernst shows, South Korean growth was based in large part on a specialization pattern that combined significant investments by large business groups (*chaebol*) in mass production of homogenous products for highly volatile markets. This strategy of combining high investment thresholds and highly volatile income streams in areas such as electronics was built on imported, expensive technology used internally by the group, rather than on a strong public innovation system involving linkages among SMEs and between such firms and larger assemblers. Korean firms are thus characterized by the capacity to ramp up quickly the production of highly capital-intensive and complex mass production lines. But they are highly dependent on large sums of capital for investment and technology procurement, and the risks associated with such dependence have been underscored by the financial crisis of the late 1990s. In contrast, the Taiwanese economy is characterized by large numbers of SMEs ("an army of ants") with little ability to raise capital for high-volume production and few legal obstacles to bankruptcy. Such firms have been forced to rely on networked linkages with each other and with larger firms. This, along with a state-supported innovation system, has resulted in a capacity for organizational innovation and product design useful for quick responses to shifts in markets and technology through flexible specialization in manufacturing, procurement, and marketing.[1] The utility of networks for facilitating inexpensive and rapid adjustments to change is highlighted in the context of crisis, and the result is to reinforce the importance of these arrangements as reflected in the volume's contributions.

Importance of Networks?

The evidence in this volume supports the proposition that those firms or industries not capable of meeting varying pressures for flexibility (Hong Kong or

Korean garment producers, machine tool firms in Malaysia's Kelang Valley) are not competitive. But saying that flexibility corresponds with market success tells us nothing about the institutional bases of such success. Is flexibility, particularly *dynamic* forms of flexibility, associated with network forms of governance? Put somewhat differently, can we address the neoclassical counterfactual argument that, while networks may correspond with success, "arms-length" market relations would have yielded even better results? The answer to this question is especially important given the charge that networks are really relics of market imperfections. Thus, the argument goes, once problems in financial markets and information provision are adequately addressed, more personalized exchanges such as those found in networks will become obsolete.

The number and range of cases included in this volume preclude a definitive response to this argument, but several pieces of evidence suggest that network governance does indeed make a difference. Particularly instructive are contrasts between Taiwan's striking and sustained success in footwear compared to South Korea's weaker performance, the more rapid growth of machine tool firms in Penang than in the Kelang Valley, and Aapico's unique position in the Thai auto industry as compared to the decline of Hong Kong clothing producers. In each of these cases, success is in part rooted in interfirm relationships whose duration and depth exceeds those connoted by the arms-length character of unfettered markets. Similarly, Singapore's position as the most advanced node within the regional (Southeast Asian) complex of disk drive production is in part rooted in closer ties in Singapore than in Malaysia, Thailand, or the Philippines (Doner and Haggard 1998) between final assemblers and suppliers and among final assemblers themselves. Equally important, the fact that networks are pervasive in Singapore, Taiwan, and Penang, where market imperfections are arguably fewer than in Thailand and the Kelang Valley, suggests that the "network as obsolete relic" view ignores key functions performed by networks in volatile markets.

But in the final analysis, the neoclassical counterfactual is best addressed by a clear understanding of the actual causal linkages between networks and performance capabilities. Do these networks in fact contribute to competitive success by more efficiently transmitting information, by reducing opportunism, by enhancing access to critical resources, and more generally by helping firms to resolve collective action problems? Our evidence is uneven and incomplete. But the cases do show, for example, that Penang's machine tool firms grew through information and support from multinational clients, often mediated by broader networks of firms and government agencies, regarding production plans and process requirements; that linkages among firms in Taiwan's footwear value chain promoted a sharing of risks and of information about issues ranging from overcapacity to new technologies and to ways of dealing with export market limitations; that disk drive producers in Singapore succeeded in process innovation in part because of the opportunity to rely on a stable group of local suppliers; and that Aapico succeeded in part by drawing on both overseas Chinese networks and long-standing ties with assembler clients and joint-venture partners. Conversely, machine tool firms in the Kelang Valley and garment producers in Hong Kong had much greater difficulty because they faced market pressures without relational support.

Network Variation?

Recall, however, the substantial sectoral variation noted above in types of flexibility pressures. Is there any correspondence between these sectoral differences and variation in kinds of networks? For example, do we find differences with regard to features such as network verticality (power), stability, and openness? Although our information regarding the features of specific networks is uneven, we can offer some preliminary observations regarding verticality and closeness. First, we find variation with regard to power symmetry (verticality), and this seems to reflect the kinds of variables typically cited by network theorists, such as number of available partners, degree of specialization, or asset-specific investments. In capital-intensive industries where suppliers must make asset-specific investments for a very small number of clients (disk drives, machine tools for semiconductors, auto parts), networks are clearly more vertical than in the case of footwear and textiles.

Second, however, power is not fixed. As they gained in experience and expertise, the disk drive suppliers in Singapore described by Wong, the Thai auto parts firm described by Deyo and Doner, and the Penang machine tool firms described by Rasiah also expanded their number of clients and capacity to influence clients' production process decisions. A similar power enhancement occurred in Taiwanese firms in design-sensitive footwear. Conversely, however, network ties can become *more* vertical over time. The Thai auto parts firm described by Deyo and Doner is clearly more reliant on and vulnerable to its clients as a result of the credit squeeze and auto market decline associated with the recent crisis. As we discuss below, a similar intensification of asymmetry, here through consolidation, may be occurring in the hard disk drive industry as well.

Third, if greater levels of asset-specific investments combined with a smaller number of alternative partners suggest greater power symmetry, they may also translate into greater stability and openness in relations among firms. This possibility is suggested in accounts of the relations between Taiwanese footwear firms and their design-sensitive clients, and between Penang machine tool firms and multinational semiconductor firms. But these are still cases of relatively vertical linkages among clients and suppliers. Can we speak of asset-specific investments and mutual vulnerability among similarly placed firms producing the same product? It is after all precisely such firms that make up a critical part of the original "Third Italy" model popularized by Piore and Sabel. The Taiwan footwear and Penang machine tool cases do illustrate the strength of network ties among competitors. In these cases, however, firms are linked less by investments specific to transactions with each other than by broader collective goods and objectives, whether industry-wide training, linkages with upstream suppliers, or strategies and support for export market penetration.

Avoiding Functionalism

The correspondence of network governance institutions with dynamic flexibility does not mean that such institutions emerge whenever they are needed. The weaknesses of Kelang Valley machine tool firms, the majority of Thai auto parts firms, and Hong Kong garment producers clearly show that they often do not. Rather, we must look to strategic and contextual factors to understand the *conditions* under which networks play such a role. Strategic considerations are at work in the efforts of Aapico management to cement long-term, trust-based relationships with client assemblers and joint-venture partners. Contextual factors include a variety of ethnic, political, and social factors which may encourage (or discourage) various modes of interfirm relations. For example, both Deyo and Doner's study of a Thai auto parts firm and Rasiah's work on Penang note the importance of shared ethnicity in reducing barriers to the exchange of information and financial resources and in promoting more "reciprocal exchange" in which "individuals know each other well and have information on each others' production opportunities and preferences. With this information firms can more readily engage in ongoing, cooperative exchanges of goods and services" (Kranton 1997: 3).

But as the Hong Kong garment and Kelang Valley machine tool firms illustrate, the simple existence of ethnic ties does not necessarily translate into such "cooperative exchanges." For one thing, as suggested in the volume's introduction, ethnicity may actually inhibit business relations outside the family or speech group. Thus, Howard Davies (1998) has argued that Hong Kong firms' "core" capacities for flexibility (fast response, effective cost leadership) bring with them "core rigidities" (low trust toward those outside the families), which inhibit movement into higher technology. Further, whether ethnic groups are able to become, in Clifford Geertz's terms, "cosmopolitan" and thus to resolve what was termed the tension between solidarity and scale may in turn depend on facilitative political institutions and coalitions. Indeed, there is no reason, except for critical incentives and support provided by political leaders and their institutions, why network relations among Taiwan's SMEs should be so much stronger than those identified by Lui and Chiu among Hong Kong firms.[2] Confirmation of the importance of political institutions and coalitions is seen as well in Deyo and Doner's depiction of the broader Thai political economy as weak in coordination functions and in the provision of industry-wide collective goods. And while the studies by Rasiah and Wong emphasize subnational political factors, it is important to acknowledge the continued importance of national variations in industry and trade policy, in collective goods provision, and in support for network governance institutions and dynamic flexibility strategies among firms.

FLEXIBILITY, GOVERNANCE, AND EQUITY

While the chapters in this volume largely focus on the institutional sources of flexibility and competitiveness among firms, the broader sociopolitical implications of our findings are addressed for the most part only implicitly. Of particular importance in this regard are the consequences of flexibility-enhancing governance arrangements for an equitable distribution of the fruits of economic growth. We here focus specifically on the implications of governance and flexibility for workers and SMEs.

The chapters confirm the largely negative social outcomes of static flexibility strategies, as major firms seek to outsource more and more production to SMEs, to rely on casual or contract labor in-house, and more generally to externalize cost and risk to workers and SME suppliers. By contrast, dynamic flexibility seeks competitiveness not by squeezing vulnerable actors, whether workers or SMEs, but rather by enhancing their capacities through improvements in organizational processes both within and across firms. Typically, dynamic flexibility requires greater autonomy and skill among all participating actors. To the extent that the relationships upon which underlying network governance relies must be ongoing and based upon significant investments by all parties, they are likely to involve longer time horizons than would be the case under purely market-based arrangements. One result is an improved bargaining position for subordinate actors. Another, and one particularly important for longer-term development, is that where the degree of autonomy and skill required for flexibility result from investments in human capital and in the upgrading of small firm capacities, these assets are in principle portable, thus suggesting opportunities for empowerment of relatively weak actors.

But even dynamic flexibility strategies tend often to be mirrored by the simultaneous consolidation of static, low-road strategies and social outcomes. The resulting dualism follows from the reorganization of transorganizational production systems by major firms as they encourage network-like relations (or, at a minimum, paternalistic variants of hierarchy) among those workers and SMEs most closely involved in core production processes, alongside more vertical or low-trust market relations for workers and SMEs in less critical production activities wherein requirements of cost reduction, capacity/numerical flexibility, and market risk can be more directly addressed. The tendency toward a strategic tiering of supplier chains by major auto assemblers in Thailand illustrates this dualism. Similarly, the restructuring of Hong Kong's garment industry (as discussed by Lui and Chiu, and by Appelbaum and Smith) illustrates both local and *transnational* dimensions of strategic dualism, with many firms moving into high-value design and brokerage niches in Hong Kong itself while externalizing low-end production to local suppliers and to mainland factories.[3] But lest we drift too far toward a deterministic account of the structural impact of corporate strategies, it must be recalled that countervailing pressures, rooted in such contextual institutions as labor unions (Deyo 1996), SME associations, and political coalitions and state policy, may encourage a broadening and opening of what would otherwise be somewhat exclusionary dynamic enclaves. Of particular relevance here is the role of communally based but open industrial networks in Penang and Taiwan in creating structural incentives for larger firms to establish more inclusive developmental supplier relations supportive of high-value production (Gereffi and Hamilton 1996).

The importance of such network-like supplier relations for SME success relates closely to an enhanced learning capacity of local firms, again reflected in the Taiwan experience. Given the importance for learning of the institutional environment within which SMEs are situated, it is clear that a densely networked sectoral economy of trading companies, equipment suppliers, technology consultants, business associations, contractors, subcontractors, and government agencies provides superior access to new information relating to export markets, new technology, innovative methods of work organization, and the like (North 1997). In this sense, an understanding of sectoral governance institutions provides a useful approach to questions of SME development and industrial upgrading.

Yet as Glasmeier et al. (1997: 9) have shown, SMEs often have their own approaches to learning and obtaining new information. Social scientists are far from a full understanding of the dynamics of these processes. Moreover, the institutions that affect SME learning are certain to be affected by the continuing economic crisis, which has placed serious demands not only on the economy but on the broader universe of social and political relationships that link actors within and across societies in the region. First, it is clear that the region has not experienced the hyperinflation that impeded long-term strategic planning among Latin American firms during corresponding periods of instability. Thus, East Asia does not offer much opportunity to test out the somewhat contrasting predictions regarding the capacity of network-based flexible production to enhance the capacity of firms to cope effectively with such conditions.[4] But macroeconomic volatility, due to wild swings in exchange rates and interest rates, remains a problem, as does general overcapacity. In this context, Deyo and Doner note the superior position of those Thai firms able to flexibly diversify out of domestic and stagnant regional markets into more dynamic export markets, as well as to more fully integrate into the supplier chains of major foreign companies able to provide access to stronger external markets, new technology, and in some cases fresh infusions of capital. Here, vertical networks have afforded some protection through a sharing, rather than downward shifting, of risk from assemblers to key suppliers. However, as Gereffi and Tam (1998: 19) have argued, and as Ernst's contribution to this volume would appear to confirm, a trend toward vertical integration in place of relational contracting could undermine the capacity for learning by doing, and thus for technological and processual upgrading, among firms located at lower rungs in the hierarchy.

The reciprocal issue relating to the impact of the crisis on flexibility and networks is similarly problematic. A credit squeeze, taking the form of high interest rates, can promote flexible production by discouraging firms from building up inventories (Kaplinsky and Posthuma 1994: 283). Yet those same interest rates can inhibit flexible production involving SMEs by weakening these firms' ability to make new investments. The exceptions are those firms, such as Aapico, already tied into multinational production networks, or Taiwanese firms, such as the footwear producers described by Cheng, which are linked to both local, horizontal networks and more vertical buyer-driven commodity chains.[5]

More generally, crisis-related pressures may have encouraged more arms-length, market-like relations among firms. This has been noted in accounts of South Korean and Japanese firms which increasingly demanded immediate payment of outstanding obligations and behaved in other ways associated less often with networks than with markets.[6] In addition, high unemployment, resulting from spiraling interest rates and overcapacity, enhanced the attractiveness of numerical flexibility based on casualized employment. This tendency toward low-road static flexibility may have been further encouraged by devalued or depreciated exchange rates whose primary export advantage was price rather than improved quality, as well as by sharp crisis-induced reductions in state assistance and collective goods provision.

In sum, on the one hand East Asia's economic crisis may weaken all firms and workers not already part of stable networks while at the same time reducing the number of those included in such networks, thus intensifying existing tendencies toward institutional, strategic, and social dualism. On the other hand, and as suggested in the chapter on Thailand, there are a host of unanswered questions relating to the ways in which the crisis has precipitated new political forces and coalitions whose impacts on economic policy, corporate strategy, and economic governance are still unclear at the time of this writing. In the long run, those larger political dynamics may play the critical role in shaping regional postcrisis political economies.

NOTES

1. For a broader and more recent treatment, see *Economist* (1998: 8).
2. The obstacles cited by Davies for low levels of trust among Hong Kong firms could also be applied to firms in Taiwan, as well as Singapore: lack of entrepot function; limited resources; need to work within technical competences available; need to overcome problems caused by large physical and psychic distance to markets; and need to protect themselves from the impact of unpredictable market changes (Davies, 1998: 14).
3. A related case is noted by Rodgers (1997) in his discussion of the relocation of low-skill production from Singapore to Indonesia alongside maintenance of relatively good employment practices within Singapore itself.
4. For example, one view is that flexible producers are better able to handle price volatility and inflation through lower inventories and shorter production runs. But another view is that negative real interest rates (caused by inflation rates being higher than the cost

of borrowing) can encourage firms to build up, rather than reduce, inventories. And inflation may compel firms to operate with short-term time horizons even when they seek long-
term collaboration (Kaplinsky and Posthuma 1994; Posthuma 1997).

5. For further evidence that linkages to multinationals have strengthened the financial
position of Thai suppliers during the crisis, see Soonruth (1998).

6. This would support Posthuma's (1997) suggestion that Latin American macroeconomic instability has tended to discourage exclusive network-like sourcing contracts and
to encourage firms to demand immediate payment for products and services.

BIBLIOGRAPHY

Business Times (Singapore).

Chiu, Stephen W. K., and Ching Kwan Lee. 1997. "After the Miracle: Women Workers
under Industrial Restructuring in Hong Kong." Paper presented at the Social Science
Research Council/Universidade Federal de Rio de Janeiro workshop on New Institutions
and Flexible Production in September, Rio de Janeiro.

Davies, Howard. 1998. "The Future Shape of Hong Kong's Economy: Why High Technology Manufacturing Will Prove to Be a Myth." In *Hong Kong's Industrial Relations*, edited
by P. Fosh et al. Routledge, 1998.

Deyo, Frederic, ed. 1996. *Social Reconstructions of the World Automobile Industry*. London:
Macmillan.

Doner, Richard, with Peter Brimble. 1998. *Thailand's Hard Disk Drive Industry*. San Diego:
Sloan Storage Research Project, University of California, San Diego.

Doner, Richard, and Stephan Haggard. 1998. "Nodes and Networks: The Regional Production System in Southeast Asia." Unpublished manuscript.

Economist. 1998. "Survey—Taiwan." 7 November.

Ernst, Dieter. 1998. "Catching-Up, Crisis and Truncated Industrial Upgrading: Evolutionary Aspects of Technological Learning in East Asia's Electronics Industry." Paper presented to the Social Science Research Council Conference on Industrial Upgrading in
October, Geneva.

Gereffi, Gary, and Gary Hamilton. 1996. "Commodity Chains and Embedded Networks:
The Economic Organization of Global Capitalism." Paper presented at the Annual
Meeting of the American Sociological Association in August, New York City.

Gereffi, Gary, and Tony Tam. 1998. "Industrial Upgrading through Organizational Chains:
Dynamics of Rent, Learning-by-Doing, and Mobility in the Global Economy." Paper pre-
sented at the Social Science Research Council Conference on Industrial Upgrading in
November, Geneva.

Glasmeier, Amy, et al. 1997. "The Relevance of Firm Learning Theories to the Design and
Evaluation of Manufacturing Modernization Programs." Unpublished manuscript, Penn-
sylvania State University.

Kaplinsky, Raphael, and Anne Posthuma. 1994. *Easternization: The Spread of Japanese Management Techniques to Developing Countries*. London: Frank Cass.

Kranton, Rachel E. 1997. "Markets vs. Networks and Personalized Exchange Arrangements: Alternative Modes of Exchange." Unpublished manuscript.

Levy, Brian, et al. 1994. "Technical Marketing Support Systems for Successful Small and Medium-Size Enterprises in Four Countries." Policy Research Paper 1400, World Bank, December.

Levy, Brian, and Wen-Jeng Kuo. 1991. "The Strategic Orientations of Firms and the Performance of Korea and Taiwan in Frontier Industries: Lessons from Comparative Case Studies of Keyboard and Personal Computer Assembly." *World Development* 19, no. 4: 363–374.

North, Klaus. 1997. *Localizing Global Production: Know-How Transfer in International Manufacturing.* Geneva: ILO.

Posthuma, Anne. 1997. "Restructuring and Changing Market Conditions in the Brazilian Auto Components Industry." Unpublished manuscript.

Rodgers, Ronald. 1997. "Organizational Flexibility through Mutual Commitment Relationships: The Case of Yokogawa Asia Pte. Ltd." Unpublished manuscript. Faculty of Business Administration, National University of Singapore.

Soonruth, Bunyamanee. 1998. "More Export Market Sharing Promoted." *Bangkok Post,* October 26.

Index

Index

factor market institutions, 16–17
FDI (foreign direct investment), 129, 139–40, 191, 209
Federation of Thai Industries (FTI), 112
financial institutions, 17; long-term financing, 110; reformed, 71–72, 98, 137; separation from industry, 58
flashlighting shoes, 47
Fleury, Alfonso, 2, 4, 28
flexibility: dynamic, 6–7, 114–15, 120, 165–67, 218–25; static, 6, 223, 225
flexible production, 3, 5–8, 25n5, 74, 212–13, 218–25; defined, 108; exploitative aspects of, 81, 90; facilitation of, 218–25; in footwear industry, 47–48; in garment industry, 63–64, 79, 86–94; in HDD industry, 191–92, 204–5, 207–8; increased with subcontracting, 165–66, 170–75; lack of, 138, 155; in the machine tool industry, 167–75; vs. mass production, 146–47; in microelectronics, 170; sustaining competitiveness, 82, 207–8; work organization, 170–75
flexible specialization, 25n5, 219
Fligstein, N., 33, 52
footwear industry, Mexico, 36
footwear industry, Taiwan, 33, 35–41, 51, 218, 220–21; athletic shoes, 42–48; market share, 34, 36
footwear industry flexible production, 47–48
foreign direct investment (FDI), 129, 139–40, 191, 209
foreign technology, 139, 141–43, 150
free-trade zones, 174–75
FTI (Federation of Thai Industries), 112

game theory, 14
Gap, The, 88–91
garment industry, 79–83; flexible production, 63–64, 79, 86–94; in Hong Kong, 60–64, 79–80, 83–84, 87–88, 94–96, 222; in Indonesia, 96; in South Korea, 79–80, 84–86, 92–94, 96–97; in Vietnam, 96
Geddes, Barbara, 18, 28
Geertz, Clifford, 222

gender differences in labor markets, 59–60
Gerakan, 183–84
Gereffi, Gary, 79, 82, 224; works, 102, 226
Gerlach, M. L., 153, 162
Gerschenkron, A., 141, 162
GINTIC Institute of Manufacturing Technology (GIMT), 210
globalization, 19, 55, 142, 155; of buyer networks, 56, 184; of competition, 192, 201, 204; of markets, 2, 4
"GM University" (automotive technology institute) (Thailand), 111
government institutions, 18–19, 57–58, 183, 185, 212; development-oriented, 84, 174–76, 194, 208–11; encouraging intra-industry coordination, 35, 38–39, 51, 173, 222; interventions, 166, 177–79; lack of support for development, 178–79; symbiotic relationships with businesses, 138–41
government research institutes (GRIs), 151–52
Granovetter, Mark, 13, 29
growth: of exports, 145, 191; immiserated, 146; sustaining, 137–38; of wages, 60
guided credit, 139

hard disk drive (HDD) industry, 192–93, 198–204, 206–7, 210–14, 221; assembly, 194–201, 207, 208; and economic policies, 208–11; flexible production, 191–92, 204–5, 207–8; subassembly, 195
Harrison, Bennett, 10, 32
Hayward, David, 13, 28
Herrigel, Gary, 16, 29
Hershberg, Eric, 73, 76
hierarchical economic governance, 7–8, 80–81, 85, 94, 96, 151
Hirst, P., 167, 188
Hitech Industrial Estate (Thailand), 115
Hollingsworth, J. Rogers, 3, 6, 13, 16, 107; works, 27, 29, 135
homeworkers, 89–90
Honda, 128, 132–33n23
Hong Kong: colonial administration of, 57–58; electronics industry, 64–67;

About the Contributors

Richard P. Appelbaum is professor of sociology at the University of California, Santa Barbara.

Lu-lin Cheng is assistant professor at the Academia Sinica, Taipei, Taiwan.

Stephen W. K. Chiu is a professor of sociology at the Chinese University of Hong Kong.

Frederic C. Deyo is professor of sociology at SUNY, Brockport, and honorary professor and NZAI research fellow at the University of Auckland.

Richard F. Doner is associate professor of political science, Emory University.

Dieter Ernst is senior fellow at the East-West Center in Honolulu.

Eric Hershberg is program director at the Social Science Research Council.

Tai Lok Lui is professor of sociology at the Chinese University of Hong Kong.

Rajah Rasiah is professor at the Institute of Malaysian and International Studies, Universiti Kebangsaan, Kuala Lumpur, Malaysia.

David A. Smith is professor of sociology at the University of California, Irvine.

Poh-Kam Wong is professor in the Faculty of Business Administration, National University of Singapore.

DATE DUE

Demco, Inc 38-293